A Mathematical Introduction
to Economics

A Mathematical Introduction to Economics

ALASDAIR SMITH

Basil Blackwell · Oxford

© Alasdair Smith 1982

First published 1982
Basil Blackwell Publisher Limited
108 Cowley Road, Oxford OX4 1JF, England

British Library Cataloguing in Publication Data

Smith, Alasdair
  A mathematical introduction to economics.
  1. Economics
  I. Title
  330   HB171

  ISBN 0-631-12888-3
  ISBN 0-631-12976-6 Pbk

Typesetting by Unicus Graphics Ltd, Horsham.
Printed in Great Britain by The Camelot Press,
Southampton.

Contents

Introduction

This book is an introduction to economics for students with a good background in mathematics. It is not an introduction to 'mathematical economics', and it certainly is not an introduction to mathematics for economists. It has some features of which the prospective reader, whether student or teacher, should have advance notice, and the main function of this introduction is to give that notice.

The book originates in a course of first-year undergraduate lectures that I gave at the London School of Economics from 1975 to 1979. The LSE is unusual in having a sufficiently large number of mathematically well-equipped undergraduates to justify the provision of a separate introductory economics course, so in revising my lecture notes for this book I have tried to keep in mind the needs of a broader group of potential readers.

In principle, the mathematical prerequisite is modest: a thorough knowledge of single variable calculus at a standard roughly comparable to English A-level mathematics. In practice, the book requires a degree of mathematical sophistication and facility unlikely to be possessed by a student who has not taken, or is not taking, some university-level courses in mathematics or mathematically-based subjects.

I do not assume any prior knowledge of economics, but the student who has already had an introductory course in economics is unlikely to find here a great deal of straightforward repetition of what he or she already knows.

There are four distinct groups of students for whom this book is intended. The first is the type of student to whom my lecture course was given: first-year undergraduates starting a degree course that emphasizes the mathematical and quantitative approach to economics, or that combines the study of economics and mathematics. For them, this book can be used as a principal text. It will not be an easy text, for the pace is fast, with few relaxing diversions, but it is an advantage of the mathematical approach to economics that it takes the student much further much faster than a conventional introduction to the subject. No doubt, most teachers will feel that an unremittingly theoretical treatment of economics deprives the student of necessary institutional and historical background and will wish to prescribe additional readings and supplementary texts, though this text is not wholly devoid of reference to the 'real world'.

Then there are undergraduates who are taking a more conventional economics course but who have mathematical ability which they wish to exploit. For them, this book can be a supplementary text, to be dipped into from time to time throughout their study of economic theory. I hope they will, occasionally at least, be surprised by the ease with which a small amount of mathematics clarifies propositions that have to be laboured through in a purely verbal approach.

The third group consists of students of mathematics, engineering or science who are taking one or two economics courses. Even though they can learn much by doing economics this way, not least that social sciences are not necessarily woolly and undemanding, I doubt that this book alone is adequate to their needs. Supplementary institutional and historical reading is recommended.

Finally there are graduate students whose previous education was in mathematically-based subjects with little or no economics and who are taking up the serious study of economics at graduate level. Such students will want to cover a great deal of ground rather fast, and will be prepared to work hard, and a mathematically oriented introduction to the subject suits their needs.

Conflicting considerations influenced my decisions on what material to include and what to exclude, but the paramount consideration was that my objective is to teach economics not to teach mathematical techniques. The first chapter is devoted to demand-and-supply analysis, where we are forced to assume the truth of propositions which are proved in the subsequent three chapters. It would have been more elegant to leave this topic to a later stage, but that would have deprived the reader of a chance to get to work on recognizably realistic economic problems at the outset, and would also have required the presentation of the most difficult mathematical material at the very beginning.

In chapters 2–4 which discuss the microeconomic theory of competitive producers' and consumers' behaviour, cost functions and expenditure functions are extensively used. In these chapters the reader will, in addition to learning a considerable amount of economics, learn of the power of some fundamentally rather simple mathematical tricks, and of the importance to much economic theorizing of the assumption that agents optimize. An optional appendix takes matters further, by introducing and using the profit function, and the student who masters all of this material

is well-equipped, and, I hope, well-motivated to study the more fundamental aspects of duality theory.

A major omission from the treatment of microeconomics is any serious
or systematic discussion of general equilibrium. A formal treatment of this
topic would require mathematical tools far more advanced than any of
those used in other topics; an informal treatment, in my view, would not
be of much interest or value. The concept of general equilibrium is introduced in chapter 5, which is concerned with welfare economics, but most
of the welfare analysis is conducted in informal, partial equilibrium,
terms. My judgement is that the mathematical and conceptual requirements of a rigorous treatment of the fundamental questions of welfare
economics would be inappropriate in an introductory book.

Just as the treatment of competitive agents' behaviour serves to introduce the reader to the elements of duality theory, so the theory of imperfectly competitive markets expounded in chapter 6 introduces some of
the concepts of game theory. Here, too, it is my hope that students will
be motivated to pursue the topic further.

Only two chapters are devoted to macroeconomics. To a greater extent
than the rest of the text, these chapters retain the character of lecture
notes. Here the mathematics has a more mundane role than in much of
microeconomics: it is used simply to work more efficiently through the
technical details of macroeconomic models than can be done in a nonmathematical treatment. The 'vision' of macroeconomics presented here
is a restricted one. Because general equilibrium theory was not treated in
the microeconomic chapters, the disequilibrium approach to macroeconomics cannot be discussed, while the 'new classical' macroeconomics,
in which rational expectations has a key role, is only briefly touched on.
Econometrics is not discussed at any point in this book, and this too
limits the scope of the macroeconomic presentation. Let me not, however,
seem too apologetic: the reader is taken far beyond the topics convention-
ally covered in an introductory book and is presented with a theoretical
framework in which the major contemporary macroeconomic issues –
Keynesians versus monetarists, stagflation, supply-side macroeconomics,
and so on – can be approached, if not finally settled.

I have already referred to the fact that my primary aim is to teach
economics. The extensive sets of problems that follow each chapter play
a vital role in this respect. Some have the function of filling in details of
the theoretical structure that are left out of the text, and some give the
student an opportunity to develop and exercise technical skills, but a large
proportion have the objective of letting the student apply economic
theory to real economic issues and to develop economic intuition. Many
of these problems can be answered using little or no mathematics. The
number of the problems may seem rather formidable, and students may
need guidance on which to select, but at the very least all problems

referred to in the text should be attempted. Answers, or hints and suggestions for obtaining answers, to some of the exercises are provided at the end of the book.

There is no mathematical introduction which lays out all the tools used in the text, nor is there an introductory chapter to define 'what economics is about' or to explain important concepts like equilibrium or the distinction between exogenous and endogenous variables. The reason for these omissions is my belief that new mathematical techniques and new concepts are more easily absorbed through practice and application.

Some sections of the text are starred: they contain more advanced material which can be omitted without loss of continuity. The starred problems are the most difficult ones.

I have adopted some conventions which may annoy the mathematical purist. If I want to maximize a function, I usually assume without question that the maximum exists; if I want to differentiate (or twice-differentiate) a function, I invariably assume without question that the function is differentiable. Where a weak inequality is being described verbally, I almost always use the words appropriate to a strong inequality, so, for example, I describe a non-decreasing function as an 'increasing' function. The first of these conventions is adopted for the sake of avoiding mathematical issues that would be unduly difficult at this stage; the second for the sake of clarity of expression. I hope no reader will suffer more than annoyance.

Equations are numbered consecutively within each chapter. The equation numbered (17) in chapter 2 is referred to in chapter 2 as equation (17), elsewhere as equation (2.17).

I have many debts. The course on whose lecture notes this book is based was originally taught at LSE by Frank Hahn and then by Steve Nickell. From them I inherited a substantial amount of material, including problem sets, and a fair proportion of that material has survived in one form or another in this book. I am grateful to my former colleagues at LSE, Steve Glaister, Richard Jackman and, especially, Bob Gould for comments, criticisms and discussion. I received extensive, useful and encouraging comments from John Hey and another, anonymous, reader. I did not always accept the advice I was given and I retain full responsibility for remaining errors and shortcomings. I am grateful to the Senate of the University of London for permission to use questions which were set in University examinations. I am required to note that where answers to problems are provided, the University of London is in no way committed to approval of such answers. Finally I am indebted for the typing of various drafts to Marianna Tappas and June Jarman.

University of Sussex   ALASDAIR SMITH

CHAPTER 1

Supply and Demand

1.1   *Introduction*

Much of this book focuses on the role of prices in determining the allocation of resources: that is in determining what goods get produced and who consumes the goods that are produced. We start therefore by looking at how prices are determined and what effect they have on production and consumption.

The fact that we focus on the price system (or the 'market mechanism') in discussing the allocation of resources should not be taken to mean that this system is the only or necessarily the best way for society to organize its economic activities. One good reason, however, for starting here is that study of the price system teaches us some important principles which can be applied to the study of other methods of economic organization.

The key to sensible analysis of how prices get determined and what their effects are is first to look *separately* at the behaviour of suppliers and consumers of goods and then consider how they will interact in the market. In later chapters we will consider in detail how people who supply goods for sale might react to prices, and also how consumers might behave. But it is convenient to start off with a fairly superficial view of consumers' and producers' behaviour so as to get as quickly as possible to the heart of the price system.

Let p be the *price* of a good. Let y be the *supply* of the good, that is, the total quantity of the good that sellers of the good want to sell. Let x be the *demand* for the good, that is, the total quantity that consumers of the good want to buy. The simple assumptions that we make about sellers' and buyers' behaviour are that: (i) the amount that sellers want to sell depends on the price, with supply increasing as price rises, that is

$$y = y(p) \qquad y'(p) > 0 \qquad\qquad (1)$$

where $y'(p)$ is the derivative of y with respect to p; and (ii) the amount demanded by consumers depends on the price, decreasing as price rises, that is

$$x = x(p) \qquad x'(p) < 0 \tag{2}$$

where $x'(p)$ is the derivative of x. The function $y(p)$ is called the *supply function* while $x(p)$ is the *demand function*.

At this stage, the only justification for assuming that supply is an increasing function of price and demand is a decreasing function of price is an appeal to common sense. If price rises, the business of supplying the good becomes more profitable and it becomes worthwhile to pay workers more to work longer hours, investment in expanding the size of the business becomes more attractive, and people engaged in other activities will be drawn away from them and into this business by the prospect of supplying goods at a high price. All of these forces will make supply rise as price rises. On the demand side, a rise in price makes consumers worse off, and makes that good more expensive relative to other goods which consumers can buy, so that a typical consumer can be expected to reduce the amount that he wants to buy. Indeed, a price rise might induce some consumers to reduce their purchases of the good to nothing. All of this will make demand fall as price rises. In chapters 2 to 4 below, more detailed and rigorous theories of suppliers' and demanders' behaviour will be developed. Among other things, we shall see more clearly that the derivation of supply and demand curves requires the assumption that both demanders and suppliers are *price-takers*. That is to say, each individual consumer and producer regards the price of a good as something over which he individually has no influence or control.

1.2   Equilibrium and stability

We can draw the graphs of the functions $y(p)$ and $x(p)$ in the same diagram. Although the usual convention in mathematics is to draw graphs with the independent variable on the horizontal axis, in this particular case the reverse convention is almost invariably adopted, and we put p on the vertical axis as in the diagram shown as figure 1.1.

The graphs of $y(p)$ and $x(p)$ are respectively called the supply curve and the demand curve. The point at which they cross is of special significance. The price p^* which is defined by

$$y(p^*) = x(p^*) \tag{3}$$

that is, the price at which the amount that sellers wish to sell is equal to the amount which consumers wish to buy, is called the *equilibrium price*, and the quantity $q^* = y(p^*) = x(p^*)$ is the equilibrium quantity.

Since the supply curve slopes up and the demand curve slopes down, it follows that there is at most one equilibrium point. (It is easy to draw

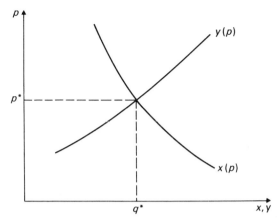

FIGURE 1.1   Equilibrium of supply and demand

supply and demand curves which do not cross at a point where both p^* and q^* are positive. Since negative prices and negative quantities are meaningless, it is left to you as an exercise to think about what might actually happen in such cases. See exercises 1.2 and 1.4.)

The significance of the equilibrium point is best seen by considering what happens at other prices. If p is different from p^*, then supply is different from demand and it is not possible for all suppliers and all demanders to do what they want to do. If p is greater than p^*, then $y(p)$ exceeds $x(p)$, supply is greater than demand. Consumers are willing to buy less than the quantity which sellers wish to sell, so sellers will be left with unsold goods. It is plausible that the reaction to this will be that the unsatisfied sellers will reduce the price. On the other hand, if p is less than p^*, demand exceeds supply and consumers will not be able to buy all they want to. It is plausible that such a shortage will cause unsatisfied consumers to offer a higher price. Thus, it *seems* that if we start from a price different from the equilibrium price, the price will over time move towards the equilibrium, as *excess demand* drives up the price and *excess supply* drives it down. If this indeed were the case we should say that p^* was a *stable* equilibrium price. Actually stability cannot be deduced from such a simple argument: we would need to look much more carefully at how suppliers and demanders behave if the market is not in equilibrium and at what might be going on in other markets.

Now markets take many different forms. For some goods, sellers and buyers actually get together in one place to trade with each other. In other cases, sellers and buyers are in constant communication by telephone or other electronic means. But for most goods, sellers and buyers are scattered around, separated from each other, and not necessarily fully informed about all that is happening. The theory described above is a plausible approximation to reality in many cases, and the informal argument about stability convincing enough to persuade us that the market price will be at or close to equilibrium. (It should be obvious, on a moment's reflection, that an equilibrium which was not stable would be of little interest.) In due course, however, we shall study several situations which do not fit in to this theory. The next section is devoted to one example of a market where the equilibrium might not be stable.

1.3   *The cobweb cycle*

In many agricultural markets, at the time suppliers make their production decisions they cannot know the market price at which they will sell their product. An egg producer, for example, has to buy, house and feed chickens before he can sell eggs. Suppose that the quantity of eggs he has for sale in any year depends on decisions he made in the previous year. If egg prices are high he wishes to sell many eggs, if prices are low, he wishes to sell little, but in making his decisions now, he has to *guess* what *next* year's prices will be. He might use this year's prices as the best guide available to next year's prices.

A simple example of such a situation is given by

$$y_t = bp_{t-1}$$

$$x_t = \alpha - \beta p_t \tag{4}$$

where b, α and β are positive constants, and the t and $t-1$ subscripts refer to different years: year t's supply depends on the previous year's price because that was the suppliers' estimate of year t's price, while consumers react to the current price. In year t, supply is y_t and if eggs cannot be stored, price will have to be at the level that ensures all of this supply is demanded. That is

$$\alpha - \beta p_t = bp_{t-1} \tag{5}$$

so that each year's price is related to the previous year's price by the equation

$$p_t = \frac{\alpha}{\beta} - \frac{b}{\beta} p_{t-1} \tag{6}$$

The price p_t which satisfies equation (5) for given p_{t-1} is a *market-clearing* price, for it makes demand equal to supply. In the model of the previous section the market-clearing price was called the equilibrium price, being the price at which both suppliers and demanders could fulfil their plans. In this model, market-clearing is not the same as equilibrium. The suppliers plan to sell y_t *at the price* p_{t-1} but this plan is only fulfilled if the price p_t is equal to p_{t-1}. Thus the equilibrium price p^* is the one satisfying $p_t = p_{t-1} = p^*$ and equation (6), so that

$$p^* = \frac{\alpha}{\beta} - \frac{b}{\beta} p^* \tag{7}$$

which implies $p^* = \alpha/(b + \beta)$, $q^* = b\alpha/(b + \beta)$. Subtracting (7) from (6) gives

$$p_t - p^* = -\frac{b}{\beta}(p_{t-1} - p^*) \tag{8}$$

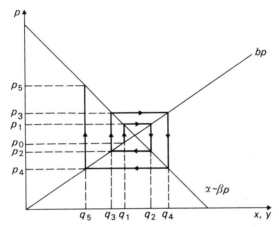

FIGURE 1.2   An unstable cobweb cycle

so that if $b > \beta$, $p_t - p^*$ is bigger in magnitude than (and of the opposite sign to) $p_{t-1} - p^*$. Each year, the price moves further away from equilibrium, so that the equilibrium is unstable. This case is illustrated in figure 1.2 where the movement of price and quantity over time traces out a pattern which shows why this phenomenon is known as a 'cobweb cycle'. It is easy to see, however, that if $b < \beta$ the cobweb cycle will be stable: prices will move towards the equilibrium price. It is left to you (see exercise 1.3) to draw the diagram for the stable case and to think of reasons why the unstable cobweb cycle is not very plausible.

1.4   *Comparative statics: the effect of a sales tax*

If the equilibrium in the market for a good is stable, the actual price and quantity should usually be close to their equilibrium values. Finding out how the market equilibrium changes in response to some change in conditions will therefore tell us approximately what will happen to the actual price and quantity. The study of how equilibrium changes as conditions change is called *comparative statics*.

Consider a market in which there is a sales tax of the amount t levied on each unit of the good sold. If the supplier receives the price p, the consumer has to pay the price π where

$$\pi = p + t \tag{9}$$

Supply is a function of p but demand is a function of π so that in equilibrium

$$y(p) = x(\pi) \tag{10}$$

For a given value of t, (9) and (10) are a pair of simultaneous equations in the two unknowns p and π. Without knowing the exact form of the functions y and x we cannot solve the equations for p and π. But we can discuss what happens as t changes.

Suppose that for some value of t, the prices p and π are at values which satisfy (9) and (10). If t were now raised, p and π would have to change in order to keep (9) and (10) satisfied. This means that (9) and (10) define p and π as *implicit functions* of t ('implicit' because we cannot in general actually solve the equations for p and π). Using the fact that both p and π are functions of t we can differentiate both sides of equations (9) and (10) with respect to t to give

$$\frac{d\pi}{dt} = \frac{dp}{dt} + 1 \tag{11}$$

$$y'(p)\frac{dp}{dt} = x'(\pi)\frac{d\pi}{dt} \tag{12}$$

where the 'chain rule' for differentiating a function is used to get (12) from (10). The reason that (11) and (12) must hold is that an equilibrium is defined by the fact that (9) and (10) hold, so when t changes, the change in π must equal the change in $p + t$ and the change in y must equal the change in x, in order for the market to stay in equilibrium.

We can solve (11) and (12) for dp/dt and $d\pi/dt$ to give

$$\frac{dp}{dt} = \frac{x'(\pi)}{y'(p) - x'(\pi)} \tag{13}$$

$$\frac{d\pi}{dt} = \frac{y'(p)}{y'(p) - x'(\pi)} \tag{14}$$

Since $x'(\pi) < 0$ and $y'(p) > 0$, it follows that $dp/dt < 0$ and $d\pi/dt > 0$. The change in quantity is given by either side of equation (12), since

$q = y(p) = x(\pi)$, and thus

$$\frac{dq}{dt} = \frac{x'(\pi) \, y'(p)}{y'(p) - x'(\pi)} \tag{15}$$

so that $dq/dt < 0$. An increase in the tax puts up the price paid by the consumer, reduces the price received by the supplier, and reduces the quantity sold.

You should note that nothing has been said above about who actually pays the tax over to the government. In fact the analysis shows that this is irrelevant to who really bears the burden of the tax. All that matters is that there is a difference between p and π, and a widening of this difference requires both p to fall and π to rise. It is the extent to which p falls and π rises that determines the extent to which the tax is paid by the supplier and the consumer respectively.

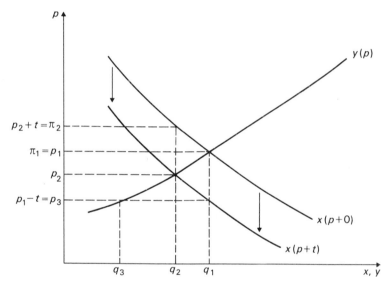

FIGURE 1.3   The effect of a sales tax

A diagrammatic treatment may help to clarify all this. Figure 1.3 is drawn with p on the vertical axis. With $t = 0$, $\pi = p$ and we have equilibrium at price p_1 and quantity q_1. The imposition of the tax t shifts the demand curve vertically downwards by the amount t. For example at the price π_2 consumers would consume q_2 in the absence of the tax. With a tax of t, only when the price p takes the value $p_2 = \pi_2 - t$ do consumers face the price π_2 at which they are willing to consume q_2.

In fact the price p_2 is the new equilibrium value of p, for at this price sellers supply q_2 which is what consumers demand at the price $\pi_2 = p_2 + t$. The difference $\pi_2 - \pi_1$ is the part of the tax which is borne by the consumers, while $p_1 - p_2$ is the part which falls on the sellers. Together they add up to t.

The irrelevance of who has the responsibility of actually paying t to the government can be seen as follows. Suppose the market is in equilibrium at (p_1, q_1) with no tax. Then sellers have imposed on them the obligation to pay t to the government. If consumers continue to pay the price $\pi_1 = p_1$, sellers will receive only $p_1 - t$ after tax, and supply will fall to q_3 while demand stays at q_1. There is excess demand which will push the equilibrium price up to p_2: the sellers *pass on* some of the tax to consumers.

You should note that the fact that in the diagram the demand curve shifts while the supply curve remains fixed is the result only of the fact that we have put p rather than π on the vertical axis. It is left to you (exercise 1.8) to draw the alternative diagram with π on the vertical axis and to show that the actual outcome is *exactly* as described above.

Although some sales taxes take the form of a fixed money tax on each unit sold (the UK tax on alcoholic drinks, for example), a commoner form of sales tax is to have tax levied at a fixed percentage rate of the seller's price. Then $\pi = p(1 + t)$ where t is the rate of sales tax. For example, if the rate of sales tax is 15%, $t = 0.15$ and π is 1.15 times p. It is left to you (exercise 1.9) to find the comparative static effects on p, π and q of a change in the tax rate in such a case.

1.5   Functions of more than one variable

It is easy to think of variables other than the price of the good which could affect supply and demand. We should expect, for example, demand to be affected by consumers' incomes as well as by price. Write this as

$$x = x(p, m) \tag{16}$$

where m is the average income of a consumer in this market. Mathematically, we say that x is a function of more than one independent variable. This is a natural extension of the concept of a function of a single variable. For example we might have

$$x = 10p^{-1}m^2 + 5m \tag{17}$$

To find the value of x we need to know the values of both p and m; and corresponding to each pair of values for p and m there is a unique value of x.

We can differentiate a function of more than one variable, with respect to one variable at a time. This gives us a *partial derivative*. For example, the partial derivative of function (17) with respect to m is found by treating p as if it were constant so that x is a function of m alone, and taking the derivative of x with respect to m to give

$$\frac{\partial x}{\partial m} = 20p^{-1}m + 5 \tag{18}$$

Similarly, treating m as constant gives

$$\frac{\partial x}{\partial p} = -10p^{-2}m^2 \tag{19}$$

The symbol ∂ rather than d is used in the derivative notation to remind us that there are other variables in the function which are being held constant, but the mathematical operation and its interpretation are the same as in ordinary differentiation. $\partial x/\partial m$ tells us the effect on x of a change in m holding p constant.

If p and m are themselves functions of other variables, we get various extensions of the chain rule of differentiation. If $p = p(z)$, then x can be written as the function of z and m defined by $x(z, m) = x(p(z), m)$ and application of the chain rule gives the result that z affects x through p so as to satisfy

$$\frac{\partial x}{\partial z} = \frac{\partial x}{\partial p}\frac{dp}{dz} \tag{20}$$

where the notation again reminds us that x is also a function of m, which is being held constant in the process of differentiation. If we have $m = m(w)$, the effect of w on x is given by

$$\frac{\partial x}{\partial w} = \frac{\partial x}{\partial m}\frac{dm}{dw} \tag{21}$$

If both p and m are functions of the same variable, say $p = p(z)$ and $m = m(z)$ then x is ultimately a function of z alone. The effect of z on x can be derived by the following simple argument. Think of the effect of z on p and m as taking place in two steps: first a change in z changes p with m constant, then it changes m with p constant. The effect of the first step on x is given by $(\partial x/\partial p)(dp/dz)$ while the effect of the second step is given by $(\partial x/\partial m)(dm/dz)$. The full effect on x is the sum of the effects of the two steps so

$$\frac{dx}{dz} = \frac{\partial x}{\partial p}\frac{dp}{dz} + \frac{\partial x}{\partial m}\frac{dm}{dz} \tag{22}$$

(where the use of the ordinary differentiation symbol on the left-hand side of (22) reflects the fact that x ultimately is a function of the single variable z).

Finally, consider the possibility that $p = p(m)$. Effectively this is the same as the previous case with $m = z$, so that $dm/dz = 1$. Thus (22) implies that

$$\frac{dx}{dm} = \frac{\partial x}{\partial p}\frac{dp}{dm} + \frac{\partial x}{\partial m} \tag{23}$$

Here it is worth noting the difference between $\partial x/\partial m$ and dx/dm: the former giving the direct effect of m on x, the latter giving the total effect when the dependence of p on m is also considered.

1.6 Comparative statics: the effect of consumer's income

If supply depends on price, as before, but demand depends on both price and consumers' income then equilibrium is defined by the equation

$$y(p) = x(p, m) \tag{24}$$

If m changes, x will change and to maintain equilibrium y will have to change, so p must change. Thus (24) means that p is an implicit function of m. As m changes, if the market is to remain in equilibrium, both sides of (24) must change at the same rate, that is

$$y'(p)\frac{dp}{dm} = \frac{\partial x}{\partial p}\frac{dp}{dm} + \frac{\partial x}{\partial m} \tag{25}$$

where the left-hand side is given by the ordinary chain rule applied to the left-hand side of (24) while the right-hand side is given by (23).

For the sake of brevity, it is frequently convenient to use subscripts to indicate differentiation, both ordinary and partial. Thus we can write y_p for $y'(p)$, x_p for $\partial x/\partial p$ and x_m for $\partial x/\partial m$.

Solving (25) for dp/dm gives

$$\frac{dp}{dm} = \frac{x_m}{y_p - x_p} \tag{26}$$

while, since the equilibrium quantity sold q is equal to both $y(p)$ and $x(p, m)$, either side of (25) gives the effect of m on q:

$$\frac{dq}{dm} = \frac{x_m y_p}{y_p - x_p} \tag{27}$$

As before, $y_p > 0$ and $x_p < 0$, while for most goods it is reasonable to assume that $x_m > 0$. Thus $dp/dm > 0$ and $dq/dm > 0$: a rise in consumer's income raises both the price and quantity sold in equilibrium.

All of this can be illustrated in a diagram. For a given value of m, a demand curve can be drawn showing that x falls as p rises. The supply curve is as before. Figure 1.4 shows the effect of a rise in m. At any value of p consumers would demand more because their income is higher. The

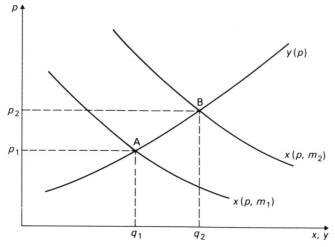

FIGURE 1.4   The effect of a rise in income

rise in income moves the demand curve to the right and shifts the equilibrium point up the supply curve from A to B.

1.7   *Exogenous and endogenous variables*

In each of the comparative statics examples we have looked at above, we have proceeded by making assumptions about how some variables are related to others. This allowed us to describe the situation by a number of equations. A common terminology is to say that we have described the situation by a 'model'.

In each of our models there are a number of variables whose equilibrium values are determined by the model; they are called *endogenous* variables. Variables whose values are determined outside the model are called *exogenous* variables. In the model of the sales tax, p, π and q are endogenous, while t is exogenous, being determined by the government. In the model including the effect of consumers' income, p and q are endogenous, while m is exogenous. Comparative statics is the analysis of the effects of changes in exogenous variables on the values of endogenous variables.

In the supply-and-demand diagram, an exogenous change appears as a shift in one (or possibly both) of the *curves*, while the change in the endogenous variables is represented by the resultant shift in the equilibrium *point*, represented by the intersection of the curves, along the other curve.

It is important to note that many different exogenous variables might have effects in particular markets. For example, the supply of an agricultural good will depend on the weather. We could model this as

$$y(p,r,s) = x(p,m) \tag{28}$$

where r is rainfall and s is sunshine (each measured in some appropriate units). Then the effects of changes in r or s on the market equilibrium can be analysed in the same way as the effects of changes in m.

Even rather nebulous things can be considered, such as a change in fashion. We could write

$$y(p) = x(p, f) \tag{29}$$

where $\partial x / \partial f > 0$. This 'dummy variable' f is simply a device to allow us to represent mathematically a shift in the functional relationship between x and p. The units in which f is measured are arbitrary. The analysis of the effects of a change in f follows exactly the same lines as the analysis of a change in income.

1.8 Comparative statics with cross-price effects

The demand or supply of one good will be affected by the prices of other goods: the demand for tea by the price of coffee, the supply of wool by the price of mutton, and so on. Therefore the equilibrium in one market will depend on the equilibria in others.

Consider, for example, the effect of a subsidy to coffee on the price of tea. Equilibrium in the tea and coffee markets respectively is defined by the equations

$$y^t(p^t) = x^t(p^t, \pi^c) \tag{30}$$

$$y^c(p^c) = x^c(p^t, \pi^c) \tag{31}$$

$$\pi^c = p^c - s \tag{32}$$

where p^t is the price of tea, p^c is the price received by suppliers of coffee while π^c is the price paid by consumers of coffee, s being the subsidy, and y^t, y^c, x^t, x^c being the supplies of tea and coffee and the demands for tea and coffee. Differentiating both sides of all three equations and substituting from the third into the first two gives

$$y_t^t \frac{dp^t}{ds} = x_t^t \frac{dp^t}{ds} + x_c^t \left(\frac{dp^c}{ds} - 1 \right) \tag{33}$$

$$y_c^c \frac{dp^c}{ds} = x_t^c \frac{dp^t}{ds} + x_c^c \left(\frac{dp^c}{ds} - 1 \right) \tag{34}$$

where $y_t^t = dy^t/dp^t$, $x_c^t = \partial x^t/\partial \pi^c$ and so on. Solving these two simultaneous equations for dp^t/ds and dp^c/ds gives

$$\frac{dp^t}{ds} = \frac{-x_c^t y_c^c}{(y_t^t - x_t^t)(y_c^c - x_c^c) - x_c^t x_t^c} \tag{35}$$

$$\frac{dp^c}{ds} = \frac{-(y_t^t - x_t^t) x_c^c - x_c^t x_t^c}{(y_t^t - x_t^t)(y_c^c - x_c^c) - x_c^t x_t^c} \tag{36}$$

and it follows that

$$\frac{d\pi^c}{ds} = \frac{-(y_t^t - x_t^t) y_c^c}{(y_t^t - x_t^t)(y_c^c - x_c^c) - x_c^t x_t^c} \tag{37}$$

It is reasonable to assume that $y_t^t > 0$, $y_c^c > 0$, $x_t^t < 0$ and $x_c^c < 0$, these being our usual assumptions. In addition, we can assume that $x_c^t > 0$ and $x_t^c > 0$. However these assumptions are not sufficient to allow us to deduce the sign of any of the expressions above. But, it is reasonable to argue that $(y_t^t - x_t^t)(y_c^c - x_c^c) - x_c^t x_t^c > 0$ even though the last part of that expression is negative, for this means that a price change has a larger effect on excess demand in its own market than on excess demand in the other market. With this additional assumption we can establish that $dp^t/ds < 0$ and $d\pi^c/ds < 0$, so a subsidy to coffee consumption reduces the price to consumers of both tea and coffee.

One interesting point to note about this analysis is that it brings out a complexity in what at first sight seems a very simple problem. 'A subsidy to coffee consumption will reduce the price to consumers even if some of the subsidy is absorbed by suppliers charging a higher price; and the lower price for coffee will reduce the demand for tea, which will push down the price of tea' *seems* a reasonable argument, but we have seen that we need to make an assumption about a quite complex expression in order for the conclusion to be correct.

A diagrammatic approach to the problem (figure 1.5) shows the nature of the complication. When we graph supply and demand for coffee against the consumer price π^c, the effect of an increased subsidy is a shift downwards of the supply curve by the amount of the increase. If p^t were

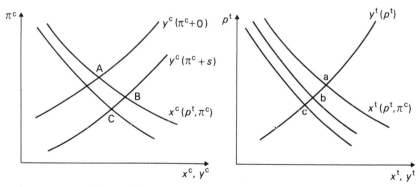

FIGURE 1.5   The effect of a coffee subsidy on the markets for tea and coffee

constant the equilibrium would move from A to B in figure 1.5. The fall in π^c will cause the x^t curve to shift downwards as the demand for tea reacts to the fall in the coffee price and the tea market equilibrium shifts from a to b in figure 1.5. The fall in p^t will reduce the demand for coffee, shifting the equilibrium to C, which in turn has an effect on the tea market, shifting it to c, which in turn.... To avoid the ridiculous conclusion that a small subsidy to coffee consumption could cause an endless downward spiral in both coffee and tea prices we need an assumption that brings the process gradually to an end. The assumption that $(y_t^t - x_t^t)(y_c^c - x_c^c) - x_c^t x_t^c > 0$ does just that. (The argument of this paragraph in fact suggests that if this condition were not satisfied, the equilibrium would not be stable.)

1.9   Elasticity

In the comparative statics problems we have looked at so far, the actual size of the effects of the exogenous changes depends on the sizes of various derivatives: (13) and (14) show that the division of the burden of a tax between sellers and buyers depends on the relative size of $x'(\pi)$ and $y'(p)$; (26) and (27) show that the effect of a rise in income depends on the sizes of y_p, x_p and x_m.

In many economic contexts, however, the size of a derivative is not a very helpful measure, principally because it depends on the units of measurement. If supply of a good is measured in tons and price is measured in dollars, the statement that $y'(p) = 4$ means that a \$1 increase in the price of the good should increase supply by approximately 4 tons. Does this mean that supply is very responsive to price changes? We do not know, for we need additional information before we can tell whether either the price change or the supply change is large: in particular, we would need to know the present price and supply. A \$1 increase in price is a large increase if the current price is \$3; it is a small increase if the price is \$300. A 4 ton increase in supply is large if the current supply is 10 tons, it is small if the current supply is 1000 tons.

An alternative measure of the responsiveness of supply to price is the *elasticity of supply* defined as

$$e_{yp} = \frac{p}{y}\frac{dy}{dp} \tag{38}$$

The point of this measure is that

$$\frac{p}{y}\frac{dy}{dp} \simeq \frac{p}{y}\frac{\Delta y}{\Delta p} = \frac{\Delta y/y}{\Delta p/p} \tag{39}$$

where Δy is the change in supply caused by a small change Δp in price, and where $\simeq$ means 'is approximately equal to'. The derivative of a function is only approximately equal to a ratio of actual changes in the dependent and independent variables, but the error in the approximation can be made as small as you like by considering a change Δp which is sufficiently small. Now the right-hand side of (39) is a ratio of *proportionate* (or percentage) changes in y and x. Thus the elasticity of supply measures the effect of changes in price or changes in supply, where each change is expressed as a proportion. For example a supply elasticity of 2 means that a 1% change in price ($\Delta p/p = 0.01$) will cause a change in quantity of approximately 2% ($\Delta y/y \simeq 0.02$).

It is easy to prove (see exercise 1.18) that

$$\frac{p}{y}\frac{dy}{dp} = \frac{d\log y}{d\log p} \tag{40}$$

We define analogously, for the demand function $x(p, m)$, the *price elasticity of demand* as

$$e_{xp} = \frac{p}{x}\frac{\partial x}{\partial p} \tag{41}$$

and the *income elasticity of demand* as

$$e_{xm} = \frac{m}{x}\frac{\partial x}{\partial m} \tag{42}$$

In the coffee and tea markets example there are *cross-price elasticities* which can be defined. The cross-elasticity of tea demand with respect to the price of coffee is

$$e_{xc}^t = \frac{\pi^c}{x^t}\frac{\partial x^t}{\partial \pi^c} \tag{43}$$

(Two minor irritants should be noted. (i) Since $\partial x/\partial p < 0$, e_{xp} will be negative. This is often taken for granted and the minus sign dropped from the statement of the elasticity. The statement 'the price elasticity of demand is 1.5' is to be interpreted as meaning that $e_{xp} = -1.5$. (ii) In contexts where it is clear that income effects and cross-price effects are not being discussed, price elasticities of demand and supply are often referred to simply as elasticities of demand and supply.)

Let us now look at how elasticities can be used to clarify the statement of some of our earlier results. In the sales tax example, results (13) and (14) can be rewritten as

$$\frac{dp}{dt} = \frac{e_{x\pi}}{(\pi/p)\,e_{yp} - e_{x\pi}} \tag{44}$$

$$\frac{d\pi}{dt} = \frac{(\pi/p)\,e_{yp}}{(\pi/p)\,e_{yp} - e_{x\pi}} \tag{45}$$

using the definitions of the elasticities and the fact that $x = y$ in equilibrium (where here we write the demand elasticity as $e_{x\pi}$ since $\pi \neq p$), and we see that writing the results in terms of the unit-free elasticities rather than the unit-dependent derivatives is achieved at the small cost of some additional complexity in the answers. However, unless the tax t is very large, the term π/p will not be very much greater than 1. Who then pays the tax? The answer is that the burden is shared by seller and consumer in the ratio of $-e_{x\pi}$ to $(\pi/p)e_{yp}$.

Some special cases are interesting. If $e_{yp} = 0$, then $d\pi/dt = 0$ and $dp/dt = -1$ so the burden of the tax falls entirely on the sellers. If, however, $e_{x\pi} = 0$, then $d\pi/dt = 1$ and $dp/dt = 0$ so the consumers bear the full burden of the tax. For given $e_{x\pi}$, the higher is e_{yp}, the more the burden of the tax falls on consumers; while given e_{yp}, the higher is $|e_{x\pi}|$ (the absolute value of $e_{x\pi}$), the more the burden of the tax falls on sellers. These results are easily illustrated in diagrams like figure 1.3. The limiting case is where either the demand curve or the supply curve is horizontal. Suppose it is the supply curve. Then there is one value of p at which suppliers are willing to supply any quantity. There is no well defined supply function $y = y(p)$, but since $dp/dy = 0$ it is natural to say that the supply elasticity is infinite. Since p is fixed and $\pi = p + t$, it follows that $d\pi/dt = 1$, and then $q = x(p + t)$. Again, a diagram like figure 1.3 illustrates the result; and also the result that if the demand elasticity is infinite, the tax falls entirely on sellers.

In the example involving income changes, results (25) and (26) can be rewritten as

$$\frac{m}{p}\frac{dp}{dm} = \frac{e_{xm}}{e_{yp} - e_{xp}} \tag{46}$$

$$\frac{m}{q}\frac{dq}{dm} = \frac{e_{xm}e_{yp}}{e_{yp} - e_{xp}} \tag{47}$$

using the definitions of the elasticities and the fact that $q = y = x$ in equilibrium. Note that the left-hand side of each equation is in elasticity form too. From (46) we see that in markets where price elasticities of both demand and supply are small, changes in consumers' income will cause large price changes.

We saw above that variables such as weather and fashion can be introduced into models of supply and demand in exactly the way consumers' income was introduced above. Thus we would expect that any exogenous change would have large effects on prices in markets where both demand and supply elasticities are small. There are good reasons to believe it is the case in many agricultural markets that demand and supply elasticities are small: and many agricultural markets do indeed exhibit substantial price variability, as the theory predicts.

1.10   *Elasticities in the short run and the long run*

In many markets it is likely that the immediate impact of an exogenous change will be different from the eventual effect. The reason is that elasticities of both demand and supply are likely to be greater in the long run than in the short run.

Consider a market for perishable goods: say fresh fish which deteriorate in quality within one day even if refrigerated. The fishmongers stock up in the morning and start selling. If demand is less than expected, they face the prospect of being left with unsold fish which cannot be stored for sale tomorrow so the price will be cut to the level at which all the stock will be sold.

This is illustrated in figure 1.6. Suppose that demand had for some time been as described by the demand curve $x_1(p)$, and equilibrium had been at A. The fishmongers are happy to sell the quantity q_1 daily at the price p_1. Now suppose that something causes the demand for fresh fish to decline: the demand curve shifts from $x_1(p)$ to $x_2(p)$. The fishmongers have the stock q_1 to sell and the price will have to be cut to p_2 because each fishmonger prefers to cut his price than be left with unsold fish. Essentially the supply curve is the vertical line y_1: the supply elasticity is zero.

But on subsequent days, the fishmongers have the possibility of varying the stock they have available for sale, and we would expect them to react to lower prices by reducing the quantity they supply. We have the supply curve $y_2(p)$ and a new equilibrium at C.

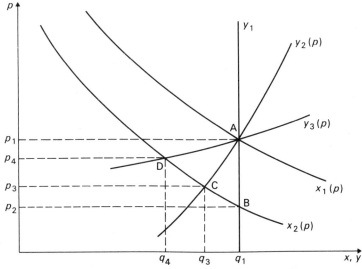

FIGURE 1.6   The market for a perishable good

Although C is an equilibrium in the sense that the fishmongers who together willingly supplied q_1 at the price p_1 now wish to supply q_3 at the price p_3, they clearly will be less happy with their situation than they were at the old equilibrium A. Faced with a lower price some may decide that they would be better off doing something entirely different. Some fish shops are closed or converted to the sale of other goods; some people who sold fish move to other occupations. The quantity supplied falls and the equilibrium point shifts along the demand curve to a point such as D. The supply curve is the more elastic curve $y_3(p)$.

A similar conclusion may well hold for the demand for many goods: at first, price increases may cause relatively small reductions in demand, as consumers' habits and plans are inflexible; but as time passes, they learn of cheaper alternative goods, and they change their plans and habits, so that they are able to reduce more substantially their consumption of the good whose price has risen. An example is the effect on consumer behaviour of rises in the price of energy (such as took place in the 1970s): it is hard to do anything immediately except pay the higher prices, but gradually people can acquire smaller cars, insulate their homes, get used to a wider range of temperatures, and so on. The demand function for energy which describes immediate consumer reaction is much less elastic than the function describing the eventual reaction.

The common use of the terms 'short run' and 'long run' should not lead one to think that the calendar is being inflexibly divided into two sorts of time period. The central idea is that elasticity of both demand and supply depend on the extent to which consumers' and sellers' present decisions are constrained by the effects of their previous decisions: the longer the time horizon relevant to whatever problem we are studying, the fewer are likely to be such constraints, the wider the range of options open to both consumers and sellers, and the larger, therefore, will be the elasticities.

1.11   Supply and demand for inputs

In many markets the suppliers of the good being traded will be firms whose business it is to produce such goods (firms can vary in shape and size from a shop owned and operated by a single person to a giant multi-national corporation), while the demanders will be individuals who wish to consume the good. There are, however, many goods which are bought by firms for use in the process of producing other goods: they are called *inputs*, in contrast with *outputs* which are the goods being produced.

Some goods are outputs of one type of firm and inputs of another type. They are called *intermediate* goods and include such things as steel plate, wheat and industrial chemicals.

Another category of goods is inputs which are not the product of some other production process: labour and land and other natural resources. They are called *factors of production*.

We shall later discuss in detail the theory of demand for inputs, both intermediates and factors. For the present, let us accept it as reasonably plausible that as the price of an input rises, firms will try to use less of it so that the demand will be a decreasing function of price, as with consumer goods.

The supply of intermediate goods should be no different from that of consumer goods; while for factors of production it is plausible that if a factor price rises, the owners of the factor will be willing to supply more of it.

Thus in input markets we can expect to have decreasing demand functions and increasing supply functions and we can apply the tools of supply and demand analysis which we have been developing above to such markets also.

1.12   *Economic rent*

There is, however, one possible outcome in the market for a factor of production which is of special interest. Some factors may be in fixed supply.

This situation is depicted in figure 1.7. Supply is fixed at q. When demand is $x_1(p)$ the equilibrium price is p_1; if demand falls to $x_2(p)$, price falls to p_2, and the income of the owners of the factor falls from $p_1 q$ to

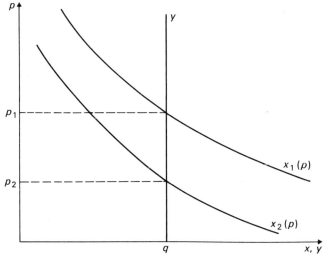

FIGURE 1.7   The market for a factor in fixed supply

p_2q. Clearly this income does not persuade the factor owners to supply q: they supply this amount whatever the price because they have no alternative. We say that their income is an *economic rent*.

That the same word 'rent' is used to denote the price paid to landlords for the use of their land is no accident. The owner of a particular type of land in a particular location has no better alternative but to rent it at whatever rent the market will bear. (He may, of course, use it himself, but this makes no real difference to the argument.) If, however, the payment received by land owners includes payments for services they provide or for improvements which they have made to their land then (since they do have the alternative of not providing services and making improvements) 'rent' and 'economic rent' are not synonymous.

We shall return to this topic later.

1.13   *Some warnings about supply and demand*

Some of the questions following this chapter are intended to give a flavour of the extraordinarily wide range of interesting and realistic economic problems that can be tackled using the simple techniques developed here. One must, however, be careful not to apply these techniques inappropriately, and three particular warnings are in order.

The first is that in the theory developed above we assume that both sellers and buyers are *price-takers*: they look at the price at which the good is being traded and they decide how much they wish to sell or buy at that price. There are many markets where this is not the case. It is unlikely that General Motors view the US car market as one in which they can choose to sell whatever number of cars they wish at the going price.

Actually it is impossible in any market for everyone to be a price-taker, for who then is responsible for the price reductions which are supposed to result from excess supply? The distinction must in reality be one of degree: between, on the one hand, 'competitive' markets where some sellers and/or buyers do set prices, but where each individual's or firm's position is so weak that they have very little choice about what price to set, and, on the other hand, markets where some sellers or buyers have considerable latitude in setting the price at which they are willing to trade. Supply and demand analysis can only be applied to the first category; and one has to judge whether any particular market is 'competitive enough' for the theory to be applicable to it.

Secondly, one must be careful about what is *a* market for *a* good. The examples above include a discussion of the egg market. But eggs come in different sizes, and are available in different places. Can we talk of the UK egg market, or should we discuss the market for size 2 brown eggs in

Cambridge separately from all the other egg markets? Obviously we can ignore trivial differences in the specification and location of different samples of the 'same' product, but judgement is required as to what differences are trivial, and this will depend on the particular purpose for which the analysis is being used.

Thirdly, the theory of supply and demand is what is called *partial equilibrium analysis*, which is to say it looks at the market for one good (or a small number of closely related goods, like tea and coffee) in isolation from the rest of the economy. In some cases this is an inappropriate way to proceed. It would, for example, be a mistake to analyse the market for labour in a whole country in a way that ignored the fact that the wages paid to workers are spent by them on goods, and the production of those goods requires the input of labour. Again, judgement is required as to when such interactions are sufficiently small to be ignored.

Indeed the need to make judgements is inescapable in the application of the theory developed here. *There is no market in the real world of which it is an exact description.* A large part of being a good economist is knowing the difference between a theoretical model which, though an inexact description of the real world, captures the essential features of the problem in hand, and theoretical models which miss crucial points. Whether the judgements made by the economic theorist in any particular case are good judgements is ultimately tested by the success or failure of the analysis in explaining observed behaviour. We should also remember that economists frequently disagree about the correct approach to particular issues or the correct answer to particular problems – though disagreement is not quite so common as the popular demonology about economics would have you believe.

Exercises

1.1   'If the demand for petrol rises (perhaps because more people have cars), this will tend to raise the price of petrol. But this contradicts the proposition that there is an inverse relationship between demand and price. Demand curves do not slope downwards.' Expose the fallacy in this argument.

1.2   Draw: (i) a supply-and-demand diagram in which $x(0) < y(0)$; (ii) one in which $p_x < p_y$, where $x(p_x) = 0$ and $y(p_y) = 0$ define p_x and p_y. In both cases, let $x'(p) < 0$ and $y'(p) > 0$. Remembering that prices and quantities cannot become negative, discuss what would be likely to happen in such markets. Is there an equilibrium price and/or quantity in either case?

1.3   Suppose that you were an egg-farmer and began to observe behaviour in the egg market that suggested that an unstable cobweb cycle was starting. What policy would you adopt if you wanted to make large profits? Does this suggest to you that unstable cobweb cycles are unlikely to persist?

1.4   Discuss: (a) the existence and (b) the stability of economically meaningful equilibria in the market described by

$$y_t = a + bp_{t-1}$$
$$x_t = \alpha - \beta p_t$$

where the subscripts refer to time periods and a, b, α, β are constants, b and β being positive. In particular, describe carefully what would actually happen in the cases where there is no equilibrium with positive price and quantity, or where the equilibrium is unstable. (Compare exercise 1.2.)

1.5   Discuss the market described by

$$y_t = bp_t^e$$
$$x_t = \alpha - \beta p_t$$
$$p_t^e = \gamma p^* + (1-\gamma) p_{t-1}$$

where p_t^e is the expected price at time t, p^* is the equilibrium price, and γ is a constant satisfying $0 < \gamma < 1$.

1.6   Suppose that the market for milk is in equilibrium at a price of p pence per pint. Analyse the effects of a subsidy of s pence per pint paid to milk producers.

1.7   Suppose the market described in figure 1.3 is in equilibrium at (p_1, q_1) when the government imposes on buyers the obligation to pay a tax t per unit bought. Describe how part of this tax will be passed on to sellers, so that the equilibrium outcome is the same as in the case discussed in the text, where the tax is imposed on sellers.

1.8   Given a diagrammatic exposition of the effect of a sales tax, but with π on the vertical axis, rather than p as in figure 1.3.

1.9   In a market in which there is a sales tax calculated as a *proportion* t of the price received by the seller so that $\pi = p(1 + t)$, analyse the comparative statics of a change in t.

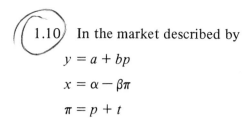

1.10 In the market described by

$$y = a + bp$$

$$x = \alpha - \beta\pi$$

$$\pi = p + t$$

derive explicit solutions for equilibrium prices and quantity as functions of t. Confirm that (13)–(15) hold. If the government wished to maximize tax revenue, at what level would it set t? What happens to equilibrium quantity if t is raised from 0 to the revenue maximizing level?

1.11 Suppose the market for wheat can be described by the following supply and demand functions:

$$y_t = 60p_{t-1} \qquad x_t = 11{,}000 - 50p_t$$

Prove that this will almost certainly give rise to fluctuations in price and quantity. Suppose that the government tries to stabilize the market by imposing a tax at the rate of s on the market price of wheat, so that the consumer price is $\pi_t = (1 + s)p_t$. Analyse mathematically the effects of this policy, show that it will stabilize the market if s is sufficiently large, and give an intuitive economic explanation of why this should be so.

1.12 Let $x(p, m) = 10p^{-1}m^2 + 5m$

(i) If $p = z^3$ and $m = e^{0.2w}$, confirm that (20) and (21) hold.
(ii) If $p = z^2$ and $m = e^z$, confirm that (22) holds.
(iii) If $p = \log_e m$, confirm that (23) holds.

1.13 In the market described by

$$y(p) = 2p$$

$$x(p, m) = 6m^2p^{-1} + m$$

solve explicitly for equilibrium price and quantity as functions of m and confirm that (26) and (27) hold.

1.14 In the market described by equation (28), discuss the effect of rainfall on the equilibrium, bearing in mind the possibility that both too little and too much rain may be harmful for crops.

1.15 (i) Analyse mathematically the effect of a rise in the demand for wool on the price of mutton. (ii) Analyse the effect of a fall in the demand for sugar on the price of coffee.

1.16 Suppose that in a city there are three types of housing: houses rented out by private landlords, houses occupied by their owners, and houses rented out by the local government (council houses). Assume that private rents and the cost of buying houses are determined freely in competitive markets. If there are fixed numbers of houses of each type, discuss the effects on private rents and on the cost of buying a house of an increase in the rents of the council houses.

Now suppose that the total number of houses is fixed, and that the number of council houses is fixed, but that other houses can change from being owner-occupied to being privately rented and vice versa. Outline the factors which will determine whether, in fact, houses will change from one type of tenure to another following the rise in council house rents.

If we now suppose that there is vacant land in and around the city which private builders can buy and use for the building of new houses, but the number of council houses remains fixed, what difference does this make to the outcome?

1.17   Is it possible for the numerator of the expression on the right-hand side of equation (36) to be negative even if the denominator is positive? How would you give an intuitive explanation of this possibility, if it does exist; or how would you explain its impossibility, if this is the case?

1.18   Prove the relationship stated in equation (40). If $y = ap^b$ where a and b are positive constants, find e_{yp}. Write the relationship $y = ap^b$ as a relationship between $\log y$ and $\log p$.

1.19   Write the results (35)–(37) in elasticity form.

1.20   Write your answer to exercise 1.9 in elasticity form.

1.21   If V is the value of goods supplied by the sellers of good y and if e is the elasticity of supply, prove that

$$\frac{dV}{dp} = y(1 + e)$$

1.22   Draw diagrams to illustrate the effect of a sales tax in the four cases: (i) $e_{yp} = 0$; (ii) $e_{yp} = \infty$; (iii) $e_{x\pi} = 0$; (iv) $e_{x\pi} = -\infty$.

1.23   For the demand function $x(p, m) = 6m^2p^{-1} + m$ find the price and income elasticities. Show that $1 < e_{xm} < 2$ and $-1 < e_{xp} < 0$, though neither is constant.

1.24   The elasticity of demand for cigarettes is constant at -1.2, the elasticity of supply is infinite. The consumer price of a packet of cigarettes is 50p of which 40p is tax. The government wishes both to discourage smoking and to raise its tax revenue. Is this possible? At what level of taxation would its tax revenue be maximized?

1.25 If the government increases the tax on alcoholic drinks with the aim of increasing tax revenue, can you deduce anything about its opinion of the price elasticity of demand for drink? (It may be easiest initially to consider the case of infinite supply elasticity.)

1.26 How would you modify your answers to exercises 1.6 and 1.14 if asked to take into account possible differences between short-run and long-run elasticities?

1.27 A government is attempting to reduce the amount of trade in illegal addictive narcotic drugs, both because of the ill-effects on consumers and because of the role of organized criminals as suppliers. Should it: (a) give limited quantities of narcotics free to registered addicts; or (b) increase the penalties for dealing in drugs and put more effort into catching offenders; or (c) do both (a) and (b); or (d) legalize the supply and consumption of narcotics? (You should think about what special features the demand of an addict might have, and remember that supply and demand analysis is applied to *market* supply and demand not to total supply and demand.)

1.28 'In 1980 the world demand for steel was low (because of continuing world recession in economic activity) and there had been major expansion of steel-producing capacity in many countries. As a result, steel prices were very low, and some producers were accused of 'dumping', that is of selling at prices below the cost of production. Such low prices could not be expected to persist in the long run.' Translate this verbal analysis into formal supply-and-demand analysis.

1.29 Suppose that the earnings of accountants are much higher than the earnings of people of similar ability in other occupations. What effect would you expect this to have in the long run on the number of people wishing to be accountants? What would happen to accountants' earnings in the long run? If the associations of accountants can control the number of people becoming accountants by raising standards in professional examinations and they wish to keep up the level of accountants' earnings, how should they react to the news that large numbers of university students wish to become accountants?

1.30   In the UK there is a tax on the employment of labour called national insurance contributions. Part of this tax is paid to the government by employers, the rest is paid by employees. The theory of supply and demand tells us that it is irrelevant who has the responsibility of actually paying the tax. Yet there is political controversy over how big the respective shares of employer and employee should be. Is there any explanation of the existence of this controversy other than simple ignorance of elementary economics by politicians?

1.31   'Immigration increases the labour supply and therefore must reduce wage rates.' Comment.

1.32   Frequently at major sporting events or popular concerts 'ticket touts' or 'scalpers' sell tickets at prices far above their original prices. What does this imply about the relation between the equilibrium price and the price set by the organization that originally sold the tickets? Is there a relationship between the equilibrium price and the 'black market' price obtained by touts? Why do you think such organizations do not sell tickets at their equilibrium price? Is it sensible for them to try to discourage the activities of touts, for example by refusing to sell tickets to known touts or by persuading the police to prosecute them?

1.33   (a) 'The price of a good is determined by what it costs to produce.'
   (b) 'The price of a good is what the consumer is willing to pay.'
   (c) 'Statements (a) and (b) cannot both be correct if the cost of production is different from what the consumer is willing to pay.'
   (d) 'We might as reasonably dispute whether it is the upper or the lower blade of a pair of scissors that cuts a paper, as whether value is governed by [what the consumer is willing to pay] or cost of production.' (Alfred Marshall, *Principles of Economics*, 1890)
   Discuss these four statements.

1.34   'In the price of every bottle of table wine sold by a wine merchant, at least 35p is accounted for by the expense of shipping, duty, and bottling so that the 55p bottle provides 20p worth of wine and the 80p bottle provides 45p worth of wine .... Broadly speaking, an 80p wine is more than twice as valuable as a 55p wine.' (A. Sichel, *The Penguin Book of Wines*, 1971) Is this good advice to the wine-drinker?

CHAPTER 2

The Theory of Producers' Behaviour

2.1 Introduction: the profit-maximizing firm

In the previous chapter we assumed, on the basis of a very brief and informal argument that the supply of a good is an increasing function of its price and the demand for an input is a decreasing function of its price. In this chapter, we develop a theory of producers' behaviour that justifies these elements of the theory of supply and demand.

The firms which produce and sell goods are in reality complex and heterogeneous organizations, whose range of activities and motivations are not easily summarized in a single theory. In our theory, however, we take a very simple view of what a firm does and why: a firm uses inputs whose quantities are denoted by $z_1, z_2, \ldots, z_n$ to produce an output whose quantity is denoted by y. The technical possibilities open to the firm are described by the *production function*

$$y = F(z_1, z_2, \ldots, z_n) \tag{1}$$

which shows the maximum quantity of output which can be produced from a set of input quantities. Different firms may have different production functions.

An example of a production function is the function

$$y = z_1^{1/2} z_2^{1/3} \tag{2}$$

which shows, for example, that with 4 units of the first input and 8 units of the second input the firm could produce 4 units of output.

The objective of the firm is assumed to be *profit maximization*. For the present we assume the firm faces *given* prices for output and inputs. If the inputs $z_1, z_2, \ldots, z_n$ have prices $w_1, w_2, \ldots, w_n$ respectively, the cost of inputs to the firm is $w_1 z_1 + w_2 z_2 + \ldots + w_n z_n$ which we write as

$$\sum_{i=1}^{n} w_i z_i$$

while if the price of output is p, the firm has sales revenue py. The firm's profits are therefore

$$py - \sum_{i=1}^{n} w_i z_i$$

and the firm tries to make this as large as possible. Recalling the relationship (1) between y and $z_1, z_2, \ldots, z_n$ we can write the firm's objective as

$$\underset{z_1, z_2, \ldots, z_n}{\text{maximize}} \; pF(z_1, z_2, \ldots, z_n) - \sum_{i=1}^{n} w_i z_i \tag{3}$$

where writing $z_1, z_2, \ldots, z_n$ below the word 'maximize' reminds us that these are the variables which the firm may choose, while the prices are given.

For the firm whose production function is (2) and which faces prices $p = 6, w_1 = 3, w_2 = 1$, (3) becomes

$$\underset{z_1, z_2}{\text{maximize}} \; 6z_1^{1/2} z_2^{1/3} - 3z_1 - z_2 \tag{4}$$

Maximizing a function of more than one variable is a little more difficult than maximizing a function of a single variable. If g is a function of x_1, x_2 then any point (x_1, x_2) at which *either* of the partial derivatives $\partial g/\partial x_1, \partial g/\partial x_2$ is not zero cannot be a maximum. For example, if $\partial g/\partial x_1 < 0$ we can increase the value of y by a small decrease in x_1 holding x_2 constant. Thus a necessary condition for the maximization of a function of more than one variable is that *all* of its partial derivatives should be zero.

Recall, however, that the derivative of a function of a single variable may be zero at points which are not maxima: if the function has a minimum or a point of inflexion, its derivative will be zero there. Similarly with functions of more than one variable the *necessary* condition that the partial derivatives all be zero is not *sufficient* to guarantee that we have found a maximum. For a function of a single variable, such as $y = f(x)$, if $f''(x_0) < 0$ as well as $f'(x_0) = 0$ then x_0 is a maximum. This is the case illustrated in figure 2.1. We say that the function $f(x)$ is *concave* in the neighbourhood of x_0.

Now consider the function $g(x_1, x_2)$. Any point in figure 2.2(a) represents a pair of values (x_1, x_2). Suppose that at the point A, $\partial g/\partial x_1$ and $\partial g/\partial x_2$ are both zero. Draw *any* straight line through A and choose *any* two points B and C on this line close to A and on opposite sides of A. We can graph the values of $g(x_1, x_2)$ along the line between B and C as in figure 2.2(b). If this graph has the same sort of concave shape as $f(x)$ in figure 2.1 for *all* lines through A then we say that $g(x_1, x_2)$ is concave in the neighbourhood of A, and clearly in this case g is maximized at A.

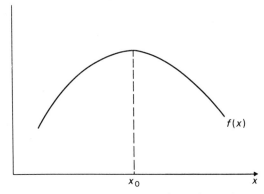

FIGURE 2.1   A concave function of x

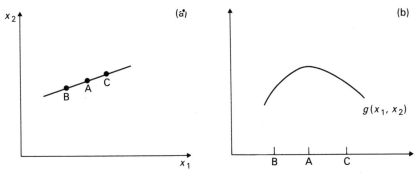

FIGURE 2.2   A concave function of (x_1, x_2)

Unfortunately this sufficient condition for maximization, that the function be concave in the neighbourhood of the point where its first derivatives are zero, does not translate into a simple condition analogous to the condition $f''(x_0) < 0$ in the case of a function of more than one variable. (It is easy to define second-order partial derivatives, but in exercise 2.2 at the end of this chapter you are asked to show from an example that the second-order partial derivatives of a function of two variables being negative is *not* sufficient to ensure that a point where the first-order derivatives are zero is a maximum.)

Returning now to the problem (4) and setting the derivatives of the function equal to zero gives

$$3z_1^{-1/2} z_2^{1/3} - 3 = 0$$

$$2z_1^{1/2} z_2^{-2/3} - 1 = 0$$

(5)

and it is easily checked that $z_1 = 4$, $z_2 = 8$ are the only values which satisfy both equations. To be sure that $z_1 = 4$, $z_2 = 8$ really do maximize profits we should check that the function in (4) is concave at this point. However, we have not yet developed a simple method of checking this, so the best we can do is calculate the value of the function at enough points where $z_1 \neq 4$ and/or $z_2 \neq 8$ to convince ourselves that we have indeed found a maximum.

In the general problem (3), setting all the partial derivatives equal to zero gives n *first-order conditions*:

$$p \frac{\partial F}{\partial z_i} = w_i \qquad i = 1, 2, \ldots, n \tag{6}$$

There is a simple economic rationale for these conditions. The right-hand side of equation (6) is the cost of using an extra unit of input i. The left-hand side is the effect on output of an extra unit of input i multiplied by the price of output. $\partial F/\partial z_i$ is called the *marginal product* of input i, and $p \, \partial F/\partial z_i$, the *value of the marginal product*, is the revenue received as a result of using an extra unit of input i. If the firm had chosen a set of inputs $(z_1, z_2, \ldots, z_n)$ at which, for example, $p \, \partial F/\partial z_1 < w_1$, it could raise its profits by reducing the amount of z_1, for this would subtract more from costs than from revenue.

There are, however, some apparently quite simple production functions for which the first-order conditions do not give solutions to the profit-maximizing problem. Try to find the profit-maximizing inputs in the following cases: (a) $y = z_1^{1/2} z_2^{1/2}$, $p = 2$, $w_1 = 1$, $w_2 = 1$; (b) $y = z_1^{1/2} z_2^{1/2}$, $p = 2$, $w_1 = 2$, $w_2 = 1$. A purely mathematical diagnosis of the trouble with these examples would show that the problem lies with the second-order conditions which we have not yet properly discussed. However, we shall see that thinking about the *economics* of the profit-maximizing firm is more helpful than a purely mathematical approach.

2.2 Vectors

When we deal with a list of variables such as $(z_1, z_2, \ldots, z_n)$ it is convenient to adopt a more compact notation. We call such a list a *vector* and write it as z. Similarly, we have a vector of input prices $\mathbf{w} = (w_1, w_2, \ldots, w_n)$. The sum $\sum_{i=1}^{n} w_i z_i$ is called a *scalar product* of vectors w, z and is written wz.

If every entry in the vector z is multiplied by the number k we obtain the vector $(kz_1, kz_2, \ldots, kz_n)$ which is written kz.

If x is the vector $(x_1, x_2, \ldots, x_n)$ and y is the vector $(y_1, y_2, \ldots, y_n)$ then x + y is the vector $(x_1 + y_1, x_2 + y_2, \ldots, x_n + y_n)$ and x − y is the vector $(x_1 - y_1, x_2 - y_2, \ldots, x_n - y_n)$.

Using this notation we can rewrite (3) as

$$\text{maximize } pF(\mathbf{z}) - \mathbf{wz} \qquad (7)$$

and (6) as

$$p\frac{\partial F}{\partial \mathbf{z}} = \mathbf{w} \qquad (8)$$

where $\partial F/\partial \mathbf{z} = (\partial F/\partial z_1, \partial F/\partial z_2, \ldots, \partial F/\partial z_n)$.

For the purposes of this book vectors can be regarded purely as a space-saving notation. If you find any expression involving vectors at all hard to follow, write it out fully in 'ordinary' notation.

2.3   Returns to scale and returns to inputs

We now need to look in more detail at the properties of production functions. In the case of a two-input production function we can draw a diagram which helps to clarify matters. In figure 2.3, the input quantities z_1 and z_2 are on the axes while the different possible values of y are drawn as contours in the graph. These contours are called *isoquants*. Thus the curved line marked $y = 10$ shows all the values of (z_1, z_2) for which $F(z_1, z_2) = 10$. This isoquant diagram also shows the $y = 20$ and $y = 30$ isoquants, and it should be obvious why the isoquants further from the origin correspond to higher levels of output. It will not be obvious why the isoquants are drawn bowed in towards the origin, but the explanation of this will have to wait.

We should be interested in how output responds to changes in inputs. There are two distinct types of input change which we shall consider. The first is exemplified by the arrow from A to B in the isoquant diagram. With z_2 constant, z_1 is being increased. A similar move is represented by a move from A to C in the diagram, where z_2 is increasing with z_1 constant.

In the general case of the production function $y = F(z_1, z_2, \ldots, z_n)$ the effect of such a move is measured by the partial derivative. If z_i changes *with all other inputs being held constant*, the change in y is given by $\partial F/\partial z_i$. This partial derivative, which can also be written $\partial y/\partial z_i$ or F_i, is the marginal product of input i.

It is generally assumed that a production function has the property that the marginal product $\partial F/\partial z_i$ should decrease as z_i increases. This property is called *diminishing returns* to input i, and is illustrated in figure 2.4 which shows the relationship between y and z_1 for given values of $z_2, z_3, \ldots, z_n$. If we think of the isoquant diagram as a contour map of a hill, where the value of y at any point is the height of the ground at that point, then

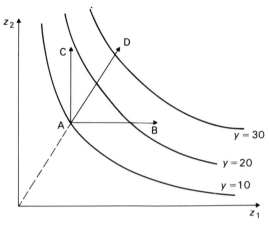

FIGURE 2.3   An isoquant diagram

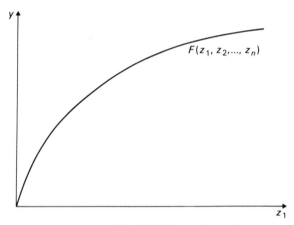

FIGURE 2.4   Diminishing returns to z_1

figure 2.4 (for $n = 2$) shows a cross-section through the hill taken along an 'east–west' line such as the one through AB.

Usually it will be obvious whether or not $\partial F/\partial z_i$ is decreasing in z_i, but in case of doubt one can differentiate $\partial F/\partial z_i$ with respect to z_i to get

$$\frac{\partial^2 F}{\partial z_i^2} = \frac{\partial}{\partial z_i}\left(\frac{\partial F}{\partial z_i}\right) \tag{9}$$

the second-order partial derivative. For diminishing returns we require $\partial^2 F/\partial z_i^2 < 0$.

It is also interesting to consider a second type of input change, where *all* inputs vary together at the same rate. This is exemplified in figure 2.3 by the arrow from A to D which, since it points directly from the origin, represents an equiproportionate increase in z_1 and z_2. In general, to apply such an increase to the input vector z we simply multiply it by a constant k to get the new vector $k\mathbf{z}$. For example, the vector $2\mathbf{z}$ has exactly twice as much of all inputs as the vector z.

If for $k > 1$

$$F(k\mathbf{z}) = kF(\mathbf{z}) \tag{10}$$

the production function is said to have *constant returns to scale*; while if

$$F(k\mathbf{z}) > kF(\mathbf{z}) \tag{11}$$

the function has *increasing returns to scale*; and if

$$F(k\mathbf{z}) < kF(\mathbf{z}) \tag{12}$$

the function has *decreasing returns to scale*. That is, if we increase all inputs by a given percentage, output will rise by (a) the same, (b) a larger, or (c) a smaller percentage as the production function has (a) constant, (b) increasing, or (c) decreasing returns to scale.

For example, the production function $y = z_1^{1/2} z_2^{1/2}$ has diminishing returns to both inputs and constant returns to scale; while the production function $y = z_1^{2/3} z_2^{1/2}$ has diminishing returns to both inputs and increasing returns to scale. These examples emphasize the point that returns to inputs and returns to scale are different properties, a point which can be reinforced by a glance back at the arrows in the isoquant diagram, figure 2.3.

2.4   *Cost minimization*

In the discussion above of the problem of profit maximization, we ran into some mathematical difficulties. Let us therefore retreat to the discussion of a more modest objective for the firm: suppose that it knows the level of output y it wishes to produce, and its objective is simply to minimize the cost of producing this output. Formally, this objective can be written as

$$\underset{\mathbf{z}}{\text{minimize }} \mathbf{wz} \tag{13}$$

$$\text{subject to } F(\mathbf{z}) = y$$

where y is a constant. This is a *constrained optimization* problem: the variables being chosen to minimize the function wz must be chosen subject to the constraint of satisfying $F(\mathbf{z}) = y$.

We follow an apparently strange procedure to solve this problem. Define a *Lagrangean function*

$$L(\mathbf{z}, \lambda) = \mathbf{wz} + \lambda(y - F(\mathbf{z})) \tag{14}$$

consisting of the function we are trying to minimize, added to the product of a new variable λ (called a Lagrange multiplier) and the function which is constrained to equal zero. The Lagrangean is a function of $n + 1$ variables, $z_1, z_2, \ldots, z_n, \lambda$. Differentiate it with respect to each of these variables and equate the derivatives to zero to give $n + 1$ equations:

$$w_i - \lambda \, \partial F / \partial z_i = 0 \qquad i = 1, \ldots, n \tag{15}$$

$$y - F(\mathbf{z}) = 0 \tag{16}$$

The values of $z_1, z_2, \ldots, z_n$ which solve problem (13) must satisfy equations (15) and (16), for the following reason. (15) can be re-written as

$$\lambda = \frac{w_i}{\partial F / \partial z_i} \qquad i = 1, \ldots, n \tag{15a}$$

Now w_i is the cost of an extra unit of input i, while $\partial F / \partial z_i$ is the product of that extra unit. Thus their ratio is the cost per unit (or _marginal cost_) of obtaining more output by using more of input i. Suppose (15a) were not satisfied so that, say, $w_1/(\partial F/\partial z_1) > w_2/(\partial F/\partial z_2)$. Then the cost of producing the fixed quantity y of output can be reduced by reducing z_1 a little and raising z_2 by enough to keep $F(z_1, z_2, z_3, \ldots, z_n)$ constant. We have established that problem (13) is not being solved if (15) is not satisfied, so that the n equations in (15) are necessary conditions for the solution of (13). That equation (16) is also a necessary condition is obvious: it is the constraint which has to be satisfied.

Thus the strange procedure of defining and differentiating the Lagrangean function can be regarded as simply a device that produces necessary conditions for the solution of the constrained optimization problem (13).

In the case where there are only two inputs z_1 and z_2 we can give a diagrammatic illustration of the solution of the cost-minimizing problem. Suppose we are faced with the specific problem

$$\text{minimize} \quad 2z_1 + \tfrac{1}{2}z_2$$
$$\underset{z_1, z_2}{}$$
$$\text{subject to } z_1^{1/2} z_2^{1/2} = 4 \tag{17}$$

In figure 2.5 the constraint $z_1^{1/2} z_2^{1/2} = 4$ is shown as the single isoquant $y = 4$. The value of cost is $2z_1 + \tfrac{1}{2}z_2$, which varies with z_1 and z_2. The straight line joining the point $z_1 = 2$, $z_2 = 0$ to the point $z_1 = 0$, $z_2 = 8$ represents all the points such that input cost is 4. Such a line is called an _isocost_ line. It is a contour of the function $2z_1 + \tfrac{1}{2}z_2$ just as an isoquant is a contour of the function $F(z_1, z_2)$. In the diagram, the isocost lines corresponding to input costs of 8 and of 12 are also drawn. The isocost lines are a series of parallel straight lines, with the isocost lines nearer the origin representing lower levels of input cost.

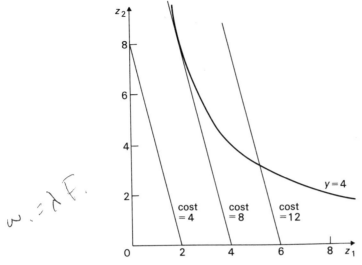

FIGURE 2.5   Cost minimization subject to $y = 4$

Now the objective specifed in (17) can be seen in diagrammatic terms as attaining the point on the given isoquant that is on the lowest possible isocost line. That point is $z_1 = 2$, $z_2 = 8$ on the isocost line $2z_1 + \frac{1}{2}z_2 = 8$. At that point the isocost line is tangent to the isoquant.

It is easily confirmed that the Lagrangean technique gives the same answer. The Lagrangean is

$$L(z_1, z_2, \lambda) = 2z_1 + \tfrac{1}{2}z_2 + \lambda(4 - z_1^{1/2}z_2^{1/2}) \tag{18}$$

whose derivatives equated to zero give the three equations:

$$2 = \tfrac{1}{2}\lambda z_1^{-1/2}z_2^{1/2}$$
$$\tfrac{1}{2} = \tfrac{1}{2}\lambda z_1^{1/2}z_2^{-1/2} \tag{19}$$
$$4 = z_1^{1/2}z_2^{1/2}$$

Eliminating λ from the first two equations gives $z_2 = 4z_1$ and substituting in the third equation we obtain $z_1 = 2$, $z_2 = 8$ (and $\lambda = 2$) as the solution of (19), and this gives a value of $2z_1 + \tfrac{1}{2}z_2$ of 8.

In general, with two inputs, the constraint $F(z_1, z_2) = y$ gives us an isoquant, which *we continue to assume without justification* is bowed in towards the origin, while a typical isocost line is given by $w_1z_1 + w_2z_2 = c$. Rewriting this equation as $z_2 = c/w_1 - (w_2/w_1)z_1$, and recalling that w_1, w_2 are constants, we see that the slope of an isocost line is constant and equal to $-w_2/w_1$, while the intercept with the z_2 axis is c/w_1 which rises with c, so that as c varies we get a series of isocost lines, parallel to each other, the lines further from the origin representing higher levels of input cost.

The solution to the cost-minimizing problem is at the point where an isocost line is tangent to the isoquant, for the tangent isocost line is the line closest to the origin that has a point on the isoquant. This solution is illustrated in figure 2.6. Now $F(z_1, z_2) = y$ defines z_2 as an implicit function of z_1. Differentiating both sides of this equation with respect to z_1, recalling that y is constant on an isoquant, and using the techniques developed in the previous chapter, gives

$$F_1 + F_2 \left(\frac{dz_2}{dz_1} \right)_y = 0 \tag{20}$$

where $(dz_2/dz_1)_y$ means the derivative of the implicit function defined by the y isoquant. Thus the slope of the isoquant is that derivative, that is

$$\left(\frac{dz_2}{dz_1} \right)_y = -\frac{F_1}{F_2} \tag{21}$$

Since F_1 and F_2 are both positive, this slope is negative: as we see also from the diagram. Since F_1 and F_2 are themselves functions of z_1 and z_2, the slope is generally different at different points along the isoquant.

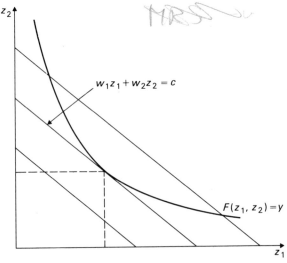

FIGURE 2.6   Cost minimization subject to $F(z_1, z_2) = y$

Thus we have established that the absolute value of the slope of the isoquant is given by the ratio of marginal products. This ratio is called the *marginal rate of substitution*, because it is the rate at which z_2 can be substituted for z_1 while keeping y constant.

The solution to the cost-minimizing problem is given then by the two requirements that the point (z_1, z_2) should be: (a) on the isoquant; (b) where the slope of the isoquant is equal to the slope of the isocost lines. These requirements translate into two equations

$$F(z_1, z_2) = y$$
$$\frac{F_1(z_1, z_2)}{F_2(z_1, z_2)} = \frac{w_1}{w_2} \tag{22}$$

which are the equations that are alternatively obtained by equating the derivatives of the Lagrangean $L(z_1, z_2, \lambda) = w_1 z_1 + w_2 z_2 + \lambda(y - F(z_1, z_2))$ to zero and then eliminating λ (see (15) and (16)).

The diagrammatic approach has the disadvantage of being confined to problems with only two inputs. However, the argument justifying the Lagrangean procedure makes it clear that the conditions derived are only *necessary* conditions for a solution to (13), but the diagram shows us what the sufficient condition is. If in figure 2.6 the isoquant were bowed out from the origin rather than in to the origin, the tangency point between isocost line and isoquant would have been a point where the cost of producing y was maximized rather than minimized. Therefore, in the two-input case the first-order necessary conditions (15) and (16) (or, equivalently, (22)) need to be accompanied by the additional requirement that the isoquant is bowed in towards the origin for the first-order conditions to give a solution to the problem.

If a production function has isoquants bowed in to the origin it is said to be *quasi-concave*. Formally, quasi-concavity requires that if A and B are any two points on the same isoquant then the straight line between A and B is either above or on the isoquant. The simplest way to check whether this condition is satisfied is to find how the marginal rate of substitution varies with z_1/z_2. In figure 2.6 as z_1/z_2 increases along the isoquant, the slope changes from being steep to being shallow; that is the marginal rate of substitution is a decreasing function of z_1/z_2:

$$\frac{d(F_1/F_2)}{d(z_1/z_2)} \leqslant 0 \tag{23}$$

A production function with this property of *diminishing marginal rate of substitution* is clearly quasi-concave; so that if (23) is satisfied by the production function, the solution to (22) is indeed the solution to the cost-minimizing problem.

When there are more than two inputs in the production function we can still define the property of quasi-concavity and this is the sufficient condition for (15) and (16) to solve (13), but there is no simple way like (23) to check quasi-concavity.

2.5   The elasticity of substitution

From (22) we see that in the two-input case the marginal rate of substitution is equated to the input price ratio to minimize costs. The marginal rate of substitution depends on the ratio of input quantities z_1/z_2. From (23), or from figure 2.6, we see that a rise in w_1/w_2 causes a fall in z_1/z_2. The size of the resulting fall depends on the shape of the isoquant – the less curved is the isoquant, the larger the change. We measure the sensitivity of the z_1/z_2 to changes in w_1/w_2 by the *elasticity of substitution*

$$\sigma = \frac{w_1/w_2}{z_1/z_2} \frac{d(z_1/z_2)}{d(w_1/w_2)} \tag{24}$$

which is, of course, negative.

The size of this elasticity determines what happens to the *share* of the firm's costs paid out to each input as the price ratio changes:

$$\frac{d(w_1 z_1/w_2 z_2)}{d(w_1/w_2)} = \frac{z_1}{z_2} + \frac{w_1}{w_2} \frac{d(z_1/z_2)}{d(w_1/w_2)} = \frac{z_1}{z_2}(1+\sigma) \tag{25}$$

Hence if $\sigma > -1$ (that is, $|\sigma| < 1$) a rise in w_i raises the share of input i; but if $\sigma < -1$ (that is $|\sigma| > 1$) a rise in w_i reduces the share of input i.

For example, if $y = (z_1^{1/2} + z_2^{1/2})^2$ then F_1/F_2 is $(z_2/z_1)^{1/2}$ so that the cost-minimizing input ratio satisfies

$$\frac{z_1}{z_2} = \left(\frac{w_1}{w_2}\right)^{-2} \tag{26}$$

and

$$\sigma = \frac{w_1/w_2}{z_1/z_2}(-2)\left(\frac{w_1}{w_2}\right)^{-3} = -2 \tag{27}$$

while

$$\frac{w_1 z_1}{w_2 z_2} = \left(\frac{w_1}{w_2}\right)^{-1} \tag{28}$$

showing that each input share is a decreasing function of its price, corresponding to the fact that the (absolute value of the) elasticity of substitution exceeds one.

2.6   The cost function and the interpretation of the Lagrange multiplier

The equations (15) and (16) are $n+1$ equations in the variables $z_1, z_2, \ldots, z_n$ and λ. When we solve those equations, we obtain values of the $n+1$ variables which will depend on the values of $w_1, w_2, \ldots, w_n$ and y in the original problem. We write the solutions as $z_1(\mathbf{w}, y), z_2(\mathbf{w}, y), \ldots, z_n(\mathbf{w}, y)$, $\lambda(\mathbf{w}, y)$ to remind ourselves of this dependence. Note also that $z_i(\mathbf{w}, y)$ is the *optimal* value of z_i given $\mathbf{w}$ and y.

The actual value of the cost of producing y when costs are minimized is therefore $\Sigma_{i=1}^n w_i z_i(\mathbf{w}, y)$. This is called the *cost function* and is written

$$c(\mathbf{w}, y) = \mathbf{w} \mathbf{z}(\mathbf{w}, y) \qquad (29)$$

where $\mathbf{z}(\mathbf{w}, y)$ is the vector $(z_1(\mathbf{w}, y), \ldots, z_n(\mathbf{w}, y))$. Again note that $c(\mathbf{w}, y)$ is the minimum cost given $\mathbf{w}$ and y. For example, with two inputs the cost function is

$$c(w_1, w_2, y) = w_1 z_1(w_1, w_2, y) + w_2 z_2(w_1, w_2, y) \qquad (30)$$

A by-product of the solution of (15) and (16) is the value $\lambda(\mathbf{w}, y)$ which the Lagrange multiplier takes. In view of the discussion of equations (15a) above, it is not surprising that this value has economic significance. If we differentiate $c(\mathbf{w}, y)$ with respect to y, we obtain

$$\frac{\partial c(\mathbf{w}, y)}{\partial y} = \sum_{i=1}^n w_i \frac{\partial z_i(\mathbf{w}, y)}{\partial y} \qquad (31)$$

But we are looking at what happens to the solution of (15) and (16) as y changes. The fact that (15) is satisfied gives

$$\sum_{i=1}^n w_i \frac{\partial z_i(\mathbf{w}, y)}{\partial y} = \lambda \sum_{i=1}^n \frac{\partial F}{\partial z_i} \frac{\partial z_i(\mathbf{w}, y)}{\partial y} \qquad (32)$$

while (16) differentiated with respect to y implies that

$$1 = \sum_{i=1}^n \frac{\partial F_i}{\partial z_i} \frac{\partial z_i(\mathbf{w}, y)}{\partial y} \qquad (33)$$

so (31), (32) and (33) together give

$$\frac{\partial c(\mathbf{w}, y)}{\partial y} = \lambda(\mathbf{w}, y) \qquad (34)$$

and we have the important result that the value of the Lagrange multiplier is the effect on cost of a change in the required output, that is it measures the *marginal cost* of output. This fits in exactly with the earlier discussion of equations (15a), where we saw that the functions which were equated to λ were interpreted as measuring marginal cost.

2.7   An example of cost minimization

Consider the cost-minimization problem of a firm whose production function is $z_1^{\alpha} z_2^{1-\alpha}$ where α is a constant satisfying $0 < \alpha < 1$, when the firm wishes to produce y and input prices are $w_1\, w_2$. The problem is

$$\text{minimize } w_1 z_1 + w_2 z_2 \tag{35}$$

$$\text{subject to } z_1^{\alpha} z_2^{1-\alpha} = y$$

The Lagrangean

$$L(z_1, z_2, \lambda) = w_1 z_1 + w_2 z_2 + \lambda(y - z_1^{\alpha} z_2^{1-\alpha})$$

gives first-order conditions

$$w_1 - \lambda \alpha z_1^{\alpha-1} z_2^{1-\alpha} = 0$$

$$w_2 - \lambda(1-\alpha)\, z_1^{\alpha} z_2^{-\alpha} = 0 \tag{36}$$

$$y - z_1^{\alpha} z_2^{1-\alpha} = 0$$

which can be simplified to

$$w_1 = \lambda \alpha y / z_1$$

$$w_2 = \lambda(1-\alpha)\, y / z_2 \tag{36a}$$

$$y = z_1^{\alpha} z_2^{1-\alpha}$$

and solved to give

$$z_1(w_1, w_2, y) = \left(\frac{\alpha}{1-\alpha}\frac{w_2}{w_1}\right)^{1-\alpha} y$$

$$z_2(w_1, w_2, y) = \left(\frac{1-\alpha}{\alpha}\frac{w_1}{w_2}\right)\left(\frac{\alpha}{1-\alpha}\frac{w_2}{w_1}\right)^{1-\alpha} y = \left(\frac{1-\alpha}{\alpha}\frac{w_1}{w_2}\right)^{\alpha} y \tag{37}$$

$$\lambda(w_1, w_2, y) = \left(\frac{w_1}{\alpha}\right)^{\alpha}\left(\frac{w_2}{1-\alpha}\right)^{1-\alpha}$$

so that

$$c(w_1, w_2, y) = \left(\frac{\alpha}{1-\alpha}\frac{w_2}{w_1}\right)^{1-\alpha}\left(w_1 + \frac{1-\alpha}{\alpha}w_1\right) y$$

$$= \left(\frac{w_1}{\alpha}\right)^{\alpha}\left(\frac{w_2}{1-\alpha}\right)^{1-\alpha} y \tag{38}$$

which confirms that (34) is true.

It remains to check that the diminishing marginal rate of substitution condition holds:

$$\frac{F_1}{F_2} = \frac{\alpha}{1-\alpha}\frac{z_1^{\alpha-1} z_2^{1-\alpha}}{z_1^{\alpha} z_2^{-\alpha}} = \frac{\alpha}{1-\alpha}\frac{z_2}{z_1} \tag{39}$$

and it is clear that (23) is satisfied, so that the functions defined by (37) and (38) do indeed describe the cost-minimizing solution.

Finally, note that from (36a) it is easily seen that $z_1/z_2 = \alpha w_2/(1-\alpha) w_1$ which implies that the elasticity of substitution has the value $|\sigma| = 1$ here; and relative factor shares $(w_1 z_1)/(w_2 z_2)$ are indeed constant at $\alpha/(1-\alpha)$.

2.8   Returns to scale and the cost function

The cost of production $c(\mathbf{w}, y)$ depends on output for the simple reason that more output requires more inputs. The exact form of the dependence of $c(\mathbf{w}, y)$ on y therefore depends on how output changes as inputs change. What information about the production function is relevant? If there are diminishing returns to inputs, we know something about what happens if only *one* changes. But if output increases, it seems likely that *all* inputs will increase (though this is not necessarily so, as we shall see) so the nature of returns to inputs does not seem relevant. On the other hand, we have no reason to believe that all inputs will increase *proportionately*, so it is not obvious that returns to scale are relevant either. It may not be obvious, but it is true, as we shall now see.

The arguments are essentially simple. With increasing returns we can more then double output by doubling the quantity of all inputs, which doubles costs. The minimum cost of producing $2y$ is therefore less than twice the cost of y. With decreasing returns, if we halve inputs we less than halve output, so the minimum cost of $y/2$ is less than half the cost of y. It is left to you, as exercise 2.15, to give a purely verbal explanation of the constant returns case.

For clarity, throughout this section from now on, the dependence of the cost-minimizing inputs $\mathbf{z}(\mathbf{w}, y)$ and of the cost function $c(\mathbf{w}, y)$ on the input prices will not be made explicit. Since the input prices are constant throughout, the functions will be written simply as $\mathbf{z}(y)$ and $c(y)$.

If the production function $y = F(\mathbf{z})$ has increasing returns to scale, then by definition $F(k\mathbf{z}) > kF(\mathbf{z})$ for $k > 1$. Therefore

$$kc(y) = k\mathbf{w}\mathbf{z}(y) = \sum_{i=1}^{n} w_i k z_i(y) > c(ky) \tag{40}$$

where the inequality follows from the fact that $k\mathbf{z}(y)$ will produce more than ky of output because of increasing returns, so the minimum cost of producing ky must be less than the cost of $k\mathbf{z}$.

If $y = F(\mathbf{z})$ has decreasing returns to scale, then $F(k\mathbf{z}) < kF(\mathbf{z})$ for $k > 1$. Since this holds for all $\mathbf{z}$, it holds for $(1/k)\mathbf{z}$, so we can write

$$F(\mathbf{z}) < kF\left(\frac{1}{k}\mathbf{z}\right),$$

that is

$$\frac{1}{k} F(\mathbf{z}) < F\left(\frac{1}{k}\mathbf{z}\right) \qquad \text{for } k > 1.$$

Thus

$$\frac{1}{k} c(y) = \frac{1}{k} \mathbf{wz}(y) = \sum_{i=1}^{n} w_i \frac{1}{k} z_i(y) > c\left(\frac{1}{k}y\right) \tag{41}$$

by essentially the same argument as (40) except that now the inequality follows from the fact that $(1/k)\,\mathbf{z}(y)$ will produce more than $(1/k)\,y$ of output because of decreasing returns.

If $y = F(\mathbf{z})$ has constant returns to scale, then $F(k\mathbf{z}) = kF(\mathbf{z})$ for $k > 1$ and this implies that

$$kc(y) = k\mathbf{wz}(y) \geqslant c(ky) \tag{42}$$

for, since $k\mathbf{z}(y)$ is a possible method of producing ky, the optimal method of production cannot cost more. But (42) holds for all k and y so applying it to $1/k$ and ky we obtain

$$\frac{1}{k} c(ky) \geqslant c(y) \tag{43}$$

But $c(ky) \leqslant kc(y) \leqslant c(ky)$ implies that

$$c(ky) = kc(y) \tag{44}$$

Given the cost function $c(y)$, we define *average cost* as $c(y)/y$. With increasing returns to scale, (40) implies that

$$\frac{c(y)}{y} > \frac{c(ky)}{ky} \qquad k > 1 \tag{45}$$

so that average cost *falls* as y rises. With decreasing returns, (41) implies

$$\frac{c(y)}{y} > \frac{c(y/k)}{y/k} \qquad k > 1 \tag{46}$$

so average cost *rises* as y rises. With constant returns, (44) implies

$$\frac{c(y)}{y} = \frac{c(ky)}{ky} \qquad k > 1 \tag{47}$$

so average cost is *constant* as y changes. The three cases are illustrated in figure 2.7.

Look back at the example discussed in the previous section: the production function has constant returns to scale and average cost is independent of y.

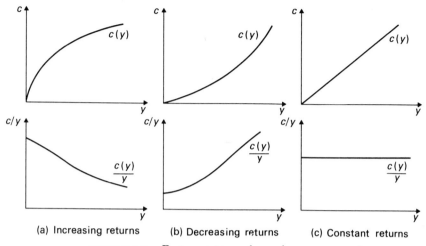

FIGURE 2.7   Returns to scale and average cost

2.9   *Profit maximization again*

The discussion of cost minimization concerns *how to produce* a given quantity y; but now we can turn to the question of *how much to produce*.

If the firm facing the profit-maximization problem:

$$\text{maximize } py - \mathbf{w}\mathbf{z}$$
$$\begin{array}{c} y, z \end{array}$$

$$\text{subject to } y = F(\mathbf{z})$$

(48)

(which is another way of writing problem (3)) has solved the cost-minimizing problem (13) and derived its cost function $c(\mathbf{w}, y)$, then problem (48) becomes the simpler profit-maximization problem:

$$\text{maximize } py - c(\mathbf{w}, y)$$
$$\begin{array}{c} y \end{array}$$

(49)

This is a one-variable maximization, whose solution is simple. For a maximum it is necessary that the derivative of profits with respect to y be zero:

$$p - \frac{\partial c(\mathbf{w}, y)}{\partial y} = 0$$

(50)

and sufficient that, in addition, the second derivative be negative:

$$-\frac{\partial^2 c(\mathbf{w}, y)}{\partial y^2} < 0$$

(51)

Although the mathematics is simple, it is worth pausing briefly to look at the economic interpretation of these conditions, which state that the firm should choose an output level where the marginal cost is equal to the price of output, and where <u>marginal cost is an increasing function of output.</u>

Consider figure 2.8. At A, marginal cost exceeds price so production of an extra unit adds more to costs than is earned by selling it at the price p. Profits can therefore be increased by reducing output. Conversely at C, it pays to raise output; while B is a point of maximum profits. Even though at D, price is equal to marginal cost, examination of how the firm should change output at points such as C and E shows that D is a point of *minimum* profits (or maximum losses).

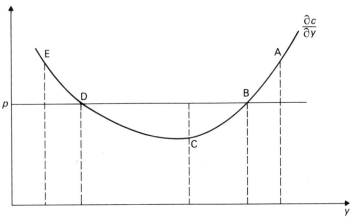

FIGURE 2.8   Profit maximization

If the sufficiency condition (51) is satisfied, then equation (50) determines the profit-maximizing value of y which will be a function of p and $\mathbf{w}$, so that we write it as $y(p, \mathbf{w})$. Clearly, the values of the z_i which minimize the cost of producing $y(p, \mathbf{w})$ are the ones which are chosen by the profit-maximizing firm, so that the profit-maximizing input vector $\mathbf{z}(p, \mathbf{w})$ is related to the cost-minimizing input vector by

$$\mathbf{z}(p, \mathbf{w}) = \mathbf{z}(\mathbf{w}, y(p, \mathbf{w})) \tag{52}$$

Recall that $z_i(\mathbf{w}, y)$ is the *optimal* value of z_i, the value chosen to minimize the cost of producing a fixed output. Now $z_i(p, \mathbf{w})$ is also an optimal value of z_i, but optimal for a different problem, being the value chosen to maximize profits when both inputs and output are variable. The two functions are different and should be carefully distinguished.

The functions $\mathbf{z}(\mathbf{w}, y)$ give the quantities of inputs which a cost-minimizing firm will wish to buy, and they are therefore called the *input demand functions of the cost-minimizing firm*. The functions $\mathbf{z}(p, \mathbf{w})$ similarly are the *input demand functions of the profit-maximizing firm*. The function $y(p, \mathbf{w})$ shows how much output a profit-maximizing firm wishes to sell: it is the *supply function of the profit-maximizing firm*.

2.10   *A profit-maximizing example*

Consider the problem of maximizing profits when $y = z_1^{1/3} z_2^{1/2}$ and prices are p, w_1 and w_2.

First we minimize the cost of producing y. The first-order conditions derived from the Lagrangean are

$$w_1 - \tfrac{1}{3}\lambda z_1^{-2/3} z_2^{1/2} = 0$$

$$w_2 - \tfrac{1}{2}\lambda z_1^{1/3} z_2^{-1/2} = 0 \tag{53}$$

$$y - z_1^{1/3} z_2^{1/2} = 0$$

which we solve to give

$$z_1(w_1, w_2, y) = y^{6/5} \left(\frac{2w_2}{3w_1}\right)^{3/5}$$

$$z_2(w_1, w_2, y) = y^{6/5} \left(\frac{3w_1}{2w_2}\right)^{2/5} \tag{54}$$

$$c(w_1, w_2, y) = 5y^{6/5} \left(\frac{w_1}{2}\right)^{2/5} \left(\frac{w_2}{3}\right)^{3/5}$$

$$\lambda(w_2, w_2, y) = 6y^{1/5} \left(\frac{w_1}{2}\right)^{2/5} \left(\frac{w_2}{3}\right)^{3/5} \qquad \left(= \frac{\partial c(w_1, w_2, y)}{\partial y}\right)$$

It is easily checked that the marginal rate of substitution diminishes. Now we can maximize profits which are

$$py - 5y^{6/5} \left(\frac{w_1}{2}\right)^{2/5} \left(\frac{w_2}{3}\right)^{3/5} \tag{55}$$

so that the first-order condition is

$$p - 6y^{1/5} \left(\frac{w_1}{2}\right)^{2/5} \left(\frac{w_2}{3}\right)^{3/5} = 0 \tag{56}$$

It is obvious that the second-order condition is satisfied. Hence the complete solution is

$$y(p, w_1, w_2) = \left(\frac{p}{6}\right)^5 \left(\frac{w_1}{2}\right)^{-2} \left(\frac{w_2}{3}\right)^{-3}$$

$$z_1(p, w_1, w_2) = \left(\frac{p}{6}\right)^6 \left(\frac{w_1}{2}\right)^{-3} \left(\frac{w_2}{3}\right)^{-3} \tag{57}$$

$$z_2(p, w_1, w_2) = \left(\frac{p}{6}\right)^6 \left(\frac{w_1}{2}\right)^{-2} \left(\frac{w_2}{3}\right)^{-4}$$

2.11 *More about second-order conditions*

Recall that in the introductory section of this chapter we wrote problem (48) in the form (3) (or, equivalently, (7)) and derived first-order conditions (6) (or (8)), but we made little progress with the discussion of second-order conditions and we encountered some problems where the first-order conditions did not give a solution.

We have now divided the problem into two steps: (13) and (49). We have two sets of first-order conditions: (15)–(16) and (50). Using the fact that $\lambda = \partial c / \partial y$ when (15) and (16) are satisfied allows us to combine (50) and (15) to give $w_i - p \, \partial F / \partial z_i = 0$ for $i = 1, \ldots, n$, which are simply the first-order conditions for the original problem.

The first-order conditions (6) were interpreted as stating that the firm would use inputs up to the level where the value of the marginal product of the input was equal to the input price. The first-order conditions (15) and (50) were interpreted as stating that the firms would equalize the marginal cost of different inputs, and then choose an output level that made this marginal cost equal to the output price. We now see that these are two ways of describing the *same* conditions.

The real difference between the two approaches is that by dividing the problem in two we have developed two sets of second-order conditions which are readily comprehensible: the quasi-concavity (diminishing marginal rate of substitution) condition for the cost-minimizing step, and the increasing marginal cost condition for the profit-maximizing step. In fact, economists usually assume that the quasi-concavity condition is satisfied and consider only examples in which it is. (If quasi-concavity were not satisfied, producers would not use several inputs in the production of output, and this would contradict our observation of what happens in reality.) On the other hand, violation of the increasing marginal cost condition raises interesting issues which we shall now discuss.

Consider the example of the production function $y = z_1^{2/3} z_2^{2/3}$. The usual procedure shows the cost function to be

$$c(w_1, w_2, y) = 4y^{3/4} \left(\frac{w_1}{2}\right)^{1/2} \left(\frac{w_2}{2}\right)^{1/2}$$

with

$$\frac{\partial c}{\partial y} = 3y^{-1/4} \left(\frac{w_1}{2}\right)^{1/2} \left(\frac{w_2}{2}\right)^{1/2}$$

which is *not* increasing in y. The first-order conditions identify the profit-*minimizing* output. This case is illustrated in figure 2.9. What should such a firm actually do? The mathematics tells us that profits increase as output is reduced from y_m to zero or as output is increased from y_m

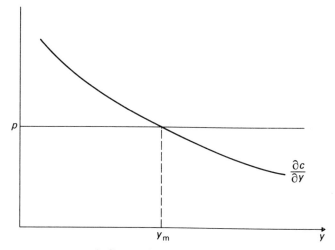

FIGURE 2.9   A firm with decreasing marginal cost

upwards. When output is zero, profits are zero; but it is not too hard to see that profits are positive if y is large enough. Thus the firm should apparently make y indefinitely large. We shall return to this case later.

Consider next the production function $y = z_1^{1/2} z_2^{1/2}$ which was the source of the troublesome examples on page 30 above. It has cost function $c(w_1, w_2, y) = 2y w_1^{1/2} w_2^{1/2}$, which does not satisfy the second-order condition since $\partial c/\partial y = 2 w_1^{1/2} w_2^{1/2}$, a constant. Since p also is a constant, the first-order condition $p = \partial c/\partial y$ can be satisfied only if prices are such that the two constants are equal. There are three possibilities, which are illustrated in figure 2.10.

In the first case, each extra unit of output adds more to cost than to sales revenue and the optimal output is zero. This is obvious if you write profit as $-(2 w_1^{1/2} w_2^{1/2} - p) y$. In the second case, the firm should make output indefinitely large, for each extra unit of output adds more to revenue than to cost, profits being given by $(p - 2 w_1^{1/2} w_2^{1/2}) y$. In the third case, profits are zero whatever the firm does – there is not a unique solution to the maximization problem.

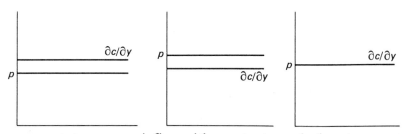

FIGURE 2.10   A firm with constant marginal cost

These examples show that we should not use first-order conditions without giving some thought to the second-order conditions. They also show that thinking about the economic meaning of cases where the second-order conditions are not satisfied allows one to make some sense of the problems involved.

The case of constant marginal cost (which it is left to you as exercise 2.21 to show arises when the production function has constant returns to scale) is particularly important, and we return to it in the next chapter.

2.12   *The properties of the firm's supply and demand functions*

We have now looked at the cost-minimizing firm and showed that it has demands for input $z(w, y)$ which are functions of input prices and of output. We can ask the question of how these demands change with changes in prices and output. The profit-maximizing firm has supply function $y(p, w)$ and input demand functions $z(w, y)$. Again, it is interesting to ask how these functions react to changes in prices.

One way to proceed would be to recall that the equations (15) and (16) implicitly define the functions $z(w, y)$ and use the methods developed in chapter 1 for solving comparative statics problems to find the properties of $z(w, y)$. Then, the equations (50) and (52) (or the equations (6)) could be used to find the properties of $y(p, w)$ and $z(p, w)$.

However, there is a much simpler type of argument available; an argument based on economic logic. Consider the cost-minimizing firm facing input prices w. Suppose these prices change from w^1 to w^2. (Note that the superscripts serve to identify different vectors and are *not* powers.) The firm will change its input choice from $z^1 = z(w^1, y)$ to $z^2 = z(w^2, y)$. Each chosen input vector minimizes the cost of producing y at the respective prices. Hence

$$w^1 z^1 \leqslant w^1 z^2 \qquad w^2 z^2 \leqslant w^2 z^1 \tag{58}$$

Adding and rearranging gives

$$(w^1 - w^2)(z^1 - z^2) \leqslant 0 \tag{59}$$

(If you are at all puzzled by (58) and (59), write the vectors and the products in 'ordinary' notation.)

Now suppose that every entry of w^1 is the same as the corresponding entry of w^2 except that w_i has changed from w_i^1 to w_i^2. Then (54) becomes

$$(w_i^1 - w_i^2)(z_i^1 - z_i^2) \leqslant 0 \tag{60}$$

and we have the result that for all i

$$\frac{\partial z_i(w, y)}{\partial w_i} \leqslant 0 \tag{61}$$

for (60) shows that if w_i rises with all other w_j constant and y constant, z_i falls or stays constant. (61) means that the *demand function of a cost-minimizing firm for any input is a decreasing function of the price of that input*.

If there are only two inputs, z_1 and z_2 then if w_1 increases, z_1 falls but to keep y constant z_2 must rise. Thus $\partial z_2(w_1, w_2, y)/\partial w_1 \geqslant 0$ and, similarly, $\partial z_1(w_1, w_2, y)/\partial w_2 \geqslant 0$, but similar results do not hold generally when there are more than two inputs.

It is, however, possible to prove one general result about the effect of other input prices on the demand for an input. The result is that for all i, j with $i \neq j$

$$\frac{\partial z_i(\mathbf{w}, y)}{\partial w_j} = \frac{\partial z_j(\mathbf{w}, y)}{\partial w_i} \tag{62}$$

The proof of this extraordinary result is postponed to chapter 4, exercise 4.7. (That it is an extraordinary result is seen by considering an example: let z_1 be tons of steel and w_1 be the price in $000 per ton of steel, let z_2 be man-hours of labour and w_2 be the wage in $ per man-hour. Now write out verbally what (62) says!)

Finally, it is left to you (exercise 2.26) to show that in general one cannot be certain that $\partial z_i(\mathbf{w}, y)/\partial y$ is positive. If $\partial z_i/\partial y < 0$, input i is said to be an *inferior* input.

The same sort of arguments as used in (58)–(60) can be applied to the profit-maximizing firm. Suppose the firm faces prices $p^1, \mathbf{w}^1$ initially, and chooses $y^1 = y(p^1, \mathbf{w}^1)$, $\mathbf{z}^1 = \mathbf{z}(p^1, \mathbf{w}^1)$, and when prices change to $p^2, \mathbf{w}^2$, the firm chooses $y^2 = y(p^2, \mathbf{w}^2)$, $\mathbf{z}^2 = \mathbf{z}(p^2, \mathbf{w}^2)$. Since in each case its choices maximize profits, we have

$$p^1 y^1 - \mathbf{w}^1 \mathbf{z}^1 \geqslant p^1 y^2 - \mathbf{w}^1 \mathbf{z}^2$$
$$p^2 y^2 - \mathbf{w}^2 \mathbf{z}^2 \geqslant p^2 y^1 - \mathbf{w}^2 \mathbf{z}^1 \tag{63}$$

Adding and rearranging gives

$$(\mathbf{w}^1 - \mathbf{w}^2)(\mathbf{z}^1 - \mathbf{z}^2) \leqslant (p^1 - p^2)(y^1 - y^2) \tag{64}$$

If $\mathbf{w}^1 = \mathbf{w}^2$, (59) implies that

$$(p^1 - p^2)(y^1 - y^2) \geqslant 0 \tag{65}$$

so that

$$\frac{\partial y(p, \mathbf{w})}{\partial p} \geqslant 0 \tag{66}$$

the profit-maximizing firm's supply function is an increasing function of the price of output.

Holding p constant and letting only one input price change shows that inequality (60) applies to the profit-maximizing firm also so that for all i

$$\frac{\partial z_i(p, \mathbf{w})}{\partial w_i} \leqslant 0 \qquad (67)$$

the demand function of a profit-maximizing firm for any input is a decreasing function of the price of that input.

It might seem obvious that $\partial y(p, \mathbf{w})/\partial w_i$ should be negative, for a rise in the price of an input will raise the cost of production, but in general one cannot be certain that $\partial y/\partial w_i \leqslant 0$. If $\partial y/\partial w_i > 0$, input i is said to be a *regressive* input.

Equation (52) states that $z_i(p, \mathbf{w}) = z_i(\mathbf{w}, y(p, \mathbf{w}))$. Therefore

$$\frac{\partial z_i(p, \mathbf{w})}{\partial p} = \frac{\partial z_i(\mathbf{w}, y)}{\partial y} \frac{\partial y(p, \mathbf{w})}{\partial p} \qquad (68)$$

and (66) implies that $\partial z_i(p, \mathbf{w})/\partial p$ has the same sign as $\partial z_i(\mathbf{w}, y)/\partial y$, but we have already observed that this sign may be either positive or negative.

There are two further results, whose proofs are relegated to an appendix:

$$\frac{\partial y(p, \mathbf{w})}{\partial w_i} = - \frac{\partial z_i(p, \mathbf{w})}{\partial p} \qquad (69)$$

and

$$\frac{\partial z_i(p, \mathbf{w})}{\partial w_j} = \frac{\partial z_j(p, \mathbf{w})}{\partial w_i} \qquad (70)$$

These results are as extraordinary as (62), for the same sort of reason. Note that (68) and (69) imply that an input is inferior if and only if it is regressive.

Finally, notice that (52) implies that

$$\frac{\partial z_i(p, \mathbf{w})}{\partial w_i} = \frac{\partial z_i(\mathbf{w}, y)}{\partial w_i} + \frac{\partial z_i(\mathbf{w}, y)}{\partial y} \frac{\partial y(p, \mathbf{w})}{\partial w_i} \qquad (71)$$

This shows that the effect of an input price change on the input demand of a profit-maximizing firm consists of two parts: the *substitution effect* $\partial z_i(\mathbf{w}, y)/\partial w_i$ which shows the effect of the change in the method of production and the *output effect* $(\partial z_i(\mathbf{w}, y)/\partial y)(\partial y(p, \mathbf{w})/\partial w_i)$ which shows the effect of the change in the level of production. We have seen above that the substitution effect is negative (equation (61)) and that the sum of the two effects is negative (equation (67)). In fact, the output effect must be negative also: usually $\partial z_i/\partial y$ is positive and $\partial y/\partial w_i$ is negative, but as stated (but not proved) above $\partial z_i/\partial y$ is negative if and only if $\partial y/\partial w_i$ is positive. If (68) and (69) are substituted in (71) we have

$$\frac{\partial z_i(p, \mathbf{w})}{\partial w_i} = \frac{\partial z_i(\mathbf{w}, y)}{\partial w_i} - \left(\frac{\partial z_i(\mathbf{w}, y)}{\partial y}\right)^2 \frac{\partial y(p, \mathbf{w})}{\partial p} \qquad (71a)$$

so that

$$\frac{\partial z_i(p, \mathbf{w})}{\partial w_i} \leqslant \frac{\partial z_i(\mathbf{w}, y)}{\partial w_i} \leqslant 0 \qquad (72)$$

It is left to you (see exercise 2.22) to go back to the example discussed in section 2.10 above and confirm that (61), (62), (66), (67), (69), (70) and (72) are indeed true in this example.

2.13   Homogeneous functions

A function $f(x_1, x_2, \ldots, x_n)$ is said to be homogeneous of degree r if

$$f(kx_1, kx_2, \ldots, kx_n) = k^r f(x_1, x_2, \ldots, x_n) \qquad (73)$$

or, in vector notation, $f(\mathbf{x})$ is homogeneous of degree r if

$$f(k\mathbf{x}) = k^r f(\mathbf{x}) \qquad (73a)$$

In fact, we have already come across this concept; for the definition of constant returns to scale is that the production function should be homogeneous of degree 1.

A function $f(x_1, \ldots, x_n, x_{n+1}, \ldots, x_m)$ is said to be homogeneous of degree r in the variables $x_1, \ldots, x_n$ if

$$f(kx_1, \ldots, kx_n, x_{n+1}, \ldots, x_m) = k^r f(x_1, \ldots, x_n, x_{n+1}, \ldots, x_m) \qquad (74)$$

For example, the function $x_1^2(x_2 + x_3)^2/x_4$ is homogeneous of degree 3; and is homogeneous of degree 4 in x_1, x_2, x_3.

The supply function $y(p, \mathbf{w})$ and the input demand functions $\mathbf{z}(p, \mathbf{w})$ are homogeneous of degree 0; that is $y(kp, k\mathbf{w}) = y(p, \mathbf{w})$ and $\mathbf{z}(kp, k\mathbf{w}) = \mathbf{z}(p, \mathbf{w})$. The proof is simple. Suppose when prices are $kp, k\mathbf{w}$ the firm does not choose $y(p, \mathbf{w})$ and $\mathbf{z}(p, \mathbf{w})$ but instead chooses $y^0, \mathbf{z}^0$. Since its choice maximizes profits it follows that

$$kpy^0 - k\mathbf{w}\mathbf{z}^0 > kpy(p, \mathbf{w}) - k\mathbf{w}\mathbf{z}(p, \mathbf{w}) \qquad (75)$$

But dividing (75) by k gives

$$py^0 - \mathbf{w}\mathbf{z}^0 > py(p, \mathbf{w}) - \mathbf{w}\mathbf{z}(p, \mathbf{w}) \qquad (76)$$

which is impossible since $y(p, \mathbf{w})$, $\mathbf{z}(p, \mathbf{w})$ are the profit-maximizing choices at the prices $p, \mathbf{w}$. (An alternative proof is to show that the solution of the first order conditions (15), (16) and (50) is unaffected by multiplying all prices by k.)

The economic interpretation of homogeneity of degree 0 is that when *all* prices change by the same proportion the firm's real situation is unchanged (in the same sense that a change from measuring prices in dollars to measuring in cents, so that all prices increase by a factor of 100, is not a real change in the firm's situation) so its behaviour is unchanged. A useful way to describe homogeneity of degree 0 is to say that only *relative* prices matter.

By similar arguments, it can be proved that the input demand functions $z(w, y)$ are homogeneous of degree 0 in w, and that the cost function $c(w, y)$ is homogeneous of degree 1 in w.

It is easy to check that the functions derived in the examples in sections 2.7 and 2.10 above satisfy these homogeneity properties. (See exercise 2.34.)

Euler's theorem states that $f(x_1, x_2, \ldots, x_n)$ is homogeneous of degree r if and only if

$$\sum_{i=1}^{n} x_i \frac{\partial f}{\partial x_i} = rf(x_1, \ldots, x_n) \tag{77}$$

The proof is omitted: it may be found in almost any book about the calculus of functions of several variables.

Euler's theorem has two important consequences for the theory of the profit-maximizing firm. If the production function $y = F(z)$ has constant returns to scale, it is homogeneous of degree 1 so that

$$\sum_{i=1}^{n} z_i \frac{\partial F}{\partial z_i} = F(z_1, \ldots, z_n) = y \tag{78}$$

But substituting the cost-minimizing equations $w_i = \lambda \, \partial F/\partial z_i$ into (78) gives

$$\sum_{i=1}^{n} w_i z_i = \lambda y \tag{79}$$

so the firm's profits are

$$py - \sum_{i=1}^{n} w_i z_i = (p - \lambda) y \tag{80}$$

Recall that λ is equal to marginal cost $\partial c/\partial y$. Recall also that a constant returns production function gives rise to a cost function with constant average cost, that is $c(y) = ay$ where a is the constant average cost, so that in fact $\lambda = \partial c/\partial y = a$, and λ is constant. Thus the results derived on page 47 and illustrated in figure 2.10 hold for any firm whose production function has constant returns to scale. In particular, if it is possible to satisfy the profit-maximizing condition $p = \lambda$ the firm's profits will be zero.

It is tempting to apply Euler's theorem to production functions with increasing or decreasing returns to scale, but results would be of limited scope since such functions are not necessarily homogeneous.

Geometric intuition suggests the second result. The isoquants of a constant constant returns production function shift *uniformly* out from the origin, as illustrated in figure 2.11. This suggests that the slope of an individual isoquant should depend only on z_2/z_1 not on z_1 and z_2 separately. This is indeed true.

By Euler's theorem, if $F(z_1, z_2)$ has constant returns then

$$F(z_1, z_2) = z_1 \frac{\partial F(z_1, z_2)}{\partial z_1} + z_2 \frac{\partial F(z_1, z_2)}{\partial z_2} \tag{81}$$

Differentiate both sides of (81) with respect to z_1:

$$\frac{\partial F(z_1, z_2)}{\partial z_1} = \frac{\partial F(z_1, z_2)}{\partial z_1} + \frac{\partial^2 F(z_1, z_2)}{\partial z_1^2} + z_2 \frac{\partial^2 F(z_1, z_2)}{\partial z_1 \partial z_2} \tag{82}$$

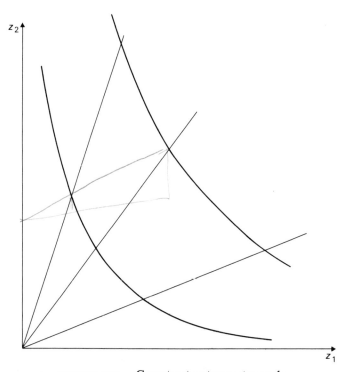

FIGURE 2.11   Constant returns to scale

where

$$\frac{\partial^2 F}{\partial z_1 \partial z_2} = \frac{\partial}{\partial z_1}\left(\frac{\partial F}{\partial z_2}\right) \tag{83}$$

the derivative of $\partial F/\partial z_2$ with respect to z_1. Now it is the case that when a function is twice-differentiable

$$\frac{\partial}{\partial z_2}\left(\frac{\partial F}{\partial z_1}\right) = \frac{\partial^2 F}{\partial z_2 \partial z_1} = \frac{\partial^2 F}{\partial z_1 \partial z_2} \tag{84}$$

(again, no proof is given of this important proposition) so that (82) implies that

$$0 = z_1 \frac{\partial}{\partial z_1}\left(\frac{\partial F}{\partial z_1}\right) + z_2 \frac{\partial}{\partial z_2}\left(\frac{\partial F}{\partial z_1}\right) \tag{85}$$

Thus Euler's theorem implies that the function $\partial F/\partial z_1$ must be homogeneous of degree 0. The same sort of proof establishes that $\partial F/\partial z_2$ is homogeneous of degree 0. Thus the slope of the isoquant, which is the marginal rate of substitution F_1/F_2, is unchanged when z_1 and z_2 change proportionately.

Although we cannot draw an isoquant diagram if there are more than two inputs the proof above applies: if $F(\mathbf{z})$ has constant returns to scale then $\partial F(\mathbf{z})/\partial z_i$ is homogeneous of degree 0 for all i. It is left to you (see exercise 2.38) to show that this means that $\mathbf{z}(\mathbf{w}, y)$ is homogeneous of degree 1 in y and to discuss the economic meaning of this.

Exercises

2.1   Find the values of x_1, x_2 at which the functions

(a) $(x_1 - 2)^2 + (x_2 - 1)^2$
(b) $(x_1 - 2)^2 - (x_2 - 1)^2$

have both partial derivatives equal to zero, but show by considering other values of x_1, x_2 that function (a) is minimized at this point but function (b) is at neither a maximum nor a minimum.

2.2   Find the partial derivatives of the function

$$f(x_1, x_2) = x_1^2 + x_2^2 - 3x_1 x_2$$

and find the point at which $\partial f/\partial x_1 = 0$ and $\partial f/\partial x_2 = 0$. Show that the second derivatives $\partial^2 f/\partial x_1^2$ and $\partial^2 f/\partial x_2^2$ are positive at this point, but, by evaluating the function at this point and also at the points $(c, 0)$, $(0, c)$ and (c, c) where c is an arbitrary number, show that the function is not minimized at the point where the partial derivatives are zero. (This shows that to have $\partial^2 f / \partial x_i^2 > 0$ for all i is not sufficient for a minimum.)

2.3 A firm with production function

$$y = z_1^{1/4} z_2^{1/2}$$

faces prices $p = 12$, $w_1 = 9$, $w_2 = 2$. Find its profit-maximizing policy. How much profit does it make?

2.4 Try to find profit-maximizing inputs in the cases (a) and (b) at the end of section 2.1.

2.5 (i) Discuss the returns to scale of the production functions

(a) $y = z_1^{1/4} z_2^{1/2}$
(b) $y = z_1^{1/2} z_2^{1/2}$
(c) $y = z_1^{\alpha} z_2^{\beta}$ where α and β are positive constants
(d) $y = (z_1^{-2} + z_2^{-2})^{-1/2}$

(ii) For each of these functions discuss whether there are diminishing returns to each input.
(iii) Is it possible to find values of α and β for function (c) such that there are increasing returns to scale *and* diminishing returns to inputs? Is it possible that function (c) has decreasing or constant returns to scale but not diminishing returns to inputs?
(iv) Draw a graph of the isoquant $y = 4$ for production function (d).

2.6 Define increasing, decreasing and constant returns to scale in terms of the relationship between $F(kz)$ and $F(z)$ when k is *less* than 1.

2.7 A producer owns two plants which produce identical products. Let y_1 be the output of the first plant and y_2 the output of the second. He wishes to produce a fixed quantity y of total output at the lowest possible cost. The cost of production in the respective plants is $c_1(y_1)$ and $c_2(y_2)$. Use a Lagrangean function to solve the problem of minimizing the cost of producing y. Is there any other way to solve the problem? Can you think of a condition that would be sufficient to ensure the solution is a minimum?

2.8 For each of the production functions in exercise 2.5 find the marginal rate of substitution and show that it is diminishing.

2.9 Discuss the properties of the production function

$$y = (z_1^2 + z_2^2)^{1/2}$$

Will the Lagrangean technique solve the cost-minimizing problem for this function?

2.10   Give a purely verbal definition of: (i) decreasing returns to scale; (ii) diminishing returns; and (iii) diminishing marginal rate of subsitution.

2.11   Find the elasticity of substitution of the production functions

(a) $y = z_1^\alpha z_2^\beta$ $(\alpha > 0, \beta > 0)$
(b) $y = (z_1^{-\alpha} + z_2^{-\alpha})^{-1/\alpha}$ $(\alpha > -1)$

What are the relative shares in each case of the inputs in the total cost of production? Verify that the relative shares satisfy the property derived from (25).

2.12   In the nineteenth century, Japanese textile manufacturers are said to have used many workers per machine so as to minimize production losses while machines were out of action waiting for such operations as repair of broken thread, replacement of empty bobbins, and so on; while British manufacturers operated the same machines with fewer workers and consequently faced longer interruptions to production. Can both be explained as rational behaviour in view of the difference between Japanese and British wages at that time?

2.13   For the production functions in exercise 2.5 if input prices are w_1, w_2 find in each case the cost-minimizing levels of inputs for a given output y. Derive the cost functions. Are the solutions truly minima in each case? Fir. average cost in each case and verify that it bears the expected relation to returns to scale.

2.14   For the production function

$$y = z_1^{1/2} + z_2^{1/2}$$

derive the cost function, checking that cost is indeed minimized. What is the elasticity of substitution? Find average cost. What property of the production function is reflected in average cost?

2.15   Give a purely verbal explanation of the fact that a constant returns production function has associated with it constant average cost of production.

2.16   If a firm calculated its cost function to be $c = 10y^2$, what could you deduce about its production function?

*2.17   The cost function $c(\mathbf{w}, y)$ is said to be a strictly convex function of

y for all $\mathbf{w}$ if, for all y_1 and y_2 satisfying $y_1 \neq y_2$ and all λ such that $0 < \lambda < 1$,

$$\lambda c(\mathbf{w}, y_1) + (1 - \lambda) c(\mathbf{w}, y_2) > c(\mathbf{w}, y_\lambda)$$

where $y_\lambda = \lambda y_1 + (1 - \lambda) y_2$. (Draw a graph of c as a function of y with this property satisfied and confirm that $\partial c / \partial y$ is increasing.)

The production function $F(\mathbf{z})$ is said to be strictly concave if, for all $\mathbf{z}_1$ and $\mathbf{z}_2$ satisfying $\mathbf{z}_1 \neq \mathbf{z}_2$ and all λ such that $0 < \lambda < 1$,

$$\lambda F(\mathbf{z}_1) + (1 - \lambda) F(\mathbf{z}_2) < F(\mathbf{z}_\lambda)$$

where $\mathbf{z}_\lambda = \lambda \mathbf{z}_1 + (1 - \lambda) \mathbf{z}_2$. (Compare the definition of concavity given on pages 28–29 and illustrated in figure 2.2.)

Consider *any* input vectors $\mathbf{z}_1$ and $\mathbf{z}_2$ and the corresponding $y_1 = F(\mathbf{z}_1)$, $y_2 = F(\mathbf{z}_2)$. Choose $\mathbf{w}$ so that $\mathbf{w}\mathbf{z}_\lambda = c(\mathbf{w}, F(\mathbf{z}_\lambda))$. Show that if the cost function is strictly convex then $y_\lambda < F(\mathbf{z}_\lambda)$ so the production function is strictly concave.

Thus show that $\partial c / \partial y$ will be an increasing function of y for all y only if the production function has diminishing returns to all inputs and decreasing returns to scale. (If $\partial c / \partial y$ is an increasing function of y only over a range of values of y then the production function has over this range diminishing returns to inputs and a property known as locally decreasing returns to scale.)

2.18   Using the cost functions derived in exercises 2.13 and 2.14 derive, *where they exist*, the profit-maximizing $y(p, w_1, w_2)$, $z_1(p, w_1, w_2)$, $z_2(p, w_1, w_2)$ corresponding to the respective production functions. Discuss in particular the outcome in the cases of the production functions (b), (c) (if $\alpha + \beta = 1$ or $\alpha + \beta > 1$), and (d) in exercises 2.5 and 2.13.

2.19   Solve the cost-minimization and profit-maximization problems for the firm with production function

$$y = (z_1^{1/3} + z_2^{1/3})^2$$

facing prices p, w_1, w_2.

2.20   A firm has cost function

$$c(y) = 200 - 10y + 0.01y^2$$

where y is the number of units of output and $c(y)$ measures in cost in £. The firm sells its product at a market price of £10 per unit. Assuming it maximizes its profits, what will be its output and profit?

Suppose now the government offers the following alternative subsidies:

(a)   a grant of £1000;
(b)   a grant of £1 per unit produced;
(c)   a grant of £5 per unit produced in excess of 1000.

If the market price is unchanged, which should the firm choose?

2.21   Prove that if the production function has constant returns to scale then marginal cost is constant and equal to average cost.

2.22   Verify that the supply functions $y(p, \mathbf{w})$ and the demand functions $\mathbf{z}(\mathbf{w}, y)$ and $\mathbf{z}(p, \mathbf{w})$ derived in exercises 2.13, 2.14, 2.18 and 2.19 satisfy (61), (62), (66), (67), (69), (70) and (72).

2.23   Discuss the reaction of a profit-maximizing firm facing given market prices to: (a) a proportional tax of 50% on its profits; and (b) a tax of 10% of the selling price on each unit of output.

2.24   Suppose that a firm produces one output from the three inputs: capital, labour and raw materials. The government imposes a 50% tax on 'profits', where profits' are defined as what is left of the revenue after labour and raw materials have been paid for. By writing down the firm's after-tax profit-maximization problem, discuss what the effect of the tax will be. Contrast this with the effect of the 50% tax on true profits in exercise 2.23.

2.25   If a firm has n inputs $z_1, z_2, \ldots, z_n$, prove that there exists at least one $j \neq i$ such that $\partial z_j(\mathbf{w}, y)/\partial w_i \geqslant 0$.

2.26   Draw a diagram to show that it is possible that $\partial z_i(\mathbf{w}, y)/\partial y < 0$.

2.27   'If the price of *one* input increases, with all other prices remaining constant, this must increase costs and therefore reduce the profit-maximizing level of output. Therefore $\partial y(p, \mathbf{w})/\partial w_i \leqslant 0$.' This argument is incorrect, because in unusual cases $\partial y/\partial w_i > 0$ as stated on page 50. By distinguishing carefully between cost and marginal cost, expose the fallacy in the argument.

2.28   Suppose that for technical reasons it is very difficult to substitute machines for workers in the building industry. A union leader argues that in consequence the union can safely press for higher wages without endangering the workers' jobs. Is he necessarily correct?

2.29   Use equation (71a) to show that a profit-maximizing firm's demand for an input will usually be more elastic the easier it is to substitute other inputs and the larger the proportion of total costs accounted for by payments to that input.

2.30   Write down the equation analogous to (71) for $\partial z_i(p, \mathbf{w})/\partial w_j$.

2.31   When the production function $F(z)$ has constant returns to scale the functions $y(p, w)$ and $z(p, w)$ do not exist for all values of p and w and (66) and (67) cannot be said to hold, since the derivatives do not always exist (and are zero where they do exist). Prove, however, that (65) and (60) hold for the profit-maximizing firm with constant returns.

2.32   Give the alternative proof of the zero-degree homogeneity of the function $y(p, w)$ and $z(p, w)$.

2.33   Prove that the functions $z(w, y)$ are homogeneous of degree 0 in w and that the cost function $c(w, y)$ is homogeneous of degree 1 in w.

2.34   Confirm that the supply, demand and cost functions derived in sections 2.7 and 2.10 and exercises 2.13, 2.14, 2.18 and 2.19 have the correct homogeneity properties.

2.35   Prove the 'only if' part of Euler's theorem.

2.36   (a) Suppose that all input prices rise proportionately except w_i which remains constant. What will happen to $z_i(w, y)$ and to $c(w, y)$?
　　(b) Suppose that all input prices rise proportionately but output price remains constant. What will happen to $y(p, w)$?
　　(c) Suppose that output price and all input prices except w_i rise proportionately. What will happen to $z_i(p, w)$?

2.37   If $y = F(z_1, z_2)$ is a production function which is homogeneous of degree α where $0 < \alpha < 1$, what can we say about its returns to scale? Use Euler's theorem to show that for any set of prices, the maximum profit will be positive.

2.38   Use Euler's theorem to prove that if $F(z)$ has constant returns to scale then $\partial F(z)/\partial z_i$ is homogeneous of degree 0 for all i. Prove that this means that $z(w, y)$ is homogeneous of degree 1 in y and discuss the economic meaning of this.

CHAPTER 3

The Firm and the Market

3.1 *Profit maximization in the short run*

An important assumption of the theory developed in the previous chapter is that the firm can freely choose its inputs. This is not always a reasonable assumption.

Consider, for example, the case of a firm which uses three inputs: raw materials, labour and machinery. The quantity of raw materials used can be varied easily, say from day to day. The size of its labour force (or the number of hours worked by each worker) can also be varied, perhaps from week to week. But the machinery may be specially designed for this firm and be of no value to any other firm; so that more machinery can be installed only after a delay of several months from the time the decision to order it is placed, while the stock of machinery can be reduced only by scrapping old machines and not replacing them.

This example may not be typical of all firms: some firms obtain materials through long-term contracts which cannot be changed at once, and have a labour force which may not be willing to accept redundancies, overtime or new recruits; while, on the other hand, some firms' machinery may be easy to buy and to sell second-hand, or may be rented.

The general point is that some of the decisions faced by a firm are made in circumstances when some inputs are fixed, and some are variable. The cost of the fixed inputs is called the *fixed cost* and the cost of the variable inputs is called the *variable cost*.

In section 1.10 we defined the difference between the 'short run' and the 'long run' as depending on whether firms (or consumers) were constrained by their past decisions in making their present decisions. In the present context there is a constraint if there are fixed inputs; so the short run is a time period within which some inputs are fixed, while in the long run all inputs are variable. It is, however, most important to recall that this terminology is a useful shorthand expression rather than a reflection of a rigid division of the future into two parts. For some firms all inputs may be variable almost immediately (consider, for example, a firm selling secretarial services using rented accommodation and equipment and non-unionized staff on weekly contracts) so that the short run is so short as to be irrelevant; while other firms have inputs which are permanently fixed (such as the embankments, cuttings and track-bed of a railway line) so that there is no true long run. Further, it is likely that the shorter the time period considered the more of the inputs are fixed, so that there is really a series of short runs.

The simplest formal model that incorporates these distinctions is one of a firm producing output y from two inputs z_1 and z_2. If z_2 is fixed the production function

$$y = F(z_1, z_2) \tag{1}$$

is a function of the single variable z_1, and the firm has no choice about how to produce. Equation (1) defines z_1 as an implicit function of y and z_2 which we write as

$$z_1 = z_1(y, z_2) \tag{2}$$

The firm's short-run cost function is

$$c(w_1, w_2, y, z_2) = w_1 z_1(y, z_2) + w_2 z_2 \tag{3}$$

so that $w_1 z_1(y, z_2)$ gives the variable cost and $w_2 z_2$ the fixed cost. Short-run average cost is $c(w_1, w_2, y, z_2)/y$, short-run marginal cost is $\partial c(w_1, w_2, y, z_2)/\partial y$ and average variable cost is $w_1 z_1(y, z_2)/y$. (Note that short-run marginal cost and average variable cost are both independent of w_2 and that short-run marginal cost is the same as marginal variable cost.) These three functions are referred to by the respective abbreviations SRAC, SRMC and AVC.

For example, if $y = z_1^{1/2} z_2^{1/2}$ with $w_1 = 2$, $w_2 = 2$ and $z_2 = 4$, the production function is $y = 2z_1^{1/2}$ so $z_1 = \frac{1}{4}y^2$ and the short-run cost function is $c = \frac{1}{2}y^2 + 8$, the variable cost being $\frac{1}{2}y^2$ and the fixed cost 8. Short-run average cost is $\frac{1}{2}y + 8/y$, short-run marginal cost is y, and average variable cost is $\frac{1}{2}y$, and these three functions are graphed in figure 3.1.

The fact that average variable cost rises with output in this example reflects the fact that as z_1 increases, y increases less than proportionately (and in turn this reflects the fact that the production function has diminishing returns to the variable input). (Contrast the long-run cost function, discussed in the previous chapter, where the shape of the average cost function depends on returns to scale, because all inputs are variable.) In fact, we could assume that returns to the variable input are not diminishing at low levels of output and only start to diminish after a certain point. A production function with this property is illustrated in figure 3.2(a): up to z_{11}, the marginal product $\partial F/\partial z_1$ is rising with z_1, and above z_{11} we have diminishing returns to z_1; while the *average* product y/z_1

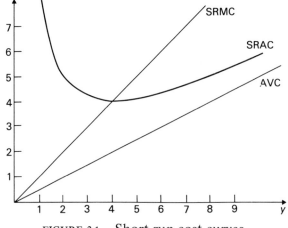

FIGURE 3.1   Short-run cost curves

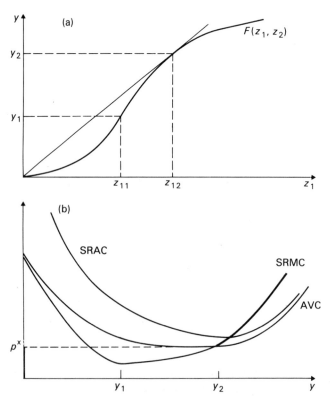

FIGURE 3.2   The short-run production function and short-run
cost curves

rises with z_1 up to z_{12} and falls thereafter. The marginal product is the slope of the $F(z_1, z_2)$ curve at a point; the average product is the slope of the line connecting the origin to that point; the two are equal at z_{12}. Now average variable cost is w_1z_1/y, which falls when average product rises and vice versa; while marginal cost is $w_1/(\partial F/\partial z_1)$, which falls when marginal product rises and vice versa. Thus we have the U-shaped SRMC and AVC curves illustrated in figure 3.2(b). The two curves intersect at y_2 corresponding to the input level z_{12}. The difference between AVC and SRAC is given by w_2z_2/y which decreases with y so that SRAC is also U-shaped.

The relationship between any average cost function and the corresponding marginal cost function is derived from

$$y \frac{d}{dy}\left(\frac{c(y)}{y}\right) = \frac{dc(y)}{dy} - \frac{c(y)}{y} \tag{4}$$

Recall that average cost is $c(y)/y$ and marginal cost is $dc(y)/dy$. Where marginal cost exceeds average cost, the right-hand side of (4) is positive, and average cost is therefore increasing; where average cost exceeds marginal cost, average cost is decreasing; and average cost is constant only when it equals marginal cost. An intuitive explanation of this relationship is that if an extra unit of output costs more than the average unit then the average cost will rise as output rises, and similarly for the reverse case.

In the case where $c(y)$ is short-run cost, (4) becomes

$$y \frac{\partial}{\partial y} (\text{SRAC}) = \text{SRMC} - \text{SRAC} \tag{5}$$

while if $c(y)$ is variable cost, (4) becomes

$$y \frac{\partial}{\partial y} (\text{AVC}) = \text{SRMC} - \text{AVC} \tag{6}$$

Thus SRMC cuts both AVC and SRAC from below at their respective minimum points. (One way to look at the connection between (5) and (6) is to observe that setting $w_2 = 0$ makes fixed costs zero, has no effect on marginal cost and makes SRAC the same as AVC so (5) becomes (6). Alternatively, as we have already seen, (6) can be established by considering the relationship between marginal and average products.)

Now suppose the firm seeks to maximize profits, but believes that z_2 is fixed. The problem is essentially the same as the long-run profit-maximization problem discussed in section 2.9, being

$$\underset{y}{\text{maximize}}\ py - c(w_1, w_2, y, z_2) \tag{7}$$

so the necessary condition for maximization is that

$$p - \frac{\partial c(w_1, w_2, y, z_2)}{\partial y} = 0 \tag{8}$$

while the second-order condition is

$$-\frac{\partial^2 c(w_1, w_2, y, z_2)}{\partial y^2} < 0 \tag{9}$$

As in the long-run problem, the firm should set a level of output that makes marginal cost equal to the output price, with marginal cost increasing.

However, we should now deal with a question that was evaded in section 2.9. In figure 3.3(a) the output level y_1 is the only one which satisfies (8) and (9) while only at y_0 is (8) satisfied without (9). Thus profits fall from 0 to y_0, rise from y_0 to y_1, and fall from y_1 onwards. Clearly y_1 is a *local* maximum, but as output falls from y_0 to 0 profits are raised, and this suggests the possibility that producing nothing may be better than producing y_1. (At the point $y = 0$, profits are still rising as output falls, but output cannot be reduced any further.) Thus we have a third condition to add to (8) and (9): we need to check that profits at y_1 exceed profits at 0. However the fixed costs $w_2 z_2$ are incurred whatever the output, so at $y = 0$ profits are $-w_2 z_2$ (that is, there are losses of $w_2 z_2$). Therefore our third condition is

$$py_1 - w_1 z_1(y_1, z_2) - w_2 z_2 \geqslant -w_2 z_2 \tag{10}$$

that is

$$py_1 - w_1 z_1(y_1, z_2) \geqslant 0 \tag{11}$$

which states that revenue should exceed *variable* cost, or price should exceed average variable cost. In the example of figure 3.3(a) this is indeed true, and in figure 3.3(b) this is illustrated in a different way, where we see profits as a function of output, with profits being maximized (losses being minimized, in fact) at y_1, with profits higher (that is losses lower) at y_1 than at 0.

By contrast, if the output price were sufficiently low so that marginal cost was equal to price at a point on the SRMC curve below the AVC curve, then (11) would not be satisfied and it is better to close down than to produce at the point satisfying (8) and (9). This case is illustrated by the price p_2 and output y_2 in figure 3.3(a).

An important feature of this argument is that (11) shows that the fixed costs are irrelevant to the decision of whether or not to produce. Or, to put it another way, whether price exceeds short-run average cost or not is irrelevant (that simply determines whether the firm makes profits or losses); it is the relation between price and average variable cost that matters. The reason is that the fixed costs are the same for either of the alternative actions (to produce or not to produce) under consideration, so do not affect the *relative* profitability of the two actions. And, of course, it is only the relative profitability of the two actions which is relevant to a choice between them.

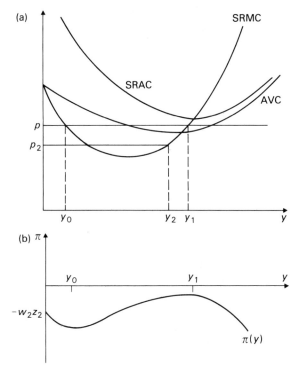

FIGURE 3.3   Short-run profit maximization

The same point is sometimes expressed by saying that fixed costs are not an *opportunity cost*. The concept of opportunity cost directs attention to the fact that economic decisions are choices between alternatives: opportunity cost is the cost of taking one action *rather than* another. Although the cost of the fixed input is $w_2 z_2$, in the sense that this expenditure is being made, the opportunity cost of using the fixed inputs in production rather than not using them is zero — for, by assumption, the expenditure of $w_2 z_2$ is made in either case, since the firm cannot remove the input from the production process and put it to some other use or sell it. By contrast, the opportunity cost of using the variable inputs, compared with not producing, is $w_1 z_1$, because this amount would be saved if output were zero.

Economists sometimes use the phrase 'bygones are bygones' to express the rule that past expenditures which cannot be reversed by sale of whatever was purchased should be ignored when decisions for the future are made. The fact that in *some* circumstances an economic decision-maker should treat some resources as being costless emphasizes the importance of correct identification of such circumstances: the opportunity cost of a resource depends on the specification of the decision problem, on the alternative actions being considered. If some machinery has no alternative use, the opportunity cost of using it in production rather than not using it is zero. If, however, the machinery could be rented out, and this alternative is being considered, the opportunity cost of using the machinery in production is the rental income that would be sacrificed. If workers can be fired if output is zero, then labour is a variable input with a positive opportunity cost; but if workers have a fixed wage and cannot be made redundant or redeployed, their labour is a fixed input with zero opportunity cost. Even in decision-making contexts where both labour and machinery are variable inputs, there may be other costs like past expenditure on research and development which cannot be saved by reducing output and these are fixed costs.

Equations (8), (9) and (11) define the profit-maximizing level of y that corresponds to given values of p, w, and z_2. (It should now be apparent why y does not depend on w_2). Equation (8) shows that the firm's short-run supply function is given by the short-run marginal cost function: if p is the value of SRMC at output level y_1, then y_1 is the profit-maximizing level of output at price p. Mathematically, (8) can be regarded as implicitly defining the function $y = y(p, w_1, z_2)$. However, this needs two qualifications: equation (9) shows that only the increasing portion of the SRMC function is relevant, while (11) shows that price must also exceed AVC. Thus it is only *the part of the increasing SRMC curve that lies above the AVC curve which is the firm's short-run supply curve*; if price is less than AVC, supply is zero. Thus the firm's supply curve is shown as the bold curve in figure 3.2(b), vertical at $y = 0$ for $p \leqslant p^*$, coincident with SRMC for $p \geqslant p^*$, with a discontinuity at the price p^* where output could be 0 or y_2. Mathematically, (9) and (11) show us that (8) defines $y(p, w_1, z_2)$ only for $p \geqslant p^*$, otherwise $y(p, w_1, z_2) = 0$. (Now you can see that in order to establish rigorously that $y(p, w_1, z_2)$ is independent of w_2 you need to show that w_2 does not enter into (8), (9) or (11); that is that it affects neither SRMC nor AVC.)

As a footnote to this section we should note that the discussion of long-run profit maximization in section 2.9 should also have included a third condition like (10) to ensure that the level of output identified by (2.50) and (2.51) is indeed better for the firm than producing nothing. Since, by definition, there are no fixed costs in the long run when all inputs are variable, that third condition in simpler than (10), being

$$py - \mathbf{w}\mathbf{z}(\mathbf{w}, y) \geqslant 0 \tag{12}$$

The three conditions together show that *the long-run supply curve is the part of the increasing LRMC curve which is above the LRAC curve* (where, obviously, LRMC and LRAC stand for long-run marginal cost and average cost, respectively). It is, in fact, easy to show that if the production function has constant returns to scale or decreasing returns to scale at all output levels then (12) is necessariiy satisfied at the value of y which satisfies (2.50) and (2.51). This is left to you to prove as exercise 3.9.

3.2 Long-run and short-run cost curves and supply functions

In the previous section we considered a firm with one fixed input and one variable input. In general, there might be several fixed inputs and several variable inputs but all arguments would be essentially unchanged. We continue therefore to confine our attention to the two-input case in analysing the important relationships between the firm's short- and long-run cost functions and short- and long-run supply functions and input demand functions.

In the long run z_1 and z_2 are chosen to minimize $w_1 z_1 + w_2 z_2$ subject to $F(z_1, z_2) = y$. In the short run z_1 is chosen to satisfy the constraint $F(z_1, z_2) = y$. Clearly

$$w_1 z_1(w_1, w_2, y) + w_2 z_2(w_1, w_2, y) \leqslant w_1 z_1(y, z_2) + w_2 z_2 \qquad (13)$$

(for if the inequality were not satisfied the $z_i(w_1, w_2, y)$ would not be the solutions to the cost-minimizing problem), that is

$$c(w_1, w_2, y) \leqslant c(w_1, w_2, y, z_2) \qquad (14)$$

and, by dividing by y, we have LRAC $<$ SRAC. (Note carefully how the arguments of the respective functions are used to distinguish short-run from long-run functions.) There is a value of y at which, in the short run, the fixed level of z_2 just happens to be the one which would have been chosen in the long run. That is, there is a value of y such that $z_2 = z_2(w_1, w_2, y)$, and at this value of y, LRAC $=$ SRAC. This relationship is illustrated in figure 3.4(a) where for given w_1, w_2, z_2 the output level y_1 satisfies $z_2 = z_2(w_1, w_2, y)$, so that SRAC $=$ LRAC at y_1, but SRAC $>$ LRAC for all other y. Further illustration is provided by the isoquant diagram in figure 3.4(b). In the short run the firm can vary output only by moving along the horizontal line $z_2 = z_2(w_1, w_2, y_1)$. In the long run it varies output along the 'expansion path' OAB described by the tangency point between isocost lines and isoquants. These two lines cross at the point A whre output is y_1 and where the short-run fixed input level is the level that would be *chosen* in the long run.

Let $f(y) = c(w_1, w_2, y, z_2) - c(w_1, w_2, y)$, the difference between short-run and long-run cost, so that $f(y) \geqslant 0$ and $f(y_1) = 0$. This function is shown in figure 3.4(c). Clearly, $f(y)$ is minimized at y_1 so that $f'(y_1) = 0$ and $f''(y_1) \geqslant 0$ (assuming that $f(y)$ is twice differentiable). Thus

$$\frac{\partial c(w_1, w_2, y_1, z_2)}{\partial y} = \frac{\partial c(w_1, w_2, y_1)}{\partial y} \qquad (15)$$

and

$$\frac{\partial^2 c(w_1, w_2, y_1, z_2)}{\partial y^2} \geqslant \frac{\partial^2 c(w_1, w_2, y_1)}{\partial y^2} \qquad (16)$$

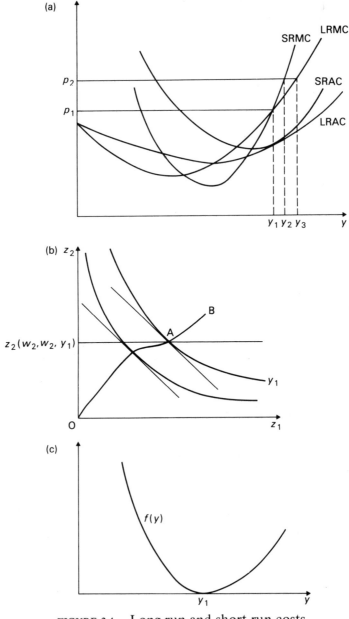

FIGURE 3.4   Long-run and short-run costs

so that, at y_1, SRMC is equal to LRMC, but the slope of SRMC is greater than the slope of LRMC. This is illustrated in figure 3.4(a) (where the relationship between the marginal cost and average cost curves reflects the fact that (5) holds for both the short-run and the long-run functions). The economic logic behind (15) and (16) is simple: since short-run cost exceeds long-run cost when $y < y_1$, is equal to long-run cost when $y = y_1$, and exceeds long-run cost again when $y > y_1$, we must have long-run cost rising faster than short-run cost (LRMC > SRMC) when $y < y_1$, while long-run cost must rise more slowly than short-run cost (LRMC < SRMC) when $y < y_1$, and at $y = y_1$ they rise at the same rate (LRMC = SRMC).

We can now consider the properties of the short-run supply function $y(p, w_1, z_2)$ defined by (8), and the short-run input demand function $z_1(p, w_1, z_2)$ defined by substituting the supply function in (2) to give $z_1(p, w_1, z_2) = z_1(y(p, w_1, z_2), z_2)$. For some purposes it is useful to consider an alternative derivation of these two functions. If we simply consider the problem

$$\text{maximize } py - w_1 z_1 - w_2 z_2$$
$$y, z_1$$

$$\text{subject to } y = F(z_1, z_2) \tag{17}$$

we derive two equations:

$$p \frac{\partial F(z_1, z_2)}{\partial z_1} = w_1 \tag{18}$$

$$F(z_1, z_2) = y \tag{19}$$

which solve to give $y(p, w_1, z_2)$, $z_1(p, w_1, z_2)$. It is fairly easy to see that these equations are just another way of writing (8) and (2), so that the solutions really are the same functions. Thus we can describe the firm in the short run as choosing an output level that makes marginal cost equal to price *or* as choosing variable input level that makes the value of the marginal product equal to the input price: these are two ways of saying the same thing.

If, initially, the firm illustrated in figure 3.4 is in long-run equilibrium at p_1, y_1, then a rise in price to p_2 will initially raise output to y_2 along the SRMC curve, but as the firm becomes able to vary all of its inputs, output will expand further along the LRMC curve to y_3. (Of course, at y_3, z_2 has changed so that the firm now has a new SRAC curve tangent to the LRAC curve at y_3 and a new SRMC curve intersecting the LRMC curve at y_3 but these new short-run curves are not shown.) Thus the long-run and short-run supply functions have the property that

$$\frac{\partial y(p, w_1, w_2)}{\partial p} \geqslant \frac{\partial y(p, w_1, z_2)}{\partial p} \geqslant 0 \tag{20}$$

Multiplying both sides of (18) by p/y changes the derivatives into elasticities, so that we have the result that *the long-run elasticity of supply is greater than the short-run elasticity*.

A more formal proof observes that the respective supply functions $y(p)$ are implicitly defined by the equations

$$p = \frac{\partial c(y)}{\partial y} \tag{21}$$

(where the other arguments in $y(\cdot)$ and $c(\cdot)$ are not written explicitly), which, differentiated with respect to p, gives

$$1 = \frac{\partial^2 c(y)}{\partial y^2} \frac{\partial y(p)}{\partial p} \tag{22}$$

so that (20) follows from (16).

Recall that in chapter 2 we proved (see equation (2.65)) the inequality

$$(\mathbf{w}^1 - \mathbf{w}^2)(\mathbf{z}^1 - \mathbf{z}^2) \leqslant (p^1 - p^2)(y^1 - y^2) \tag{23}$$

for the profit-maximizing firm choosing $(y^1, \mathbf{z}^1)$ when facing prices $(p^1, \mathbf{w}^1)$ and switching to $(y^2, \mathbf{z}^2)$ when prices change to $(p^2, \mathbf{w}^2)$. This inequality was used to prove that the (long-run) supply of y is an increasing function of p and the (long-run) demand for z_i is a decreasing function of w_i. The same inequality describes the choices of the cost-minimizing firm except that it faces the constraint that $y^1 = y^2$. It was stated, but not proved, that the input demand function of the cost-minimizing firm was less elastic than that of the profit-maximizing firm.

Clearly (23) holds in the short run also, with the modification that now a part of the z vector is constrained to be constant. In the two-input case (23) becomes

$$(w_1^1 - w_1^2)(z_1^1 - z_1^2) \leqslant (p^1 - p^2)(y^1 - y^2) \tag{24}$$

(though the generalization to several variable inputs and several fixed inputs should be obvious). With w_1 constant the left-hand side is zero, and we have an alternative proof of the fact that short-run supply is an increasing function of output price. Holding p constant makes the right-hand side zero so that

$$(w_1^1 - w_1^2)(z_1^1 - z_1^2) \leqslant 0 \tag{25}$$

that is, the short-run input demand function has the property that

$$\frac{\partial z_1(p, w_1, z_2)}{\partial w_1} \leqslant 0 \tag{26}$$

Since the imposition of the constraint on y in the cost-minimizing problem reduces the elasticity of input demand compared with the long-run profit-maximizing problem, and since the imposition of the constraint on z_2 in short-run profit maximization reduces the elasticity of output supply compared with the long run, it will come as no surprise to learn that *the short-run elasticity of demand for a variable input is less than the long-run elasticity*. The proof is relegated to the appendix.

We clearly have the following relationship between long-run and short-run demand and supply functions (compare (2.52))

$$y(p, w_1, w_2) = y(w_1, p, z_2(p, w_1, w_2))$$

$$z_1(p, w_1, w_2) = z_1(w_1, p, z_2(p, w_1, w_2)) \tag{27}$$

Thus,

$$\frac{\partial y(p, w_1, w_2)}{\partial p} = \frac{\partial y(w_1, p, z_2)}{\partial p} + \frac{\partial y(w_1, p, z_2)}{\partial z_2} \frac{\partial z_2(p, w_1, w_2)}{\partial p}$$

$$\frac{\partial z_1(p, w_1, w_2)}{\partial w_1} = \frac{\partial z_1(w_1, p, z_2)}{\partial w_1} + \frac{\partial z_1(w_1, p, z_2)}{\partial z_2} \frac{\partial z_2(p, w_1, w_2)}{\partial p}$$

(28)

and we see the long-run effect of a price change divided in each case into a short-run effect and what could be called a 'capacity adjustment' effect. The formal similarity between the equation (28) and equation (2.71) should be clear.

Finally, it is left to you as exercise 3.11 to prove that the short-run supply function $y(w_1, p, z_2)$ and the short-run input demand function $z_1(w_1, p, z_2)$ are both homogeneous of degree 0 in the prices w_1, p.

3.3   An example

Consider the production function $y = z_1^{1/2} + z_2^{1/2}$. It is easily checked that it has decreasing returns to scale.

In the long run the conditions for cost minimization are

$$w_1 = \tfrac{1}{2}\lambda z_1^{-1/2}$$
$$w_2 = \tfrac{1}{2}\lambda z_2^{-1/2}$$

(29)

$$y = z_1^{1/2} + z_2^{1/2}$$

which solve to give

$$z_1(w_1, w_2, y) = [yw_2/(w_1 + w_2)]^2$$
$$z_2(w_1, w_2, y) = [yw_1/(w_1 + w_2)]^2$$

(30)

$$c(w_1, w_2, y) = y^2 w_1 w_2/(w_1 + w_2)$$

It is easily checked that the second-order conditions for cost minimization and profit maximization are both satisfied, so that profit-maximizing supply is determined by

$$p = \frac{\partial c(w_1, w_2, y)}{\partial y} = \frac{2y w_1 w_2}{w_1 + w_2}$$

(31)

which gives the long-run supply function

$$y(p, w_1, w_2) = p(w_1 + w_2)/(2w_1 w_2)$$

(32)

and the long-run demand functions

$$z_1(p, w_1, w_2) = (p/2w_1)^2$$
$$z_2(p, w_1, w_2) = (p/2w_2)^2$$

(33)

Profits are

$$\frac{p^2(w_1 + w_2)}{2w_1 w_2} - \frac{p^2_-}{4w_1} - \frac{p^2}{4w_2} = \frac{p^2(w_1 + w_2)}{4w_1 w_2} > 0 \tag{34}$$

so that it is indeed better to produce the profit-maximizing output than to shut down.

In the short run with z_2 fixed we have the cost function

$$c(w_1, w_2, y, z_2) = w_1(y - z_2^{1/2})^2 + w_2 z_2 \tag{35}$$

which, it is possible to show by some tedious manipulation, is greater than $c(w_1, w_2, y)$ unless $z_2 = z_2(w_1, w_2, y)$. Short-run profit maximization requires

$$p = 2w_1(y - z_2^{1/2}) \tag{36}$$

(since it is obvious that $\partial^2 c / \partial y^2 > 0$) so the short-run supply function is

$$y(p, w_1, z_2) = p/2w_1 + z_2^{1/2} \tag{37}$$

and the short-run input demand function is

$$z_1(p, w_1, z_2) = (p/2w_1)^2 \tag{38}$$

In this case, the short-run and the long-run input demand functions are the same, but there is a difference in the supply functions. The long-run supply response is greater than the short-run, for

$$0 < \frac{\partial y(p, w_1, z_2)}{\partial p} = \frac{1}{2w_1} < \frac{1}{2w_1} + \frac{1}{2w_2} = \frac{\partial y(p, w_1, w_2)}{\partial p} \tag{39}$$

Observe that all the demand and supply functions are homogeneous of degree zero in prices.

3.4   The firm and the industry

Up until this point we have considered the firm in isolation from the rest of the economy. The outside world impinges on the firm only through the prices of output and inputs, which prices the firm assumes are fixed. But there are typically many rather similar firms producing the same output, and we have to consider how they interact.

When we analyse a whole *industry*, that is all of the firms which produce the same type of output, it is no longer generally plausible to take the price of output as given. Instead we assume that the industry faces a demand function $x(p)$ for the product, with the negative derivative $x'(p) < 0$ reflecting the fact that consumers will buy less as the price rises, and more as the price falls. There is no contradiction between the assumption that *each* individual firm takes prices as given independently of *its own* actions, and the assumption that the price of output must fall if *all* the firms in the industry raise their output. (There is a simple analogy to voting in large organizations: the outcome of an election is determined by the votes of individuals each of whom individually has only one insignificant vote.)

Just to prevent matters getting too complicated we will assume that input prices are unaffected by changes in input demand even by a whole industry. So even if all car manufacturers expand their production and thus need more labour and more steel, they can buy these inputs at unchanged prices, because their demand for labour and for steel even in aggregate is only a small part of the total demand for these inputs.

Mathematically, it is then simple to develop the concept of a supply function for the industry. If there are F firms labelled $f = 1, \ldots, F$, with the supply function of firm f being $y^f(p)$ (where the arguments of the function other than output price are left implicit) then total supply is

$$y(p) = \sum_{f=1}^{F} y^f(p) \tag{40}$$

Graphically, for given input prices and quantities of fixed inputs, this is equivalent to the horizontal addition of supply (marginal cost) curves, as illustrated in figure 3.5. (We could not do this if input prices were not assumed to be unaffected by the industry's actions.)

Now we can consider how to determine the output of an industry, on the assumption that it is composed of profit-maximizing firms which take prices as given, and on different assumptions about technology and potential entry into the industry. We shall see that the question of entry is important. It may be that there is nothing whatsoever to stop a new firm starting up production in competition with existing firms in an industry. In such a case, we say there is 'free entry' into the industry. (Of course, the existing firms may own the best sites and have superior knowledge gained through experience, so the costs of different firms may be different.) On the other hand, there may be barriers to the entry of

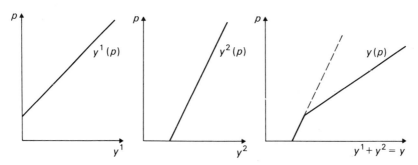

FIGURE 3.5   Addition of supply curves

new firms — a firm can offer a certain product for sale only if it has obtained a government licence, or if its employees have passed a professional examination, or if it has paid a bribe to the local gangsters. Consider the following cases.

Case 1: All firms have identical U-shaped long-run average cost curves and there is free entry to the industry. A typical firm is depicted in figure 3.6(a). At price p_1 the firm is in equilibrium and produces y_1: its long-run supply curve is the upward sloping part of the LRMC curve above LRAC, while its short-run supply curve is the upward sloping part of the SRMC curve above AVC (this last curve not being shown in the diagram). When we add together the respective curves of all of the firms in the industry we get the short-run supply curve SRS and the long-run supply curve LRS_{F1} shown in figure 3.6(b). Given the demand curve $x(p)$ we see that indeed the price p_1 is an equilibrium *for these firms*, since $x(p_1)$ is equal to the sum of all of the firm's supplies.

However, since $p_1 > \text{LRAC}$ at y_1, the firm is making profits. By assumption, other firms are free to enter this industry and the prospect of making

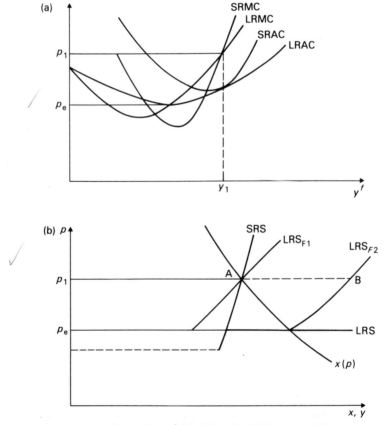

FIGURE 3.6   A market with identical firms and free entry

profits will attract other firms into the industry. With an increased number of firms' supply curves to add up we get the new long-run supply curve LRS_{F2}. Clearly p_1 is no longer the equilibrium price, since at p_1 supply is at B and demand at A, so price must fall to restore equilibrium. As price falls, each firm reduces its output, a little in the short run, more in the long run, so the whole industry slides down its long-run supply curve. This process must continue until the price falls to p_e, and each firm produces y_e. From figure 3.6(b) we see that this requires that there are just enough firms in the industry so that the new long-run supply curve is LRS_{F2} which intersects the demand curve at C. Thus in long-run equilibrium after new entry, each firm produces at the lowest point on its long-run average cost curve, and sells at a price that exactly covers this cost, and the number of firms is determined by how much will be demanded by consumers at this price. The long-run supply curve with free entry is given by the horizontal LRS curve.

If we had started with a price below p_e, we would have observed losses, exit from the industry and a rising price until equilibrium was established at p_e.

A good exercise to test your understanding of this analysis is to discuss the effect of a change in demand for the industry's product.

(It is easy to see that the analysis of this case would be unchanged even if the firms do not have identical average cost curves, so long as the minimum value of LRAC is the same for all firms.)

Case 2: All firms have U-shaped long-run average cost curves, not generally identical. What will happen in this case follows fairly directly from the previous case. If, for example, we had started off at p_1 in the previous case, but a limited number of new entrants had LRAC curves whose minimum point was at $p_a > p_e$, while all other potential entrants had minimum LRAC at $p_b > p_a$, then the long-run supply curve would be the 'stepped' curve shown in figure 3.7, where LRS_{F1} is the long-run supply curve of the original group of firms, and LRS_{F2} is the long-run supply curve with the second group added in.

In general, the long-run supply curve will slope upwards, as higher prices are needed to attract the higher-cost firms. At the long-run equilibrium price, the firms in the industry supply what is demanded, but all other firms would make losses at this price and do not produce. There may be some 'marginal' firms which make zero profits by producing at the minimum point on their long-run average cost curves.

All firms in the industry which have lower costs than the marginal firms will make positive profits, as there are no new entrants to bring price down.

Note that this case includes, as an extreme case, an industry into which entry of any new firms is barred. (One simply regards all potential entrants as facing prohibitively high costs.)

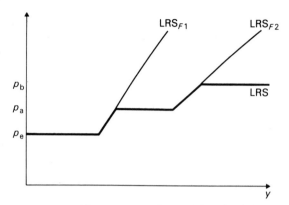

FIGURE 3.7   Free entry of non-identical firms

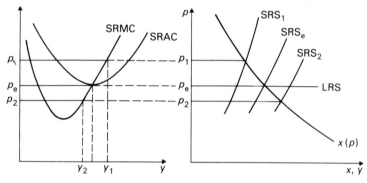

FIGURE 3.8   Identical constant returns firms

Case 3: All firms have identical horizontal long-run average cost curves.
Here we return to the previously problematic case of constant returns to
scale. If $p >$ LRAC = LRMC, the typical firm illustrated in figure 3.8(a)
produces y_1 in the short run and seeks to expand, because higher output
means higher profits. Also new firms will be attracted in by the profits,
if entry is possible. Each firm's short-run supply curve moves outwards,
and new firms enter, so the industry's short-run supply curve moves right,
as illustrated in figure 3.8(b). The process continues until the short-run
supply curve reaches SRS_e and the price is driven down to p_e.

If we start with $p <$ LRAC = LRMC, the typical firm produces y_2 (or
0 if $p <$ AVC) and firms tend to contract or to leave the industry. The
industry's short-run supply curve shifts inwards from SRS_2 until SRS_e is
reached at price p_e.

It is impossible to predict what size the firms will be at the end of this
process or how many firms there will be: that depends on how fast each
firm can change its fixed inputs and enter or leave the industry. Note also
that it does not matter whether or not there is free entry, since the exist-

ing firms can expand and contract with no loss of long-run efficiency. All firms will produce at the minimum point on their SRAC curves and all have the same cost of production.

Now the problem of profit-maximization under constant returns to scale, a problem which came up several times in chapter 2, is resolved. It is indeed the case that if $p \neq$ LRMC there is no finite positive profit-maximizing output level; while if $p =$ LRMC, any output level maximizes profits and maximum profits are zero. We now see, however, that when $p \neq$ LRMC, profit-maximizing *short-run* output is determinate and expansion of contraction and entry or exit will push p towards LRMC. When $p =$ LRMC, the profit-maximizing output of the individual firm and the number of firms are indeterminate and the actual output of each firm will depend on its previous history, but the total output of the industry will be determined by demand.

Case 4: A given number of firms have decreasing returns to scale and there is no new entry into the industry. The individual firm's equilibrium and the market equilibrium are shown in figure 3.9. Firms are making profits (the more efficient making more profits), but the existing firms do not wish to expand, nor is there new entry. The absence of new entrants could be because all potential entrants face high costs of entry, or because of some legal or institutional barrier to new entry.

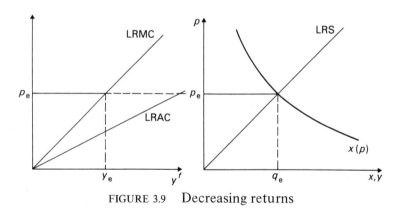

FIGURE 3.9   Decreasing returns

Case 5: All firms have decreasing returns to scale and there is free entry. Initially, the market would look like the one discussed as case 4, but the existence of profits would attract new entrants and the price would get driven steadily downwards as the LRS curve became flatter and flatter. So long as the price is positive, profits are being made, so eventually there would be an indefinitely large number of firms each producing infinitesimally small levels of output, with total output being what is demanded at a zero price. If you find this outcome implausible, as you ought to, you should think about which assumptions are the source of this implausible conclusion.

Case 6: All firms have increasing returns to scale. Here the LRAC curve slopes downwards and the LRMC curves lies below it. In the short run, output is determinate as shown in figure 3.10, but in the long run firms would expand, the price would fall, and the largest firms would have the lowest costs and so be the most profitable. Indeed, eventually there would be only one firm since firms can reduce costs by amalgamating. But such a firm would be foolish to believe that it faced a price which was fixed independently of what the firm produced. Thus there is an inconsistency here between the assumption that we have made about the production functions and the assumption we have made about firms' beliefs. We shall have to develop a separate theory to account for the behaviour of firms who believe that their actions do influence market price.

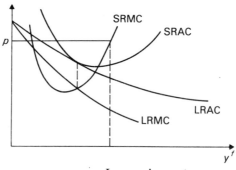

FIGURE 3.10   Increasing returns

These simple models of industrial organization are meant to provide a first step towards a comprehensive analysis rather than a definitive theory. There is no explanation of whether and when the different cases might arise; and connected with this, but more fundamentally, there is no explanation of what is the function of organizing production through firms. Nevertheless some useful conclusions have been reached.

Let us call a profit-maximizing firm that takes prices as given independently of its own actions a *competitive firm*; and an industry consisting of competitive firms with no barriers to the entry of new firms a *competitive industry*. If all the firms in a competitive industry and all potential entrants have the same minimum average cost of production, let us say the industry is in a state of *perfect competition*. (This terminology is not the same as used in all textbooks. The fact that different people use different definitions is unimportant. What matters is understanding the concepts.)

If we exclude cases 5 and 6 as implausible, we can categorize the other four cases as follows. Cases 1 and 3 satisfy all the conditions of perfect competition and in the long run profits are zero. In cases 2 and 4, the firms are competitive, the industry may or may not be competitive, but there may be positive long-run profits for some firms because of the absence of free entry of firms *with equally low costs*. Thus we have the following conclusions

(i) The supply curve of an industry consisting of competitive firms will slope upwards in the short run and slope upwards or be horizontal in the long run.

(ii) In an industry consisting of competitive firms, the marginal cost of output will be the same in all firms and will equal the price of output.

(iii) In a competitive industry in the long run, all firms producing positive output will make non-negative profits, while firms which choose to produce nothing would make non-negative losses if they started production.

(iv) In a perfectly competitive industry, all firms make zero profits in the long run and produce at a point which minimizes the average cost of production.

As a footnote to this section, we should observe that the analysis assumes that each firm's costs depend on the level of its own production. This excludes the possibility of what are called *external economies and diseconomies* where a firm's costs depend on the production of other firms, for example because as a by-product of the activities of some firms the labour force available to all firms becomes more skilful. This sort of phenomenon is of great economic interest, but to permit its introduction into the theory at this stage would complicate matters considerably (we would, for example, have to contemplate the possibility of downward sloping supply curves) so we leave this aside for the present.

*3.5   The industry's demand for inputs

The firm's supply curve is (a part of) its marginal cost curve, reflecting the equation of marginal cost and output price, and we obtain the industry's supply curve by adding the firms' supply curves. The firm's demand for an input satisfies the condition that the value of the marginal product is equal to the input price: $w_i = p \, \partial F / \partial z_i$. Thus both in the short run and the long run the demand curve for input z_i is given by the value of the marginal product $p \, \partial F / \partial z_i$. We have seen that in both the short and the long run z_i falls as w_i rises so we have the curves illustrated in figure 3.11. The curve VMP_L is $p \, \partial F / \partial z_1$ where z_1 and z_2 are chosen to maximize profits, while VMP_S is $p \, \partial F / \partial z_1$ with z_2 fixed.

It is tempting to say that the industry's demand curve for an input will be the horizontal sum of the firms' demand curves, but this is incorrect.

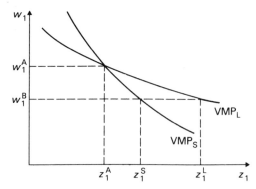

FIGURE 3.11   The firm's short-run and long-run input demand

The reason is that when w_1 changes, say from w_1^A to w_1^B in figure 3.11, each firm would change its input demand, from z_1^A to z_1^S or z_1^L, if all other prices *including the price of output* were unchanged. But if all firms are changing their output levels it is extremely unlikely that the output price will remain constant. The normal outcome is that a fall in the price of an input will raise output of each firm so reducing output price, which will tend to reduce the firms' demands for inputs, thus reducing the original expansionary effect of the initial input price change. It is pretty clear that the industry's demand curve will nevertheless be downward sloping. A formal proof is as follows. Consider an industry facing fixed prices $w_1, w_2, \ldots, w_n$ for inputs and facing a demand function for output that implies that p is a decreasing function of y. Each firm satisfies inequality (23) and thus adding all of the firms' inputs and outputs to get the industry's inputs and output we see that (23) holds for the industry as a whole. Suppose now that w_1 changes from w_1^1 to w_1^2 with all the other w_i constant. We have the inequality

$$(w_1^1 - w_1^2)\,(z_1^1 - z_1^2) \leqslant (p^1 - p^2)\,(y^1 - y^2) \tag{41}$$

for the change in the industry's demand for input 1 and supply of output. Now if $y^1 > y^2$ is must be that $p^1 < p^2$, while $y^1 < y^2$ implies $p^1 > p^2$, so the right-hand side of (41) is negative. Thus

$$(w_1^1 - w_1^2)\,(z_1^1 - z_1^2) \leqslant 0 \tag{42}$$

and the industry's demand for the input is a decreasing function of the input price.

   The fact that the industry's demand curve for an input is not the sum of individual firms' demand curves is easily seen in the case of an industry in which all F firms have identical production functions with constant returns to scale. The firms have identical cost functions which are linear in output:

$$c^f = c(\mathbf{w})\,y^f \tag{43}$$

since this is the only type of cost function that has marginal cost and average cost equal and independent of y^f. In long-run equilibrium, price equals marginal cost so

$$p = c(\mathbf{w}) \tag{44}$$

The firm's demand function for z_i will depend on $\mathbf{w}$ and y^f and will also be linear in y^f (see the last paragraph of chapter 2, and exercise 2.38) so it can be written as

$$z_i^f = \psi_i(\mathbf{w}) y^f \tag{45}$$

where ψ_i is some function of $\mathbf{w}$.

Now if w_i rises with *all* other prices constant, $c(\mathbf{w})$ rises and the firm sees $c(\mathbf{w}) > p$ so that it reduces output to zero and z_i^f falls to zero. Clearly the firm's long-run demand function for input i is infinitely elastic with respect to w_i — its demand curve is horizontal. (The second term in equation (2.71), the firm's output effect, is infinite for a firm with constant returns.)

For the industry, however, p is endogenous. Let y be total output $y^1 + y^2 + \ldots + y^F$ and let z_i be total demand $z_i^1 + z_i^2 + \ldots + z_i^F$ for input i. The demand function for the product is $x(p)$. Thus we have in equilibrium

$$z_i = \psi_i(\mathbf{w}) y \tag{46}$$

$$y = x(p) \tag{47}$$

and (44), (46) and (47) give

$$z_i = \psi_i(\mathbf{w}) x(c(\mathbf{w})) \tag{48}$$

so that

$$\frac{\partial z_i}{\partial w_i} = \frac{\partial \psi_i(\mathbf{w})}{\partial w_i} x(p) + \psi_i(\mathbf{w}) \frac{dx}{dp} \frac{\partial c(\mathbf{w})}{\partial w_i} \tag{49}$$

and

$$\frac{w_i}{z_i} \frac{\partial z_i}{\partial w_i} = \frac{w_i}{\psi_i} \frac{\partial \psi_i}{\partial w_i} + \left(\frac{p}{x} \frac{dx}{dp} \right) \left(\frac{w_i}{p} \frac{\partial c(\mathbf{w})}{\partial w_i} \right) \tag{50}$$

Thus the industry's elasticity of demand for input i is the sum of two terms. The first term is an elasticity associated with the substitution effect (which can be shown in the two-input case to be related to but not the same as the elasticity of substitution defined in section 2.5). The second term is the elasticity of demand for the product multiplied by the elasticity of unit cost with respect to w_i. (In fact, using the result (A6) proved in the appendix to chapters 2 and 3, we can prove that

$$\frac{\partial c(\mathbf{w})}{\partial w_i} = \psi_i(\mathbf{w}) \tag{51}$$

so that the second term becomes the elasticity of demand for the product multiplied by the share of input i in the cost of producing the product.) This second term, which measures in elasticity form the output effect for the industry, is finite so the industry's elasticity of demand for the input is finite, even though each individual firm has an infinite output effect and infinitely elastic demand for the input.

3.6   *The meaning and function of profits*

In several cases discussed in this chapter the long-run equilibrium of the industry is one in which firms make no profits. In other cases, profits to at least some firms are positive in the long run. In the short run, firms can make either profits or losses. This raises several questions.

The first is that firms in the real world seem to make positive profits as a rule, with losses as the exception, which seems to contradict the argument that zero profits for all firms should be the long-run equilibrium in many cases. However, what accountants call 'profits' is not the same as what is called 'profits' in our theory.

The firm is owned by individuals. Suppose that the owners supply some of the inputs, so that the firm buys only the remaining inputs. Specifically, suppose the firm uses two inputs z_1 and z_2, but that part of z_2, say z_2^A, is supplied by the owners of the firm and the remainder, z_2^B, bought by the firm, where $z_2 = z_2^A + z_2^B$. Typically the accountants' definition of profit is revenue less the cost of inputs *bought* by the firm:

$$\pi^A = py - w_1 z_1 - w_2 z_2^B \qquad (52)$$

From the viewpoint of the owners of the firm this is not a sensible measure of the return to producing output, for the alternative course of action available to them is to produce nothing *and* to sell z_2^A on the market. The return to producing output is therefore given by the *difference* between what is earned by employing z_2^A in the firm and what is earned by selling it in the market, that is by

$$\pi^A - w_2 z_2^A = py - w_1 z_1 - w_2 z_2 = \pi \qquad (53)$$

our definition of profit. Definition (52) is a definition of profit which ignores the opportunity cost of the owners' inputs.

Thus when in our theory we say that profits are positive in the long run, we mean that revenue exceeds the cost of *all* marketable inputs used in production. This situation arose in a competitive industry (recall the discussion of section 3.4) when some firms had lower costs of production than others, or when potential entrants were kept out of the industry, by prohibitively high costs or by legal barriers. Why would one firm have lower costs than another? This could happen only if the firm has access to some special knowledge or skill or input which other firms do not have *and cannot buy*.

Recall that in section 1.12 we looked at the market for a factor of production which was in fixed supply, observed that the income of such a factor plays no role in encouraging supply of the factor, and called such income economic rent. The discussion of the previous paragraph shows that long-run profit is economic rent. The owner of a special sort of input is receiving a reward for that input, and the reward is a rent since the input cannot be transferred to another use.

Whether economic rent turns up as profit, or as wage, or as land rent depends on circumstances. Suppose, for example, that there are many steel producers competing with each other, but that there is one particular location that is better than all others for steel production, but only one plant can be located there. If the owner of this site sets up a steel-producing firm then this firm will have lower cost than its competitors and so will make long-run profits say of £1 million per year. If, on the other hand, the land owner simply rents the site to the highest bidder, then some steel producer will be willing to pay rent of £1 million per year for the site. His costs will then be just as high as his competitors' costs, all firms will make no profits in the long run, but the land owner will receive £1 million per year of economic rent. Similarly, if there is one person with unique skill in producing steel, she will receive payment for this skill. If she owns a steel-producing firm, this payment will appear as profit; if she works for a steel-producing firm which she does not own, the payment will appear as a wage that is higher than the wage paid to other workers. In either case, she is receiving economic rent on this special skill which is in fixed supply.

The case where long-run profits are the result of a legal (as opposed to a cost) barrier to entry by new competitors is essentially the same. In the UK many of the transactions involved in buying and selling houses have usually to be conducted through lawyers. This is not because lawyers have unusual skill in conducting these transactions: it is because the law makes it difficult for non-lawyers to set up in competition with lawyers (and the lawyers' trade union can control the number of people who become lawyers). The result is that the price paid for the service provided is substantially higher than the work or skill required would justify: the lawyers are earning profit because the entry of competitors is barred; that is, they are earning economic rent. The fact that entry is restricted artificially by law makes no essential difference to the analysis.

We should note also that short-run profits too are associated with inputs which are in fixed supply and are therefore rents. In the short run, the firm hires variable inputs at their market price, and (as we saw above) variable cost is therefore opportunity cost. It owns given amounts of the fixed inputs, and so the rest of the revenue, that is profits without fixed costs subtracted, is economic rent. The opportunity costs of the fixed inputs, their alternative earnings, are zero. Whatever revenue is earned in excess of variable cost plays no role in encouraging the supply of fixed inputs, for that supply is fixed in the sense that the fixed inputs will be used in the industry so long as revenue exceeds variable cost. Short-run profits do, however, have the effect of drawing more inputs into the industry in the long run (as losses would have the effect of driving them out) so causing rents to disappear as supply becomes variable.

Figure 3.12 illustrates the market for a good. As before, suppose that all input prices are fixed. Each firm supplies output at a level such that price equals marginal cost. Thus an extra unit of output will add the same amount to cost irrespective of which firms produce it. The supply curve is the industry's marginal cost curve.

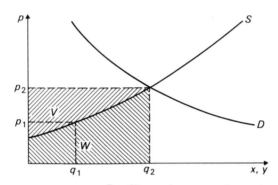

FIGURE 3.12   Profits and economic rent

Mathematically, total cost is the sum of individual firms' costs:

$$c = \sum_{f=1}^{F} c^f(\mathbf{w}, y^f) \tag{54}$$

where $c^f(\mathbf{w}, y^f)$ is the cost function of firm f, and where profit maximization implies that

$$p = \frac{\partial c^f(\mathbf{w}, y^f)}{\partial y} \qquad f = 1, \ldots, F \tag{55}$$

while total output is given by

$$y = \sum_{f=1}^{F} y^f \tag{56}$$

It is left to you as exercise 3.24 to confirm that these equations imply the results stated in the previous paragraph: that c is a function of $\mathbf{w}$ and of y with $\partial c/\partial y = p$.

If we integrate the function $\partial c(\mathbf{w}, y)/\partial y$ with $\mathbf{w}$ constant we obtain

$$\int_0^{y_2} \frac{\partial c(\mathbf{w}, y)}{\partial y} \, dy = c(\mathbf{w}, y_2) - c(\mathbf{w}, 0) \qquad (57)$$

which, since $c(\mathbf{w}, 0)$ is fixed cost, gives the variable cost of producing y_2. (In the long run, $c(\mathbf{w}, 0) = 0$.) In graphical terms, the integral of a function is represented by the area under the graph of the function, and since the supply curve S in figure 3.12 represents marginal cost as a function of y, the area marked W represents the total (variable) cost of producing q_2. The revenue received by suppliers is $p_2 q_2$, represented by the whole area $V + W$, so that profit is

$$p_2 q_2 - \int_0^{q_2} \frac{\partial c(\mathbf{w}, y)}{\partial y} \, dy = \int_0^{q_2} \left(p_2 - \frac{\partial c(\mathbf{w}, y)}{\partial y} \right) dy \qquad (58)$$

which is represented by the area V. Revenue has been divided into opportunity cost (the variable cost of production, area W) and economic rent (profit, V).

This argument can be adapted to show that economic rent arises in factor markets not only when supply is fixed but so long as supply is not infinitely elastic. Suppose that figure 3.12 represents the market for a factor of production: say the market for bus-drivers. The height of the supply curve at any point shows the opportunity cost of supplying an extra unit at this point. For example, at the wage p_1 there is a person who is just indifferent to becoming a bus-driver. At a slightly lower wage she would prefer another occupation, not necessarily because the other job offers a wage of p_1, for the two jobs may differ in their pleasantness, or their non-wage benefits. All we can say is that p_1 is the price needed to persuade the worker to forego the benefits offered by the alternative job. Thus this supply curve too is a marginal (opportunity) cost curve. If the market is in equilibrium at q_2 the total opportunity cost to the workers who are supplying this labour is the integral of marginal cost from 0 to q_2 and is represented in the diagram as the area W. Since the total wage bill is $p_2 q_2$, represented by the whole area $V + W$, so the area V represents the total payment to workers in excess of their opportunity cost. The worker who was just willing to supply her labour at p_1 is actually receiving a wage of p_2, and the sum $p_2 - p_1$ is economic rent since its size does not affect her willingness to supply this unit of labour. The total economic rent, represented by area V, is the sum (the integral, that is) of such rents over the whole labour force in this market. So in this case, as in the previous one, we have divided revenue into opportunity cost (W) and economic rent (V).

All of this raises several further questions about the morality of the system described in the theory. Is it morally right that the owners of some firms should make profits as a result of the luck of inheriting a special skill or a special piece of land? We now see that we can equally well ask whether it is morally right that the owner of a special skill, say the skill to sing well or to kick a ball accurately, should earn high wages. The question is essentially the same. Do we need such inequalities in order to allocate resources so as to produce as efficiently as possible the goods that people 'really need'? Are there other and better ways of allocating resources that avoid the potential inequalities implied by the existence of profit? These are all important, sensible and relevant questions, but we postpone discussion of them to a later chapter.

Exercises

3.1   Derive a relationship like (4) between marginal product $\partial F/\partial z_1$ and average product $F(z_1, z_2)/z_1$.

3.2   Why is the short-run supply function $y(p, w_1, z_2)$ independent of w_2?

3.3   What is the opportunity cost to society (that is, to people other than the car-driver) of allowing a car to use road or a bridge: (a) if it is congested; and (b) if it is uncongested?

3.4   Suppose that an aircraft manufacturer has spent an enormous amount on research and development to produce a supersonic passenger aircraft, and has produced a small number of actual aircraft. Discuss carefully what calculations should be made in arriving at the decisions: (i) whether to produce more aircraft; and (ii) whether to operate the aircraft already produced.

3.5   A government operates a programme to employ and train young people who would otherwise be unemployed. Should it require that projects in this programme are acceptable only if they earn enough revenue at least to cover the costs of paying the workers' wages and the costs of other inputs?

3.6   '... On the face of it, some of the proposals [for tunnels under or bridges across the English Channel between England and France] would be certain to reduce greatly the usage of existing equipment and will lead to under-use or premature abandonment. May we expect that it will be demonstrated how such costs have been allowed for in the calculation of "profitable returns" on some of the new proposals?' (Extract from letter in the *Financial Times* of March 2, 1981.) Comment.

3.7   A government embarked in the past on a large programme of training school-teachers, but as the increased number of trained teachers
becomes available for employment, it turns out that, because of an
unexpected fall in the birth rate, the number of children in schools has
fallen. Is it correct to argue that since the teacher-training programme is
a fixed cost, in deciding how many teachers to employ, the government
should recognize that the employment of a teacher has no opportunity
cost?

3.8   Prove that if the firm's production function has constant returns to
scale or decreasing returns to scale at all output levels then profits will
necessarily be non-negative at the output level which makes long-run
marginal cost equal to price. (A diagrammatic approach is probably best.)

3.9   Discuss how the answers to exercises 2.23 and 2.24 would be
different in the short run from the long run.

3.10   Find the long-run average cost and marginal cost functions of a
firm with production function

$$y = (z_1^{-1} + z_2^{-1})^{-1}$$

and input prices $w_1 = 1$, $w_2 = 4$. Find the short-run average cost, average
variable cost and marginal cost functions if z_2 is fixed at 300. Sketch all
these functions in a diagram, confirming that (14), (15) and (16) are
satisfied.

3.11   Prove that a firm's short-run supply function $y(w_1, p, z_2)$ and input
demand function $z_1(w_1, p, z_2)$ are homogeneous of degree 0 in the prices
w_1, p_1,. Confirm that these properties hold in the case of a firm with the
production function of the previous exercise.

3.12   Discuss the homogeneity properties of the short-run cost function
$c(w_1, w_2, y, z_2)$.

3.13   Explain why in the example discussed in section 3.3 the short-run
and the long-run input demand functions for z_1 are the same. (Hint:
consider $\partial F/\partial z_1$.)

3.14   Suppose that all firms in an industry have identical U-shaped long-
run average cost curves and there is free entry. The market is in equilibrium with zero profits when a sudden change in consumers' tastes shifts
the demand curve outwards. Trace the effects on the firms and on the
industry. (For the sake of simplicity, assume that all inputs are variable
so there are no short-run cost curves to worry about.)

3.15   Show that the analysis of case 1 in section 3.4 would be unchanged if firms had different cost curves, so long as the minimum value of long-run average cost is the same for all firms.

3.16   Consider an industry in which all firms have U-shaped LRAC curves, but one firm has lower costs than the rest, which are all identical. In long-run equilibrium, the price of the industry's product will equal the minimum value of long-run average cost for the rest of the firms, but show that, in general, the single low-cost firm will not produce at the minimum point on its LRAC curve. Show nevertheless that forcing it to produce at this point would raise the total cost of supplying goods to consumers. Is it possible that the low-cost firm will produce less than the others?

3.17   The US motor-car industry consists of a small number of companies and there is evidence that the largest, General Motors, can produce cars more cheaply than the others. What does this suggest about returns to scale in motor-car manufacturing? What policy would be adopted in (a) the short run, (b) the long run by a motor-car company that believed that the price at which it could sell its cars was fixed independently of the number it sold? Do you think US motor-car manufacturers have this belief?

3.18   Do you think the assumptions of case 5 in section 3.4 are implausible?

3.19   Consider the industry consisting of firms with long-run cost functions as follows:

$$\left.\begin{array}{l} 80 \text{ firms have } c(y) = 3600 - 10y + 0.01y^2 \\ 80 \text{ firms have } c(y) = 4900 - 10y + 0.01y^2 \\ 140 \text{ firms have } c(y) = 6400 - 10y + 0.01y^2 \end{array}\right\} \text{ for } y > 0$$

where y is the level of output; and all firms have $c(0) = 0$. By finding what the industry would supply at the prices 1, 2, 3, 4, 5, 6, and 7, graph the industry's supply curve.

3.20   Suppose an industry has a fixed number of firms with identical constant returns to scale production functions, but there is also a further group of firms with constant returns but a higher level of cost than the first group. What will the market equilibrium be?

3.21   Consider an industry producing a product y from inputs z_1 and z_2 where p, the output price, depends on the quantity y sold and w_1, the price of z_1, depends on the quantity bought by the industry as a whole.

Generalize the argument of equations (41) and (42) to show that if p is a decreasing function of y and w_1 is an increasing function of z_1, then the industry's demand for z_2 will be a decreasing function of w_2.

3.22   In a competitive industry there are 100 firms each of which has the cost function

$$c(y) = \begin{cases} 10y & y \leqslant 10 \\ y^2 - 10y + 100 & y \geqslant 10 \end{cases}$$

There are a further 100 firms with the cost function

$$c(y) = \begin{cases} 12y & y \leqslant 10 \\ y^2 - 8y + 100 & y \geqslant 10 \end{cases}$$

(a) Sketch the industry's supply curve.
(b) If the market demand curve is described by

$$Y = 2400 - 100p$$

where Y is demand and p is price in dollars, find the price, the total output of the industry and the outputs of the individual firms in equilibrium.
(c) If a tax of \$1 is imposed on sales of the good, what will happen to the price paid by consumers, to the price received by firms and to output? What would be the effects of a rise in tax to \$4?

3.23   Suppose that a firm finds itself in the position of making losses, even though the price of its output exceeds average variable cost. Suppose that no bank or other institution is willing to continue to lend it money to cover its short-run losses and the owners of the firm have no money of their own to meet the losses. The firm is therefore forced to become bankrupt. Yet economic theory tells us that it should continue to produce. Does this mean that it is a mistake for the banks to let such a firm go bankrupt? (You should think about what happens to the firm's fixed inputs when it goes bankrupt and closes down, and thus about the circumstances in which it would be rational for a bank to make bankrupt a firm which is in debt to it.)

3.24   Confirm that (54), (55) and (56) imply that $c = c(\mathbf{w}, y)$ with $\partial c / \partial y = p$.

CHAPTER 4

The Theory of Consumers' Behaviour

4.1 *Preferences and utility functions*

When we set about discussing the behaviour of producers, we made a simple assumption about their motivation, the assumption that firms seek to maximize their profits. This assumption is undoubtedly an oversimplification, but it is nonetheless a natural one to make.

We now turn to an examination of the motivation and behaviour of consumers. There is no obvious single objective, like profit, that a consumer might be assumed to have: a typical consumer might like to have more good food, a bigger house, longer vacations, and so on. It would not be sensible to assume that individuals seek to maximize their money income, because (except in the case of a pathological miser) money is not an end in itself, it is desired in order to be spent on what the individual really wants, and even if we believed that people sought as much money as possible, that would still leave unanswered the more interesting questions about consumer behaviour, of how the consumer is to spend his money. In any case, it is not reasonable to assume that people want as much money as possible: many people forego opportunities to gain money in order to spend more time with their families, or in bars and brothels, or in other 'leisure' activities.

Our problem then is that a typical individual has preferences for and between a wide range of goods, and there is no obvious way to represent formally his desire to behave in a way that satisfies these preferences as best he can. We adopt a mathematical approach which seeks to model the behaviour of a consumer who is trying to satisfy his multi-dimensional desires, but only gradually as we go along will the justification for our approach emerge, so you are entitled to be very sceptical at the outset. (And it is no bad thing if you remain somewhat sceptical at the end.)

We make the assumption that a typical consumer faced with the choice of how much to consume of n different goods has preferences which can be represented by a *utility function*

$$U = U(x_1, x_2, \ldots, x_n) = U(\mathbf{x}) \tag{1}$$

which associates a value of 'utility' with the consumption of the 'basket' or 'bundle' of goods consisting of x_1 units of the first good, x_2 units of the second, ..., and x_n units of the nth good. The actual value of 'utility' has no significance: all that we are interested in is whether the consumer *prefers* one bundle to another, and this is indicated by the one bundle having a higher value of 'utility' than the other. If two bundles have the same level of 'utility', the consumer is *indifferent* between them.

In the case of $n = 2$, we can represent the utility function in an indifference curve diagram, like figure 4.1. The contours of the utility function represent the different bundles (x_1, x_2) which have the same level of utility because the consumer is indifferent between them. They are called *indifference curves* (and are analogous to the isoquants of the production function).

The indifference curves drawn in figure 4.1 have two properties which reflect two standard assumptions about consumer preferences:

(i) $U(k\mathbf{x}) > U(\mathbf{x})$ for $k > 1$, the consumer prefers more goods to less goods, so the indifference curves further away from the origin give higher utility than those closer to the origin;

(ii) the utility function is quasi-concave (see p. 37), so the indifference curves are bowed in towards the origin.

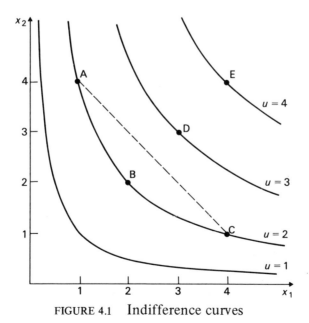

FIGURE 4.1   Indifference curves

For the utility function $U(x_1, x_2)$ the slope of the indifference curve $U(x_1, x_2) = u$ is

$$\left(\frac{dx_2}{dx_1}\right)_u = -\frac{U_1}{U_2} \tag{2}$$

(compare (2.21)), and U_1/U_2 is called the (consumer's) marginal rate of substitution. Then assumption (ii) implies that the utility function has the property of diminishing marginal rate of substitution:

$$\frac{d(U_1/U_2)}{d(x_1/x_2)} \leqslant 0 \tag{3}$$

(look back at the discussion of (2.23) if this is not immediately clear). The marginal rate of substitution measures the amount of x_2 that the consumer needs to compensate him for the loss of a unit of x_1, that is, to keep him on the same indifference curve: it is a measure of the relative value attached by the consumer to a unit of x_1. We would expect that as x_1/x_2 gets larger, so that the consumer has more x_1 and less x_2, then this value should be smaller. This is what (3) states.

An example of a utility function is

$$U(x_1, x_2) = x_1^\alpha x_2^{1-\alpha} \qquad (0 < \alpha < 1) \tag{4}$$

and, in fact, it is this function (with $\alpha = \frac{1}{2}$) which is illustrated in figure 4.1. At the point A the consumer has the bundle (1,4) which gives him utility 2; the bundle (2,2), at point B, gives him the same utility; while the bundle (4,4), at point E, gives utility 4. This shows that he is indifferent between A and B, and prefers E to both A and B; recall that the actual values of utility of 2 and 4 have no significance – it would be wrong, for example, to say that he likes E twice as much as A or B. Notice also how properties (i) and (ii) are satisfied: the points B(2,2), D(3, 3) and E(4,4) lie on successively higher indifference curves; while all points on the line between A(1,4) and C(4,1) lie above the indifference curve $u = 2$.

4.2   Utility maximization and demand functions

The point of representing preferences by a utility function is that when the consumer is faced with a limited budget to spend on buying goods, the problem of choosing the bundle which he prefers most out of all those available to him becomes, mathematically, a problem of maximization subject to a constraint.

If the consumer has money income m available to spend on goods, and if the prices of the respective goods are given by the vector $p = (p_1, p_2, \ldots, p_n)$, his *budget constraint* is

$$p_1 x_1 + p_2 x_2 + \ldots + p_n x_n \leqslant m \tag{5}$$

or, in vector notation, $\mathbf{px} \leqslant m$. The consumer has no power to change m or $\mathbf{p}$. Assumption (i) about the utility function means that the consumer will spend all of his income so (5) will be an equality. Thus the consumer's problem of choosing the best point that satisfies (5) can be written as

$$\text{maximize} \quad U(\mathbf{x})$$
$$\text{x}$$
$$\text{subject to} \quad \mathbf{px} = m \tag{6}$$

The fact that the Lagrangean function gave rise to a method of solving the constrained minimization problem (2.13) suggests that it should be used for this constrained maximization problem.

The Lagrangean is

$$L(\mathbf{x}, \lambda) = U(\mathbf{x}) + \lambda(m - \mathbf{px}) \tag{7}$$

and equating to zero its derivatives with respect to the $n + 1$ variables $\mathbf{x}, \lambda$ gives

$$\partial U / \partial x_i - \lambda p_i = 0 \qquad i = 1, \ldots, n \tag{8}$$

$$m - \mathbf{px} = 0 \tag{9}$$

These equations will give solutions for the $n + 1$ unknowns $\mathbf{x}, \lambda$ which will depend on the values of $\mathbf{p}$ and m, so we write the solutions as $\mathbf{x}(\mathbf{p}, m)$, $\lambda(\mathbf{p}, m)$. The reason why the solutions to (6) must satisfy (8) and (9) is seen by writing (8) as

$$\lambda = \frac{\partial U / \partial x_i}{p_i} \qquad i = 1, \ldots, n \tag{8a}$$

The right-hand side of (8a) is the effect on utility of spending an extra dollar on good i if p_i is the price in dollars, for the quantity bought will be $1/p_i$. We could call this the 'marginal utility of money spent on good i'. Then (8a) requires that this marginal utility should be the same for all goods, that is for each of the possible uses of money. If this were not satisfied, the consumer could raise his utility by re-allocating money from goods with low marginal utilities of money to ones with high, showing that utility is not being maximized. Thus (6) is not being solved if the equations (8) are not being satisfied: they are necessary conditions for solution of (6). That (9) is also necessary is obvious.

In the two-good case, we can give a diagrammatic representation of these conditions, and also show what sufficiency condition will ensure that the necessary conditions do indeed find the solution to the maximization problem.

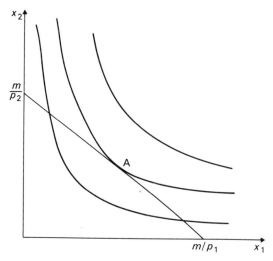

FIGURE 4.2   Utility maximization

The problem is

$$\underset{x_1, x_2}{\text{maximize}} \quad U(x_1, x_2)$$

$$\text{subject to} \quad p_1 x_1 + p_2 x_2 = m$$

(10)

In figure 4.2, the constraint $p_1 x_1 + p_2 x_2 = m$ appears as a straight line — the 'budget line'. Maximizing $U(x_1, x_2)$ is equivalent to finding an indifference curve as far away from the origin as possible. The solution is the point A: the highest attainable indifference curve is tangent to the budget line at this point. The slope of the budget line is $-p_1/p_2$; and the slope of the indifference curve is $-U_1/U_2$. Thus at the tangency point we have

$$U_1/U_2 = p_1/p_2$$

(11)

and also, of course,

$$p_1 x_1 + p_2 x_2 = m$$

(12)

The Lagrangean method would have given us (8) and (9) with $n = 2$; (12) is the same as (9), and (11) is obtained from (8) by eliminating λ.

However, it is clear that the argument used to justify (11) as a utility-maximizing condition relies on the indifference curves being bowed in towards the origin — the property of diminishing marginal rate of substitution assumed above. It is easy to see that if this condition were not satisfied, a point of tangency between the budget line and an indifference curve would not necessarily be a point of maximum utility, so the first-order conditions derived from the Lagrangean might not solve the problem. When there are more than two goods, quasi-concavity is still a sufficient condition, but it cannot be checked in a simple way like (3).

The functions $x_1(\mathbf{p}, m), x_2(\mathbf{p}, m), \ldots, x_n(\mathbf{p}, m)$ derived from (8) and (9) are called the consumer's *demand functions*: they define the quantities the consumer wishes to buy as functions of the prices of all goods and of the consumer's income.

4.3   Three examples

Consider the consumer with utility function $U^1(x_1, x_2) = x_1^\alpha x_2^{1-\alpha}$, facing prices p_1, p_2 and income m. The Lagrangean is

$$L(x_1, x_2, \lambda) = x_1^\alpha x_2^{1-\alpha} + \lambda(m - p_1 x_1 - p_2 x_2) \tag{13}$$

giving first-order conditions

$$\alpha x_1^{\alpha-1} x_2^{1-\alpha} - \lambda p_1 = 0$$

$$(1-\alpha) x_1^\alpha x_2^{-\alpha} - \lambda p_2 = 0 \tag{14}$$

$$m - p_1 x_1 - p_2 x_2 = 0$$

which are conveniently rewritten as

$$\alpha \frac{U}{x_1} = \lambda p_1$$

$$(1-\alpha) \frac{U}{x_2} = \lambda p_2 \tag{15}$$

$$m = p_1 x_1 + p_2 x_2$$

The first two equations imply that $p_1 x_1 = \alpha U/\lambda$ and $p_2 x_2 = (1-\alpha) U/\lambda$, so the third equation implies that $m = U/\lambda$ and we obtain the demand functions

$$x_1 = \alpha m/p_1 \qquad x_2 = (1-\alpha) m/p_2 \tag{16}$$

Note that the consumer's expenditure on good 1, $p_1 x_1$, is the fixed fraction α of his income, while $p_2 x_2$ is the fixed fraction $1-\alpha$ of m.

Our second example is the consumer with utility function $U^2(x_1, x_2) = x_1^{1/2} + x_2^{1/2}$. The Lagrangean is

$$L(x_1, x_2, \lambda) = x_1^{1/2} + x_2^{1/2} + \lambda(m - p_1 x_1 - p_2 x_2) \tag{17}$$

giving first-order conditions

$$\tfrac{1}{2} x_1^{-1/2} = \lambda p_1$$

$$\tfrac{1}{2} x_2^{-1/2} = \lambda p_2 \tag{18}$$

$$m = p_1 x_1 + p_2 x_2$$

Dividing the first equation by the second eliminates λ and gives the demand functions

$$x_1 = \frac{p_2 m}{p_1(p_1 + p_2)} \qquad x_2 = \frac{p_1 m}{p_2(p_1 + p_2)} \tag{19}$$

Finally, consider the consumer with utility function $U^3(x_1, x_2) = \alpha \log x_1 + (1 - \alpha) \log x_2$. The Lagrangean

$$L(x_1, x_2, \lambda) = \alpha \log x_1 + (1 - \alpha) \log x_2 + \lambda(m - p_1 x_1 - p_2 x_2) \tag{20}$$

gives first-order conditions

$$\alpha/x_1 = p_1$$

$$(1 - \alpha)/x_2 = p_2$$

$$m = p_1 x_1 + p_2 x_2$$

which solve to give the demand functions

$$x_1 = \alpha m/p_1 \qquad x_2 = (1 - \alpha) m/p_2 \tag{22}$$

which are exactly the same as (16). The first consumer and the third consumer behave identically.

This is no accident: it is the result of the fact that their utility functions satisfy the relationship $U^3(x_1, x_2) = \log U^1(x_1, x_2)$. Thus they have the same indifference curves: at all values of x_1, x_2 such that U^1 is the constant u, U^3 must have the constant value $\log u$. All that is different is the value of 'utility' that is associated with their respective indifference curves, but as is emphasized above, utility is only a device for representing preferences, and its value is of no significance, in the theory. It is only the preferences that matter, and *our two consumers behave the same way because they have the same preferences*.

Figure 4.3 illustrates this by depicting the indifference curves corresponding to both U^1 and U^3 when $\alpha = 1/3$, and both consumers face $p_1 = 1, p_2 = 2$ and $m = 30$ so that $x_1 = x_2 = 10$.

It is left to you as an exercise to derive the first-order conditions for the consumer with utility function $f(U(x))$ where f is a function whose derivative is always positive, and to show that he will have the same demand functions as the consumer whose utility function is $U(x)$.

This demonstration of the meaninglessness of 'utility', in the present context, should warn one to be careful of discussions of the theory of consumer behaviour which put a great deal of weight on ideas of utility and marginal utility. Certainly we can loosely interpret the equations $U_i/\lambda = p_i$ as saying something like 'a good is purchased in a quantity such that its marginal utility is equal to its price' (where $1/\lambda$ is a scaling factor that translates utility into money terms), but such statements are at best a convenient shorthand: the approach developed above is much superior.

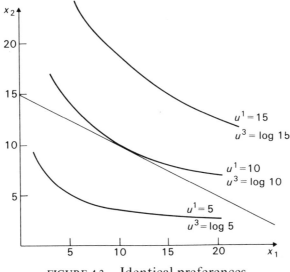

x_2

20

15

10

5

$u^1 = 15$
$u^3 = \log 15$

$u^1 = 10$
$u^3 = \log 10$

$u^1 = 5$
$u^3 = \log 5$

5   10   15   20 x_1

FIGURE 4.3   Identical preferences

4.4   *Expenditure minimization and compensated demand functions*

It is useful to look at an alternative problem that a consumer might face, the problem of minimizing the expenditure required to attain a given indifference curve:

$$\text{minimize} \quad \mathbf{px}$$
$$x \tag{23}$$

$$\text{subject to} \quad U(\mathbf{x}) = u$$

This problem is formally identical to the producer's cost-minimization problem discussed in section 2.4, so without further discussion, we know that the solutions to (23) will be functions $\mathbf{x}(\mathbf{p}, u)$. These functions, analogous to the firm's input demand functions, are called the consumer's *compensated demand functions*. The reason for this terminology will emerge shortly. Analogous to the firm's cost function we have the consumer's *expenditure function*:

$$e(\mathbf{p}, u) = \mathbf{px}(\mathbf{p}, u) \tag{24}$$

We know, from the theory of the cost-minimizing firm, that the compensated demand functions are homogeneous of degree 0 in prices and the expenditure function is homogeneous of degree 1 in prices.

The $\mathbf{x}(\mathbf{p}, u)$ are, as in the theory of the cost-minimizing firm, derived by the Lagrangean technique. Writing the Lagrange multiplier used in the solution of (23) as μ, to avoid confusion with the multiplier used in the utility-maximization problem (6), we have $n + 1$ first-order conditions for

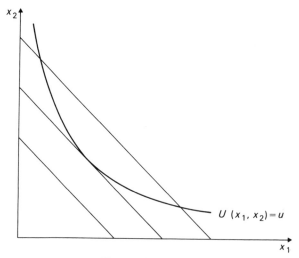

FIGURE 4.4   Expenditure minimization

the solution of (23):

$$p_i = \mu\, \partial U/\partial x_i \qquad i = 1, \ldots, n \tag{25}$$

$$u = U(\mathbf{x}) \tag{26}$$

These equations define $x_1, x_2, \ldots, x_n$ and μ as functions of $\mathbf{p}$ and u.

In the two-good case, this solution is illustrated in figure 4.4. Equation (26) gives the indifference curve corresponding to the fixed utility level u; expenditure levels $p_1 x_1 + p_2 x_2$ are represented by a series of parallel lines, with lower expenditure closer to the origin; and the lowest expenditure level compatible with utility level u corresponds to the budget line tangent to the indifference curve. The tangency condition is given by equations (25) since eliminating μ gives $p_1/p_2 = U_1/U_2$. Again, diminishing marginal rate of substitution is a sufficient condition. The analogy with the cost-minimizing firm is exact.

Now we can prove a remarkable property of the expenditure function. (The firm's cost function has the exactly analogous property which it is left to you as exercise 4.7 to state and prove.) Consider what happens to the function $\mathbf{x}(\mathbf{p}, u)$ and thus to the expenditure function if p_i changes. (Compare the discussion in section 2.6 of what happens to the cost function as y changes.) As p_i changes, the consumer continues to minimize his expenditure so that the x_i and μ change to keep (25) and (26) satisfied. From (24) we have

$$\frac{\partial e(\mathbf{p}, u)}{\partial p_i} = x_i(\mathbf{p}, u) + \sum_{j=1}^{n} p_j \frac{\partial x_j(\mathbf{p}, u)}{\partial p_i} \tag{27}$$

But (25) implies that $p_j = \mu \, \partial U/\partial x_j$ for all j so that

$$\sum_{j=1}^{n} p_j \frac{\partial x_j(\mathbf{p}, u)}{\partial p_i} = \mu \sum_{j=1}^{n} \frac{\partial U(\mathbf{x})}{\partial x_j} \frac{\partial x_j(\mathbf{p}, u)}{\partial p_i} \qquad (28)$$

and the fact that $U(\mathbf{x}) = u$ implies that the right-hand side of (28) is zero. Thus

$$\frac{\partial e(\mathbf{p}, u)}{\partial p_i} = x_i(\mathbf{p}, u) \qquad (29)$$

the derivative of the expenditure function with respect to the price of a good is equal to the quantity demanded of that good.

This result is remarkable for the following reason. If the x_i's were constant rather than being functions of prices, then (29) would obviously be correct since $e = \sum_{j=1}^{n} p_j x_j$. But each of the x_j depends on prices, including p_i, so we have n further effects of p_i on e. We have proved that these extra effects must always add up exactly to zero!

A further remarkable result follows immediately from (29):

$$\frac{\partial x_i(\mathbf{p}, u)}{\partial p_i} = \frac{\partial x_j(\mathbf{p}, u)}{\partial p_i} \qquad (30)$$

since $\partial^2 e/\partial p_j \, \partial p_i = \partial^2 e/\partial p_i \, \partial p_j$. (It is left to you as an exercise to prove the analogous result for the cost-minimizing firm; a result which was stated as (2.62) but not proved.)

Since we have derived the demand functions corresponding to the utility function $x_1^{\alpha} x_2^{1-\alpha}$, it is worth deriving also the compensated demand functions. The derivation is formally identical to the cost-minimizing example done in section 2.7 so we obtain the compensated demand functions

$$x_1(p_1, p_2, u) = \left(\frac{\alpha}{1 - \alpha} \frac{p_2}{p_1}\right)^{1-\alpha} u, \qquad x_2(p_1, p_2, u) = \left(\frac{1 - \alpha}{\alpha} \frac{p_1}{p_2}\right)^{\alpha} u \quad (31)$$

and the expenditure function

$$e(p_1, p_2, u) = \left(\frac{p_1}{\alpha}\right)^{\alpha} \left(\frac{p_2}{1 - \alpha}\right)^{1-\alpha} u \qquad (32)$$

It is easily checked that these functions satisfy (29).

4.5   *The Slutsky equation and comparative statics*

We can now look at the relation between the demand functions $\mathbf{x}(\mathbf{p}, m)$ and the compensated demand functions $\mathbf{x}(\mathbf{p}, u)$. Clearly, if the consumer is solving the expenditure-minimizing problem with utility u and actually spending m, then the same bundle of goods maximizes utility subject to a budget of m and gives a value of utility of u. (Diagrammatically, the indifference curve u represents the highest utility level compatible with the budget line m, as well as that budget line representing the lowest expenditure compatible with the indifference curve.) Hence, $x_i(\mathbf{p}, u) = x_i(\mathbf{p}, m)$ if $m = e(\mathbf{p}, u)$; that is

$$x_i(\mathbf{p}, u) = x_i(\mathbf{p}, e(\mathbf{p}, u)) \tag{33}$$

Differentiating (33) with respect to p_i gives

$$\frac{\partial x_i(\mathbf{p}, u)}{\partial p_i} = \frac{\partial x_i(\mathbf{p}, m)}{\partial p_i} + \frac{\partial x_i(\mathbf{p}, m)}{\partial m} \frac{\partial e(\mathbf{p}, u)}{\partial p_i} \tag{34}$$

Using (29) and rearranging gives

$$\frac{\partial x_i(\mathbf{p}, m)}{\partial p_i} = \frac{\partial x_i(\mathbf{p}, u)}{\partial p_i} - x_i \frac{\partial x_i(\mathbf{p}, m)}{\partial m} \tag{35}$$

Equation (35) is called the *Slutsky equation*: it divides the *price effect* on demand (the term on the left) into a *substitution effect* (first term on the right) and an *income effect* (second term). In elasticity terms, the Slutsky equation becomes

$$\frac{p_i}{x_i} \frac{\partial x_i(\mathbf{p}, m)}{\partial p_i} = \frac{p_i}{x_i} \frac{\partial x_i(\mathbf{p}, u)}{\partial p_i} - \frac{p_i x_i}{m} \frac{m}{x_i} \frac{\partial x_i(\mathbf{p}, m)}{\partial m} \tag{36}$$

so the price elasticity of demand is the substitution elasticity minus the product of the income elasticity and the proportion of income spent on the good.

All of this can be expressed in some useful terminology. The consumer's *money income* is m. His *real income* (or 'standard of living') is represented by u. His *cost of living* (that is, cost of attaining a certain standard of living) is e. Now the economic interpretation of the Slutsky equation is straightforward. A rise in p_i with money income constant has two effects: it makes good i relatively more expensive than other goods, and it reduces the consumer's real income, by reducing the quantities of goods he can buy with the money income m. The substitution effect is the first effect: what a rise in p_i would do to x_i if the consumer's real income was unchanged. The income effect is the second: (29) shows that x_i measures the effect on the cost of living of a rise in p_i, so it measures the reduction in the real value of the fixed money income m, and multiplying by $\partial x_i / \partial m$ gives the effect on demand.

A diagrammatic illustration of this is possible in the two-good case, and it may help to explain the terminology 'substitution effect' and 'compensated demand function'. Instead of the infinitesimal changes, the effects

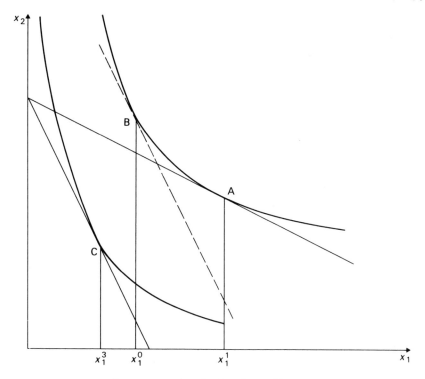

FIGURE 4.5   Income and substitution effects: the utility
approach

of which are indicated by the derivatives in the Slutsky equation, we show
in figure 4.5 the effect of a finite rise in p_1. The budget line was originally
the line tangent to an indifference curve at A. A rise in p_1 with p_2 and m
constant leaves the intercept with the x_2 axis unchanged (at m/p_2), but the
intercept with the x_1 axis shifts towards the origin (being m/p_1), and we
have the new budget line tangent to an indifference curve at C. The
budget line has changed its slope, and shifted in towards the origin. These
two changes can be separated. The broken line shows what the consumer's
budget line would be if, after p_1 rose, he also received sufficient extra
money income to keep him on the same indifference curve. The extra
money income *compensates* him for the price rise by keeping his real
income unchanged. His chosen point shifts from A to B and his consumption of good 1 falls from x_1^1 to x_1^0. This is the substitution effect, which is
measured by the derivative of the compensated demand function. If the
consumer now lost the compensating money income, his budget line
would shift in towards the origin, from the broken line through B to the
parallel line through C, his chosen point shifts from B to C, and his consumption of good 1 changes from x_1^0 to x_1^3. This is the income effect of the
price change.

We can appeal to the formal identity of the theory of the cost-minimizing firm and the theory of the expenditure-minimizing consumer to prove one comparative-static result. An argument identical to the one which gave (2.61) implies that

$$\frac{\partial x_i(\mathbf{p}, u)}{\partial p_i} \leqslant 0 \tag{37}$$

that is, the *substitution effect is negative*, or the *compensated demand function for any good is a decreasing function of the price of that good*. This result is illustrated in figure 4.5 where B is to the left of A.

However, a search for further general comparative-statics results is fruitless. It is easy to show by example that $\partial x_i(\mathbf{p}, m)/\partial m$ may be either positive or negative. Figure 4.5 shows a case where both $\partial x_1/\partial m$ and $\partial x_2/\partial m$ are positive, but it is easy to modify the diagram to give the required example. Indeed, it should be clear there is nothing extraordinary about a consumer choosing to consume less of a particular good as his income rises. Since, however, a richer person has more money to spend than a poorer person, $\partial x_i/\partial m$ is 'more likely' to be positive than negative. (You are asked in exercise 4.13 to show precisely what 'more likely' means.) A good whose consumption rises with income, so that $\partial x_i/\partial m > 0$, is called a *normal* good; while if consumption falls with income, so that $\partial x_i/\partial m < 0$, the good is an <u>inferior</u> good.

From (35) and (37) it follows that, if $\partial x_i/\partial m > 0$, then $\partial x_i(\mathbf{p}, m)/\partial p_i < 0$: *a normal good has a negative price effect*, or *the demand function of a normal good is a decreasing function of the price of that good*. If, however, $\partial x_i/\partial m < 0$, the price effect is divided into a negative substitution effect and a positive income effect so that it is of ambiguous sign. If the income effect outweighs the substitution effect, the demand for the good will *increase* with price. A good for which this happens is called a *Giffen good*, and it is left to you in exercise 4.16 to show that this is more likely to happen when a large proportion of the consumer's income is spent on the inferior good.

It is left to you (see exercise 4.17) to prove that when $i \neq j$

$$\frac{\partial x_i(\mathbf{p}, m)}{\partial p_j} = \frac{\partial x_i(\mathbf{p}, u)}{\partial p_j} - x_j \frac{\partial x_i(\mathbf{p}, m)}{\partial m} \tag{38}$$

Now recall equation (30). If $\partial x_i(\mathbf{p}, u)/\partial p_j = \partial x_j(\mathbf{p}, u)/\partial p_i > 0$, goods i and j are said to be *substitutes*; while if the inequality goes the other way, they are said to be *complements*. Butter and margarine are likely to be substitutes, while butter and bread are likely to be complements. It is left to you (exercise 4.18) to prove that if there are only two goods they must be substitutes.

If $\partial x_i(\mathbf{p}, m)/\partial p_j > 0$, good i is said to be a *gross substitute* for good j; with the reverse inequality, good i is a *gross complement* for good j. Note from (38) that in general $\partial x_i(\mathbf{p}, m)/\partial p_j \neq \partial x_j(\mathbf{p}, m)/\partial p_i$.

We have already noted that the compensated demand functions are homogeneous of degree 0 in prices and the expenditure function is homogeneous of degree 1 in prices. It is easy to show that the demand functions $\mathbf{x}(\mathbf{p}, m)$ are homogeneous of degree 0 in prices and income.

It is left to you as exercise 4.9 to go back to the demand functions and compensated demand functions derived from the utility function $x_1^\alpha x_2^{1-\alpha}$ and confirm that (35), (37) and (38) hold.

4.6   Revealed preference

There is an alternative approach to the theory of consumers' behaviour which makes no reference to the concept of utility. The key to the alternative approach is the assumption that the consumer makes choices in different situations which are *consistent* with his having fixed preferences. If in one situation both A and B are possible choices and he chooses A, we say that his choice reveals that he prefers A to B. Consistency then requires that in any other situation in which both A and B are available he should *not* choose B: for such a choice would reveal that he preferred B to A, contradicting his earlier revealed preference.

Suppose the consumer is faced by the budget constraint depicted in figure 4.6 by a solid line and chooses to consume the bundle labelled X. His choice reveals that he prefers X to any other point on or below the budget line, for all such points are possible choices given his income. Suppose now that changes in prices and income shift his budget constraint

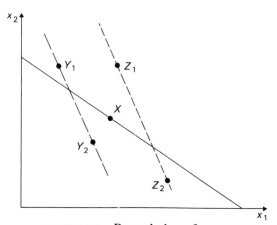

FIGURE 4.6   Revealed preference

to the one shown by the broken line through Y_1. He will now choose a point such as Y_1 or Y_2, depending on his preferences. If his choice were Y_1, nothing is revealed about his preferences: when he chose X, Y_1 was unavailable, being above his budget line; and when he chose Y_1, X was unavailable. If, however, his choice were Y_2 in the new situation, we would know that he prefers X to Y_2, for that preference was revealed by his choice of X in the first situation, when Y_2 was also available. We would also know that the shift in his budget line has made him worse off.

Suppose by contrast, the budget line had shifted to the position shown by the broken line through Z_1. Consider the point Z_2 which lies on the new budget line but below the original line. Note that X lies below the new budget line. When he chose X, Z_2 was available; and since X and Z_2 are both available in the new situation, it would be inconsistent for him now to choose Z_2. Only a choice such as Z_1 which lies above the original budget line is consistent, and since X is still available, the choice of Z_1 reveals that he prefers Z_1 to X. The shift in the budget line has made him better off.

The logic of these examples can be applied to give some general propositions. Suppose the consumer faced with the prices $\mathbf{p}^1$ and income m^1) chooses consumption bundle $\mathbf{x}^1$ (such that $\mathbf{p}^1\mathbf{x}^1 = m^1$); while when prices change to $\mathbf{p}^2$ and his income changes too, he chooses $\mathbf{x}^2$. (For simplicity, ignore the trivial possibility that $\mathbf{x}^1 = \mathbf{x}^2$.) If $\mathbf{x}^2$ was available when he chose $\mathbf{x}^1$, he has revealed a preference for $\mathbf{x}^1$ over $\mathbf{x}^2$, so that $\mathbf{x}^2$ can be consistently chosen only if $\mathbf{x}^1$ were not available: that is

$$\mathbf{p}^1\mathbf{x}^2 \leqslant \mathbf{p}^1\mathbf{x}^1 \Rightarrow \mathbf{p}^2\mathbf{x}^2 < \mathbf{p}^2\mathbf{x}^1 \tag{39}$$

Symmetrically,

$$\mathbf{p}^2\mathbf{x}^1 \leqslant \mathbf{p}^2\mathbf{x}^2 \Rightarrow \mathbf{p}^1\mathbf{x}^1 < \mathbf{p}^1\mathbf{x}^2 \tag{39a}$$

There are thus three possibilities. If $\mathbf{p}^1\mathbf{x}^2 \leqslant \mathbf{p}^1\mathbf{x}^1$ and $\mathbf{p}^2\mathbf{x}^2 < \mathbf{p}^2\mathbf{x}^1$, the consumer reveals a preference of $\mathbf{x}^1$ over $\mathbf{x}^2$, and is better off in the first situation. If $\mathbf{p}^2\mathbf{x}^1 \leqslant \mathbf{p}^2\mathbf{x}^2$ and $\mathbf{p}^1\mathbf{x}^1 < \mathbf{p}^1\mathbf{x}^2$, the consumer prefers $\mathbf{x}^2$ to $\mathbf{x}^1$ and is better off in the second situation. If $\mathbf{p}^1\mathbf{x}^2 > \mathbf{p}^1\mathbf{x}^1$ and $\mathbf{p}^2\mathbf{x}^1 > \mathbf{p}^2\mathbf{x}^2$, we are unable to deduce from the consumer's behaviour which of the two bundles he prefers and in which situation therefore he is better off.

Revealed preference theory can be used to give an alternative division of the price effect into income and substitution effects. Consider figure 4.7 which depicts the same price change as figure 4.5: as p_1 rises with m and p_2 constant the budget line becomes steeper and closer to the origin and the chosen consumption bundle shifts from A to C. Suppose now we want to compensate the consumer for the effect of the price rise on his income, but do not know anything about the consumer's preferences other than what is revealed by his behaviour. In particular, we do not know the shape of the indifference curve through A. If we give him

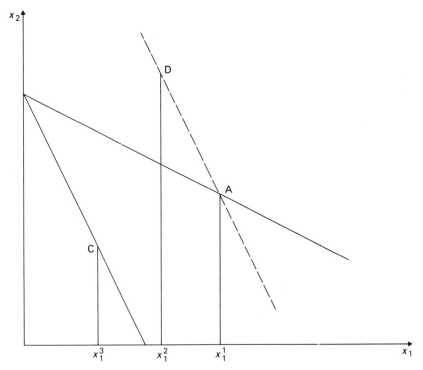

FIGURE 4.7   Income and substitution effects: the revealed
preference approach

enough income so that he can still purchase A, his budget line will be the
broken line through A parallel to the line through C. Since he can still
buy A, he cannot be worse off than he was originally; so he has been
compensated. In fact, he will choose to consume at a point such as D on
the part of the new budget line lying above the old line. This reduction in
consumption of x_1 from x_1^1 to x_1^2 is the substitution effect of the rise in p_1,
and consistency ensures that it is indeed a reduction, so that the substitution effect is negative. (Actually, it is possible that D coincides with A, so
that strictly we should say that the substitution effect is non-positive.)
The shift from D to C, the change in x_1 from x_1^2 to x_1^3, is the income effect;
and we have no theoretical reason to suppose it is positive or negative.

In general, suppose prices shift from $\mathbf{p}^1$ to $\mathbf{p}^2$, and consumption shifts
from $\mathbf{x}^1$ to $\mathbf{x}^3$ when income m^1 is unchanged. We compensate the consumer for the price change by giving him income m^2 which satisfies
$m^2 = \mathbf{p}^2\mathbf{x}^1$. In fact, at prices $\mathbf{p}^2$ with income m^2, the consumer chooses $\mathbf{x}^2$.
Since $m^2 = \mathbf{p}^2\mathbf{x}^1 = \mathbf{p}^2\mathbf{x}^2$, (39a) implies that $\mathbf{p}^1\mathbf{x}^1 < \mathbf{p}^1\mathbf{x}^2$ (unless $\mathbf{x}^1 = \mathbf{x}^2$,
in which case, of course, $\mathbf{p}^1\mathbf{x}^1 = \mathbf{p}^1\mathbf{x}^2$). Hence

$$\mathbf{p}^1\mathbf{x}^1 - \mathbf{p}^2\mathbf{x}^1 \leqslant \mathbf{p}^1\mathbf{x}^2 - \mathbf{p}^2\mathbf{x}^2 \qquad\qquad (40)$$

But now suppose that the only difference between $\mathbf{p}^1$ and $\mathbf{p}^2$ is in p_i. Then (40) gives

$$(p_i^1 - p_i^2)(x_i^1 - x_i^2) \leqslant 0 \tag{41}$$

and we have the general result that the substitution effect is negative.

If we combine figures 4.5 and 4.7 we can see that there is a difference between the revealed preference approach and the utility approach in the way they divide the price effect into income and substitution effects. The points A, B, C and D in figure 4.8 are exactly as in figures 4.5 and 4.7. We can see at once that if we give the consumer enough income after the rise in p_2 to allow him still to consume at A then he will actually consume at D which is on a higher indifference curve than A. We have overcompensated him for the price rise: the smaller amount of compensation that would have enabled him to consume at B would have been enough to keep his real income constant. It is, however, left to you as exercise 4.22 to show that this is only the case when we look at non-infinitesimal price changes: the income effect of an infinitesimal price change is the same on either definition, so that the division of the price effect into substitution and income effects is the same, and equations (35) and (37) could equally well have been derived from the revealed preference approach.

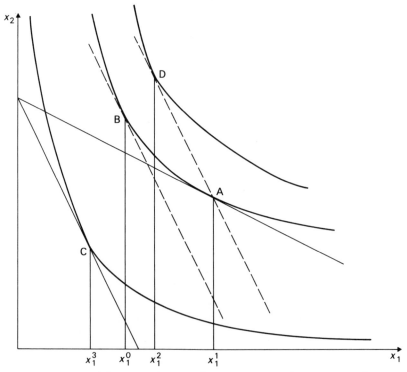

FIGURE 4.8   The revealed preference and utility approaches compared

Finally, let us consider some situations where the income change required to compensate for price changes is actually calculated and paid. Suppose that the government calculates that the 'cost of living' of retired people has risen by 10% and that their social security pensions should therefore be raised by 10%. Let us make this familiar-sounding statement more precise. The government finds out what bundle of goods is consumed by a 'typical' pensioner. Then, as prices rise, with some prices rising more than others, it calculates that the cost of this bundle has risen by 10%. A 10% rise in money income would thus be needed if the typical pensioner is to be able to buy what he bought before the price rise. However, figure 4.8 shows that compensation which permits the purchase of the original bundle also normally permits the purchase of bundles which are actually better than the original. That figure 4.8 does not present a misleadingly simple case is shown by the fact that, in general, if $p^2x^2 = p^2x^1$ it follows from an earlier argument that x^2 is preferred to x^1. (There are two trivial exceptions to this statement: two circumstances in which x^2 is the same as x^1. It is left to you to find what these circumstances are — see exercise 4.21.) Thus the 10% rise in income following a 10% rise in the 'cost of living' makes the typical pensioner *better* off than before. The intuition behind this result is simple: the 10% rise in the cost of living will usually involve a rise in some prices of more than 10% and a rise in others of less than 10%. That is, *relative* prices change. The pensioner *can* buy what he bought before and be as well off as before, but he should *substitute* away from goods whose prices have gone up more and towards goods whose prices have gone up less and thereby become better off.

Why then do governments calculate the income increase that would be needed to enable the pensioner to buy the previous bundle of goods rather than the (smaller) income increase that would enable the pensioner to stay on his old indifference curve? The answer is obvious: the government can find out what a typical pensioner buys, but it cannot find out what a typical pensioner's indifference curves are.

The same argument applies to a trade-union negotiating for a cost-of-living increase in wages; or to a comparison of the cost of living in two different countries. If we calculate the income needed in the second year or the second situation to buy the goods consumed in the first year or the first situation (this is called 'using a base-weighted index' of the cost of living) we are overestimating the income needed truly to maintain the typical consumer's standard of living.

4.7 *The individual's supply of labour*

It is easy to extend the theory of the consumer to give a very simple model of the supply of labour. Let x be the vector of goods consumed weekly by the individual and let L be the number of hours he works in a week. Since in total there are 168 hours in a week, he is not working for $168 - L$ hours. This we called leisure, denoted by

$$N = 168 - L \qquad (42)$$

and we can treat leisure as another 'good' which contributes to his enjoyment of life so that the utility function is

$$U = U(\mathbf{x}, N) \qquad (43)$$

If we suppose the consumer has money income m, derived from sources other than work, then if the wage rate is w, the total income available for expenditure on $\mathbf{x}$ is $wL + m$ so that his budget constraint is

$$\mathbf{px} = wL + m \qquad (44)$$

Using (42) we can write this as

$$\mathbf{px} + wN = 168w + m \qquad (45)$$

Thus the individual's objective is to maximize (43) subject to (45). Note how (45) shows that the opportunity cost of leisure is w: the consumer starts the week with money m and 168 hours, each of which can be sold for w, and every hour of leisure that he takes costs w just as every unit of good i costs p_i.

The case where there is only one good x in $\mathbf{x}$ is illustrated in figure 4.9. The budget line ends at $N = 168$, $x = m/p$ since the individual cannot work fewer than 0 hours, and at this point he would spend m/p on x. The

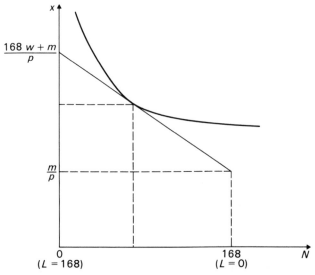

FIGURE 4.9   The individual's supply of labour

slope of the budget line is w/p, often referred to as the 'real wage' since it measures in goods (as opposed to money) what is gained from an extra hour of work. Clearly the optimal point, as usual, is the tangency point where $U_N/U_x = w/p$.

In general, maximizing (43) subject to (45) gives Lagrangean first-order conditions

$$\partial U/\partial x_i = \lambda p_i \qquad i = 1, \dots, n \tag{46}$$

$$\partial U/\partial N = \lambda w \tag{47}$$

and, of course, (45). From these $n + 2$ equations in $\mathbf{x}, N$ and λ we derive consumer demand functions $x(\mathbf{p}, w, m)$ and $N(\mathbf{p}, w, m)$, the last being the demand for leisure and from the fact that $L = 168 - N$ we have a *labour supply function*

$$L = L(\mathbf{p}, w, m) = 168 - N(\mathbf{p}, w, m) \tag{48}$$

The most interesting feature of this simple theory is that when leisure is a normal good, the income and substitution effects act in *opposite* directions, so that the effect of w on $L(\mathbf{p}, w, m)$ is ambiguous. (Contrast the demand functions $x(\mathbf{p}, w, m)$: it is easy to confirm that, as before, the effect of p_i on x_i is ambiguous only when x_i is an inferior good.) This arises because w appears on both sides of (45), and it is easily illustrated in figure 4.10, which shows the effect of a rise in w. The chosen point shifts from A to C. Since C lies on a higher indifference curve than A there has

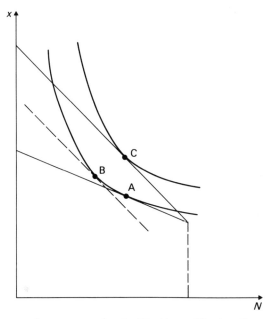

FIGURE 4.10   Income and substitution effects of a wage rise

been a rise in real income which can be compensated by a reduction in money income m which shifts the budget line in towards the origin parallel to the new budget line until the chosen point B is on the old indifference curve. The shift from A to B is the substitution effect: the rise in the wage rate implies a rise in the relative cost of leisure so that demand for leisure falls and labour supply rises. The shift from B to C is the income effect, which implies (since leisure is assumed to be a normal good) a rise in the demand for leisure and a fall in the supply of labour. The sum of the two changes could give either a decrease or an increase in labour supply.

This analysis is used to explain the effects of income tax on workers' supply of labour. A tax rise is effectively a reduction in the wage rate. The substitution effect reduces willingness to work: 'it's not worth working so hard if one loses most of the money in tax' is a common way of expressing this. But the income effect raises labour supply: 'one has to work harder to have enough money to spend after paying tax'.

By looking at a different constrained optimization problem we could derive compensated demand functions and an expenditure function incorporating labour supply as well as goods demand (or, equivalently, incorporating leisure as one of the goods demanded). The whole analysis is straightforward and is left to you to develop if you wish.

For some purposes, it is helpful to take a revealed preference approach to this class of problem. Again, the extension of the revealed preference analysis developed above is perfectly straightforward and is not spelled out here.

It should be emphasized that this is a very simplistic model. The most apparent departure from reality is that there are few jobs which pay an hourly wage *and* allow the worker to choose his hours of work. (This can at least partly be countered by the observation that workers can choose between taking different jobs that each involve fixed but different hours.) More important, perhaps, is the objection that the labour which a worker supplies is not a homogeneous one-dimensional quantity measured in hours and paid at a fixed rate, but rather involves the complications of varying skill, enthusiasm, effort and job satisfaction. The theory sketched above is therefore the beginning of a theoretical treatment of the issues involved in labour supply rather than the last word.

Note, however, that it is relatively easy to introduce some complications. Overtime payments involve a higher wage rate for hours of work beyond a certain point. A 'progressive' income tax means a higher tax rate, so a lower after-tax wage rate, after income reaches a certain level. Such multiple wage rates give rise to kinked budget lines as illustrated in figure 4.11, which shows how the budget line would look with a progressive income tax. (A 'regressive' income tax, or an overtime system would give rise to a different sort of kink.)

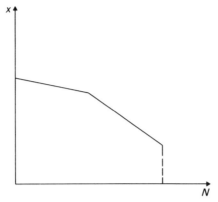

FIGURE 4.11   A kinked budget line

4.8   *Market demand and labour supply*

All of this chapter has been concerned with individual behaviour, but just as we derived market supply functions for a good by adding together different firms' supply functions, so we can derive the market demand function for a good by adding together individuals' demand functions. Thus if there are H individuals, indexed by the superscripts $h = 1, \ldots, H$, with demand functions $x_i^h(\mathbf{p}, m^h)$ for good i, the market demand is given by

$$\sum_{h=1}^{H} x_i^h(\mathbf{p}, m^h)$$

If we assume away the Giffen case then since each individual's demand is a decreasing function of p_i, we can say that the market demand is a decreasing function of p_i. In diagrammatic terms, we are summing horizontally a set of downward-sloping individual demand curves to get a downward-sloping market demand curve.

It is, however, less easy to rule out 'perverse' behaviour of labour supply. We saw that the possibility that a worker will work less as the wage rises is not a curiosity depending on an unlikely set of assumptions, but a real possibility. In such a case the individual's labour supply curve would bend backwards, as illustrated in figure 4.12 for $w > w_0$. Clearly aggregate labour supply might also therefore bend backwards. In the case of a particular occupation, however, any tendency for this to be observed might be at least partly counteracted by the fact that higher wages should attract new workers into the occupation.

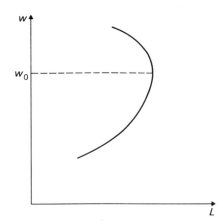

FIGURE 4.12   Backward-bending labour supply

Exercises

4.1   Use assumption (i) of section 4.1 to prove that indifference curves cannot cross each other.

4.2   Derive the demand functions corresponding to the utility functions

(i) $\log x_1 + \log x_2$
(ii) $x_1^2 x_2$
(iii) $x_1^\alpha x_2^\beta x_3^\gamma$

where in (iii) α, β, γ are all positive and $\alpha + \beta + \gamma = 1$.

4.3   Which of the following utility functions represent the same set of preferences:

(i) $x_1^{1/2} x_2^{1/2}$
(ii) $x_1^2 x_2$
(iii) $\log x_1 + \log x_2$?

4.4   Derive the first-order condition for utility maximization for a consumer whose utility function is $f(U(\mathbf{x}))$ where f is a function whose derivative is always positive, and show that the resulting demand functions are the same as for the consumer whose utility function is $U(\mathbf{x})$. Explain why.

4.5   Prove that the consumer's demand functions are homogeneous of degree 0 in **p** and m. Give a verbal explanation.

4.6   Show in a diagram that if the utility function is not quasi-concave, the first-order conditions would not necessarily solve the utility-maximization problem.

4.7 State and prove the results for the cost-minimizing firm which correspond to (29) and (30).

4.8 Derive the compensated demand functions and the expenditure functions corresponding to the utility functions

(i) $x_1^{1/2} + x_2^{1/2}$
(ii) $\alpha \log x_1 + (1 - \alpha) \log x_2$

and confirm that (29) and (33) hold (recall that the demand functions were derived in section 4.3).

4.9 For the utility function $x_1^{\alpha} x_2^{1-\alpha}$ confirm that (35), (37) and (38) hold.

4.10 Prove that the substitution effect is negative.

4.11 Prove that the compensated demand functions are homogeneous of degree 0 in prices and that the expenditure function is homogeneous of degree 1 in prices. Give a verbal explanation.

4.12 Draw a diagram to show the possibility of a good being inferior.

4.13 It is necessarily the case that $\Sigma_{i=1}^n p_i x_i(\mathbf{p}, m) = m$. Use this fact to show that not all goods can be inferior. Make more precise the statement in section 4.5 that a good is 'more likely' to be normal than inferior.

4.14 Suppose that all the goods which a consumer buys are normal goods to him, and that the price of each good rises by 10% with the consumer's money income unchanged. What will be the effect on his consumption pattern?

4.15 Draw a diagram to illustrate the Giffen good case.

4.16 Other things being equal, an inferior good is more likely to be a Giffen good if consumers spend a high proportion of their income on it. Give a verbal explanation of this, give a geometrical explanation in terms of the diagram used to answer exercise 4.15, and use (36) to give a mathematical explanation.

4.17 Prove (38).

4.18 Prove that if there are only two goods they must be substitutes, but draw a diagram to show that they need not be gross substitutes.

4.19   In the utility function

$$U(x_1, x_2) = (x_1 - a_1)^\alpha (x_2 - a_2)^{1-\alpha}$$

α is a constant satisfying $0 < \alpha < 1$, and a_1 and a_2 are positive constants. Derive the demand functions, compensated demand functions and expenditure function corresponding to this utility function. (You will find this easier if you follow very closely what was done in the case of the function $x_1^\alpha x_2^{1-\alpha}$.)

Give an interpretation to the constants a_1 and a_2 and find whether the goods are substitutes and gross substitutes.

Confirm that the Slutsky equation holds.

4.20   You observe a consumer in two situations:

(i)   with an income of £80 he buys 20 units of good x at a price of £1 each and 3 units of good y at a price of £20 each;
(ii)   with an income of £160 he buys 30 units of good x at a price of £4 each and 2 units of good y at a price of £20 each.

Is his behaviour in the two situations consistent with his having unchanging preferences?

4.21   Show that there are two sets of circumstances (one arising from the nature of the price and income changes, the other arising from the nature of the consumer's preferences) in which a change in prices and income which satisfies $m^2 = p^2 x^1$ will lead to no change in consumption so that $x^2 = x^1$.

*4.22   The result analogous to (29) is obvious when it is the revealed preference concept of income compensation for price changes which is used. Thus show that the income effect of a rise in p_i is given by $-x_i(\partial x_i/\partial m)$ whichever concept of compensation is used, so that the Slutsky equation could equally well have been derived from the revealed preference approach.

4.23   A civil servant is moved from London to Brussels. The government calculates the income he will need in order to 'maintain his previous standard of living' and pays him that income in Belgian francs. Is the civil servant better off or worse off?

4.24   An individual's preferences are described by the utility function

$$U(x_1, x_2, N) = \log x_1 + 2 \log x_2 + 9 \log N$$

where x_1 and x_2 are the quantities of goods consumed per day, L is the number of hours worked per day and $N = 24 - L$. The goods' prices are

p_1 and p_2. His income is partly derived from work, at a wage rate of w per hour, but he also has an 'unearned' income of m per day. Derive the individual's demand functions for the goods and his supply function of labour. Show that if $m = 0$, he works a fixed number of hours per day independently of prices; but that if $m > 0$, the substitution effect of a wage rise outweighs the income effect.

4.25 Consider the individual whose behaviour is described by the maximization of $U(x, N)$ subject to a budget constraint where N is leisure and x is consumption of a single good. The government considers two ways of taxing his income:

(i) a 'progressive' tax in which the first slice of income is taxed at a low rate, the rest at a higher rate;
(ii) a 'regressive' tax in which the tax on the first slice is high and on the rest lower.

If the rates in the two systems are chosen so as to make the individual's real income the same in both cases, in which system does he supply more labour?

(Answer this question first using a utility definition of real income and then using a revealed-preference definition.)

4.26 Mr Doolittle has an 'unearned' income of £40 per week but chooses to work for 20 hours per week at a wage of £2 per hour. On losing that job he finds another which pays £1.80 per hour and decides to work for 25 hours per week at this job.

(i) Is his behaviour consistent with unchanging preferences?
(ii) In which situation is he better off?
(iii) Is it possible to deduce whether leisure is a normal good or an inferior good for him?
(iv) If during his second employment, his 'unearned' income rises to £44 per week because of the death of his rich aunt, but he continues to work for 25 hours per week, would you conclude that this sad event has led to a change in his tastes?

4.27 It is sometimes alleged that as the wages of coal-miners in Britain have risen, the rate of absenteeism has also risen. Could you explain such a phenomenon?

CHAPTER 5

Welfare Economics in Competitive Markets

5.1 *Introduction*

Having developed a theory which aims to *describe* how a competitive market allocates resources, we are now in a position to start to *evaluate* the market mechanism. We have seen how the price system regulates supply and demand of both inputs and outputs, drawing firms into particular industries, controlling how they produce and how much they produce, and allocating goods to consumers. Does the price system do this job well? Welfare economics consists of the study of questions of this nature.

A common argument runs as follows: in a competitive market firms produce the quantity at which marginal cost is equal to price, while consumers will buy products so long as the price is less than or equal to what they are willing to pay. The marginal cost is the cost of the extra resources needed to produce an extra unit of the good. The market rations the goods which are produced, allocating goods to those individuals who are willing to pay at least the cost of supplying the good to them, and denying goods to those individuals who are not willing to pay that cost and prefer to spend their income on other goods. A similar argument is clearly possible for goods which are the output of one industry and the input of another; or for labour, supplied by individuals, used by firms. Thus goods get allocated to those who are willing to pay for them, and resources get allocated to the uses in which they are most valued.

This argument is illustrated in figure 5.1, in a supply and demand diagram for good i. The supply curve $y_i(p_i)$ and demand curve $x_i(p_i)$ intersect at the equilibrium price and quantity p_i^*, q_i^*.

The supply curve is the sum of producers' marginal cost (MC) curves so that when $y_i < q_i^*$, $MC_i < p_i^*$, while when $y_i > q_i^*$, $MC_i > p_i^*$. The demand curve is determined by the behaviour of consumers, and we have seen that the typical consumer should satisfy the relation

$$p_i = \frac{1}{\lambda} \frac{\partial U}{\partial x_i} \qquad (1)$$

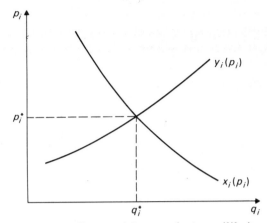

FIGURE 5.1   Competitive market equilibrium

(see (4.8)) which could loosely be described as stating that price should equal 'marginal utility' (MU). (Note that λ is independent of i, and remember that the actual value of utility is irrelevant.) Thus for $x_i < q_i^*$, $MU_i > p_i^*$, while when $x_i > q_i^*$, $MU_i < p_i^*$, where MU_i stands for $(1/\lambda)(\partial U/\partial x_i)$.

It is not desirable to have $q_i < q_i^*$, for then $MC_i < MU_i$, and there are individuals who are willing to pay for a unit of the good more than the cost of supplying them. Conversely at $q > q_i^*$, $MC_i > MU_i$ and q_i is too high. The market equilibrium quantity $q_i = q_i^*$ is the optimal quantity.

There are several features of this argument that require attention. (i) We should note that it applies to a competitive market, in which both suppliers and demanders take the price as given independently of their individual actions. When we look at markets which are not competitive in this sense, we shall see that the story is then different. This will be considered in the next chapter. (ii) We are assuming that consumers behave rationally so as to satisfy their desires as effectively as possible, and we are accepting consumers' own judgement as to what is good for them. We should think of the possibility that consumers act irrationally or unwisely; or that they are influenced by misleading information about products about which they are imperfectly informed. Equally, it is possible that a producer may be imperfectly informed of the technical possibilities open to him. The fact that we have nothing more to say about these issues does not mean that they are unimportant. (iii) What a producer pays for inputs may not be the true cost of production: for example, if he does not have to pay to clean up pollution caused by his activities. A similar point applies to consumers: smoking cigarettes in the presence of non-smokers imposes costs on the non-smokers which the smoker may not take into account. (iv) 'Utility' has no meaning as such, and therefore 'marginal utility' is not comparable between individuals. When one consumer chooses to spend money on one good rather than another, we can assume (subject to the qualifications in (ii) above) that he prefers the chosen good (his 'marginal utility' per dollar spent on the chosen good is higher). But the fact that one individual is willing to pay more for a good than another individual may reflect their relative wealth rather than their relative need. (v) There is an element of question-begging in the argument. In using the concept of marginal cost we are implicitly assuming that the market's valuation of inputs is correct: that is, to show that one market operates optimally we seem to be *assuming* that other markets operate optimally. Also the individual's consumption of other goods enters his 'marginal utility'. We must look at all markets together. The next section does this, and in the process casts light on the issue raised in (iv).

5.2   *Pareto efficiency*

Consider an economy in which there are n goods consumed by individuals but labour is the only factor of production supplied by individuals, so that individuals behave as described in section 4.7. (It is easily seen that the assumption that labour is the only factor supplied by individuals could be relaxed without making any essential changes to the arguments below. This assumption is made purely for expositional simplicity.) Individual h consumes goods in quantities given by the vector $x^h = (x_1^h, \ldots, x_n^h)$ and supplies labour L^h, and there are H individuals in the economy. A complete description of all consumption and labour supply in the economy is given by the $(n + 1)H$ vector $a = (x^1, x^2, \ldots, x^H, L^1, L^2, \ldots, L^H)$ and such a vector is called an *allocation*. (Note that a does not sum the supplies and demands of the different households; it lists each individual consumption vector and labour supply, one after another.) An allocation a^* is said to be *Pareto efficient* if there does *not* exist some other possible allocation a^0 such that: (i) each individual h prefers (x^{h0}, L^{h0}) to (x^{h*}, L^{h*}) or is indifferent between them; and (ii) there is one individual k who prefers (x^{k0}, L^{k0}) to (x^{k*}, L^{k*}). That is, a^* is Pareto efficient if it is impossible to make someone better off without making someone else worse off.

(Sometimes we say that a is *Pareto superior* to a^1, if everyone prefers his situation in a to his situation in a^1 or is indifferent between them, and at least one individual prefers his situation in a. Thus a^* is Pareto efficient if there is no feasible allocation which is Pareto superior to it.)

Consider the following example. There are two individuals X and Y who each initially own some apples and some bananas. There is no labour supply and no production. X's marginal rate of substitution between apples and bananas at the initial allocation is 1: the exchange of one apple for one banana would leave him indifferent. Y's marginal rate of substitution is 4: he would be indifferent to the exchange of four apples for one banana. Clearly if Y gives two apples to X in exchange for one banana, they are *both* better off. The initial allocation is therefore not Pareto efficient.

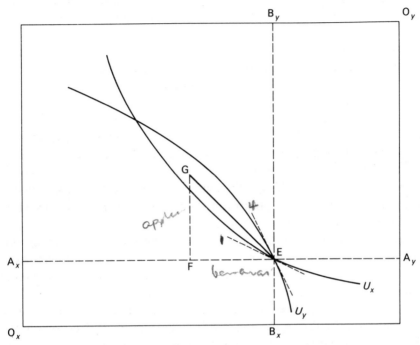

FIGURE 5.2   A Pareto-inefficient allocation

This can be seen diagrammatically in figure 5.2, which is a type of diagram called an 'Edgeworth box'. X has $O_x A_x$ apples and $O_x B_x$ bananas and O_x is the origin for his indifference curves. Y's origin is O_y, his indifference map has been rotated through 180° and he has $O_y A_y$ apples and $O_y B_y$ bananas. The height and width of the box thus measure the total quantities of apples and bananas available to X and Y, and E represents the initial allocation. The indifference curve U_x through E reflects X's preferences and has slope 1, his marginal rate of substitution, at E. Similarly, U_y is Y's indifference curve through E and has slope 4 at this point. By trading at the rate of 2 apples for 1 banana they can shift from the initial allocation to the new allocation at G. X gives EF bananas to Y in exchange for the FG apples which Y gives to X. At G they are both better off because G lies above U_x (viewed from O_x) and above U_y (viewed from O_y). It should be obvious that it is the fact that their marginal rates of substitution were initially different that has made it possible to find a trade that makes them both better off.

*5.3   The efficiency of competitive general equilibrium

In chapter 1 we saw the uses of partial equilibrium analysis. Equilibrium in a single market (or a small number of closely related markets) occurred when demand and supply of the good were equal, and all agents expectations were fulfilled. Now we turn briefly to consideration of *general equilibrium*, which exists when *all* the markets in an economy are in equilibrium. Thus in the economy in which there are n goods and labour, we suppose that at the prices $(\mathbf{p}, w) = (p_1, p_2, \ldots, p_n, w)$ all $n + 1$ markets are in equilibrium and let the resulting allocation be $\mathbf{a}$.

In partial equilibrium, there was no difficulty about the existence of equilibrium. The intersection of the downward-sloping demand curve and the upward-sloping supply curve determines the equilibrium, and even when such an intersection does not occur at a positive price and quantity we can still usually say what the equilibrium outcome will be. We saw that the question of stability of equilibrium is trickier, and the argument which suggested that the partial equilibrium should usually be stable was a rather informal argument.

Things are much more difficult when we consider general equilibrium. To prove the existence of a set of prices which will equate supply and demand simultaneously in a number of markets is a non-trivial exercise. To find conditions under which such an equilibrium will be stable, in the sense that the actual price vector will converge over time to the equilibrium price vector, is harder still. These issues have received much attention from mathematical economists, and if you continue to study economics you will soon encounter the work that has been done in this area. They are not discussed in this book because a discussion of them would require mathematical tools considerably more sophisticated than those we have been using here.

Let us therefore simply *assume* that the economy has somehow arrived at an equilibrium price vector and allocation. Suppose that $\mathbf{a}$ is not Pareto efficient, so that there exists an allocation $\mathbf{a}^0$ which makes one individual better off and no one worse off. Since $\mathbf{a}$ is chosen by individuals in a situation where individual h faces the budget constraint (see section 4.7)

$$\mathbf{p}x^h = wL^h + m^h \tag{2}$$

where m^h is his non-labour money income, it follows that, for all h,

$$\mathbf{p}x^{h0} - wL^{h0} \geqslant \mathbf{p}x^h - wL^h \tag{3}$$

while, for the individual k who strictly prefers his part of the $\mathbf{a}^0$ allocation,

$$\mathbf{p}x^{k0} - wL^{k0} > \mathbf{p}x^k - wL^k \tag{4}$$

since a rational individual would choose the vector that makes him better off if it were not more expensive, and will choose the cheaper of the vectors between which he is indifferent. (Reread section 4.6 if you do not understand this.) Adding these inequalities gives

$$\mathbf{p}\mathbf{x}^0 - w L^0 > \mathbf{p}\mathbf{x} - wL \qquad (5)$$

where $\mathbf{x} = \Sigma_{h=1}^H \mathbf{x}^h$, the aggregate consumption vector in allocation $\mathbf{a}$, $L = \Sigma_{h=1}^H L^h$, and so on.

The right-hand side of (5) is consumers' expenditure on goods less their labour income in the competitive equilibrium, and from (2) this must equal the sum of consumers' non-labour incomes m^h. Since labour is the only factor supplied by individuals, the incomes m^h must come from individuals' shares in the income of firms from profits (including rents of any factors owned by firms). Thus the right-hand side of (5) is the total profit made by firms.

(An alternative way to arrive at the same conclusion is to observe that firms' revenue is consumers' expenditure while firms' expenditure is consumers' labour income.)

By assumption, however, $\mathbf{a}^0$ is a feasible allocation so that $(\mathbf{x}^0, L^0)$ is a feasible set of outputs and inputs for the firms in the economy to undertake. The right-hand side of (5) is the total profit that would be made by firms at the prices $(\mathbf{p}, w)$ by producing $\mathbf{x}^0$ from L^0. It exceeds the profit actually made in the competitive equilibrium. Therefore there is at least one firm that would, at these prices, make more profit by switching its production plan to what it would do in the alternative allocation $\mathbf{a}^0$. This contradicts the fact that price-taking firms maximize profits in the competitive equilibrium. Hence the original supposition that there exists a feasible allocation $\mathbf{a}^0$ satisfying (3) and (4) must be mistaken, and therefore a *competitive general equilibrium is Pareto efficient*.

Loosely speaking, what this proof establishes is that if it were possible to make one individual better off without making others worse off then some firm could increase its profits by making the appropriate re-allocations between individuals. In the example illustrated in figure 5.2, a firm could buy 1 banana from X in exchange for $1\frac{1}{2}$ apples and sell the banana to Y for $3\frac{1}{2}$ apples, thereby making both X and Y better off and giving the firm a profit of 2 apples.

A crucial feature of the proof that a competitive general equilibrium is Pareto efficient is the assumption that all individuals and firms (all 'agents', for short) face the same prices. If different agents face different prices for the same good, an inefficient allocation of resources will result. For example, in the case illustrated in figure 5.2, if for some reason X believed that the price ratio of apples for bananas is 1 while Y believed that a banana costs the same as 4 apples then both would wish to remain at E, which would be the equilibrium but is inefficient.

A more general example is the case where, in our n-goods-plus-labour general equilibrium, taxes are imposed on transactions between producers and consumers. The government imposing the taxes has no real role to play, and does not itself spend any of the proceeds, so the net tax revenue is simply handed back to individuals. (Note that a subsidy can be regarded as a negative tax, so that the government may not actually be raising any revenue from these 'taxes'.) Firms receive prices $\mathbf{p}^t$ for goods and pay the wage rate w^t for labour, but individuals have to pay the prices $\mathbf{q}^t$ for goods and receive the wage rate ω^t. Taxes on goods are therefore $\mathbf{t} = \mathbf{q}^t - \mathbf{p}^t$ and the tax on labour is $\tau = w^t - \omega^t$.

At these prices, firms make profit $\mathbf{p}^t \mathbf{x}^t - w^t L^t$, while total net tax receipts are $\mathbf{t} \mathbf{x}^t + \tau L^t$, where $\mathbf{x}^t$ is production (and aggregate consumption) and L^t is labour supplied. Total non-labour income is now the sum of profit and tax revenue so it is

$$\sum_{h=1}^{H} m^{ht} = \mathbf{p}^t \mathbf{x}^t - w^t L^t + \mathbf{t} \mathbf{x}^t + \tau L^t = \mathbf{q}^t \mathbf{x}^t - \omega^t L^t \tag{6}$$

Now consider an alternative allocation. The government abolishes all taxes on transactions but announces that it will confiscate all profits. It will then redistribute the proceeds so that each individual is at least as well off as in the original allocation. Is this feasible? In the initial allocation, individual h consumed $\mathbf{x}^{ht}$ and supplied labour L^{ht} so revealed preference theory tells us that if the new prices are $\mathbf{p}, w$, income of

$$m^h = \mathbf{p} \mathbf{x}^{ht} - w L^{ht} \tag{7}$$

will be sufficient to ensure individual h is at least as well off as before. This will require total payments from the government of

$$\sum_{h=1}^{H} m^h = \mathbf{p} \mathbf{x}^t - w L^t \tag{8}$$

However, in the new allocation firms are following the production plan $(\mathbf{x}, L)$ which may differ from $(\mathbf{x}^t, L^t)$. Since the new plan is chosen by firms at prices $(\mathbf{p}, w)$ and the old plan is feasible it follows that the new plan must be more profitable at these prices. Therefore

$$\mathbf{p} \mathbf{x} - w L \geqslant \mathbf{p} \mathbf{x}^t - w L^t \tag{9}$$

The left-hand side of (9) is total profit in the new allocation, so it is the amount available for redistribution by the government, and combining (9) and (8) we see that the government does indeed have enough to pay the sums m^h to the respective individuals. If the inequality in (9) is strict, at least one individual can be given more than the m^h which satisfies (7). Also we know from revealed preference theory that income of m^h as defined by (7) will normally make the individual better off than before. Thus we have the results that there is an equilibrium without taxes on transactions that makes everyone at least as well off as in the taxed equilibrium, and, except in exceptional cases, at least one individual better off, so that the *taxes on transactions cause inefficiency*.

5.4   *Income redistribution*

The general equilibrium model presented in the previous section has dealt with problem (v) raised in the first section, by looking at all markets together. But problem (iv) reappears in a slightly different form. The fact that an equilibrium is Pareto efficient, so that no one can be made better off without someone else being made worse off, does not rule out the possibility of extreme inequalities between individuals. Consider, for example, an economy in which there are some individuals who have inherited no property, have no shares in the ownership of firms and are capable of supplying very little labour. In the competitive equilibrium such individuals will be very poor because they have little to offer on the competitive markets, while those who are more favourably placed may be able to lead extremely luxurious lives. The fact that the equilibrium is Pareto efficient tells us merely that the poor can be made better off only at the expense of the rich. In short, the market leads to an efficient *allocation of resources* but may also lead to a *distribution of income* which would be regarded as inequitable by some.

Suppose that all members of a society agree that the free market income distribution is unjust, and should be altered. What can be done?

The obvious answer is to take money from the rich and give it to the poor. The concluding section of chapter 3 argued that some of the wages of those who are lucky enough to find themselves with a skill which is in demand can be regarded as economic rent, just as can the profits of firms lucky enough to find themselves, whether in the short run or the long run, in a situation where positive profits can be made. If we simply confiscate some of the rents of the lucky, and transfer the proceeds to the unlucky, then allow everyone to produce and trade freely we will achieve a new competitive equilibrium, efficient but with a more equal income distribution.

A simple example of such a redistribution is in figure 5.3 which is the same sort of diagram as figure 5.2. Suppose X and Y find themselves with the initial 'endowments' of goods indicated by E_1. If they trade with each other at the price ratio given by the slope of the line $E_1 H_1$ they will both wish to trade to the point G_1 for that is the point at which each of their indifference curves are tangent to the budget line: X wishes to sell $E_1 F_1$ bananas and buy $F_1 G_1$ apples, and these are the quantities which Y wishes to buy and sell respectively so both markets are in equilibrium. That this is Pareto efficient is shown by the fact that the indifference curves are

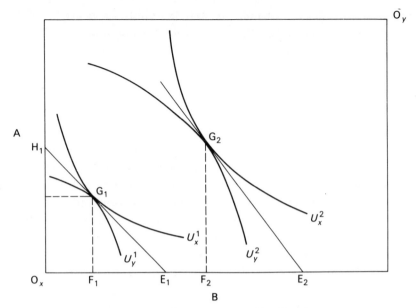

FIGURE 5.3   Lump-sum redistribution

tangent to each other at G_1. (It is fairly easy to see that if we had chosen a different price, we would not in general be in equilibrium.) But at this equilibrium X faces a budget line that is close to O_x while Y faces a budget line far from O_y, so it seems that Y is much better off than X. Suppose that $E_1 E_2$ of Y's bananas were confiscated and given to X so that their endowments were shifted to E_2, and then they were permitted to trade. The new equilibrium would be at a point such as G_2, which is Pareto efficient but with X better off and Y worse off than at G_1.

However, there are enormous problems in implementing such redistribution in reality (leaving aside the problem of whether the individuals within a society can agree on how much redistribution they want). We have already discussed in the theory of the firm how it is difficult to separate true profits (rents) from the normal payments to the inputs supplied by the firm's owners. If a firm seems to earn high profits, because of being in the right market at the right time, this may be the result of skilful decisions rather than luck. And if the skilful are well paid for their work, may this not reflect the effort they put into their work and the effort they put into their education rather than their being born lucky? It is the difficulty of making this sort of separation that makes it virtually impossible to tax true profits without also taxing, and thereby discouraging, initiative, investment and work.

A proper investigation of the problem of devising methods of changing the distribution of income without interfering too much with the efficiency of the market would require further techniques which are far beyond the scope of this book. The conflict between equity and efficiency will reappear in many policy issues we discuss, but from now on this and other issues will be discussed in the simpler, single market, model of section 5.1. That is to say, we are shifting back from general equilibrium to partial equilibrium analysis.

5.5   Consumer surplus and the effect of taxes

Consider the demand curve $x(p)$ illustrated in figure 5.4. It is convenient to think of this as expressing price as a function of quantity: $p = p(x)$. This *inverse demand function* measures consumers' marginal willingness to pay for the good: $p(x)$ is the price per unit of the good that some consumer is willing to pay for a little more of the good when x units are already being consumed. Thus the total benefit which consumers receive from consuming x_1 units of the good is

$$B(x_1) = \int_0^{x_1} p(x)\, dx \tag{10}$$

for this has the property that $B'(x) = p(x)$ – the price measures the benefit to the consumers of extra consumption of the good – as well as the obvious property that $B(0) = 0$. This is represented graphically as the whole area under the demand curve between 0 and x_1; the sum of the areas marked A, B and D in figure 5.4. However, quantity will be x_1 if price is p_1, so consumers' expenditure is $p_1 x_1$, represented by the areas B and D in the diagram. Total benefit to consumers thus exceeds expenditure by the area A, which is called *consumer surplus* and is measured

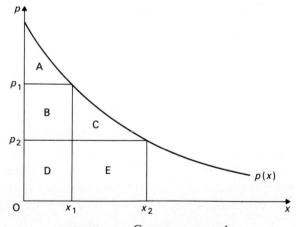

FIGURE 5.4   Consumer surplus

mathematically as

$$CS(x_1) = \int_0^{x_1} p(x)\, dx - p_1 x_1 = \int_0^{x_1} (p(x) - p_1)\, dx \qquad (11)$$

If price were now to fall to p_2, consumer surplus would become the sum of the areas marked A, B and C. The increase in consumer surplus comes in two parts: area B represents the increased consumer surplus due to the fall in price of the goods already being consumed at price p_1, while C is the consumer surplus associated with the new consumption of $x_2 - x_1$.

This argument is exactly analogous to the argument used in section 3.6 (see especially figure 3.12) that when the supply curve in a competitive market measures the marginal cost of production, the area under the supply curve measures total variable cost so that the area between the horizontal line at market price and the supply curve is profit (plus fixed cost).

Obviously this is a very informal argument. It is worth taking a moment to look in a direction in which the argument could be made more rigorous. Suppose a typical consumer faces prices $\mathbf{p}$ for n goods and makes utility-maximizing choices which result in a utility level u. From equations (29) we know that his expenditure function $e(\mathbf{p}, u)$ and compensated demand functions $\mathbf{x}(\mathbf{p}, u)$ have the property

$$x_i(\mathbf{p}, u) = \frac{\partial e(\mathbf{p}, u)}{\partial p_i} \qquad (12)$$

Suppose that p_i were to fall from p_{i1} to p_{i2} with all other prices unchanged. A measure of the benefit to the consumer of this price change is the reduction in expenditure which would leave him on the same indifference curve that he was on before the price change. We are, in the terminology of chapter 4, compensating him for the price change, and the *compensating variation* in his money income is $e(\mathbf{p}_1, u) - e(\mathbf{p}_2, u)$, where the price vectors $\mathbf{p}_1$ and $\mathbf{p}_2$ differ only in their ith entry, and where, if $p_{i1} > p_{i2}$, $e(\mathbf{p}_1, u) > e(\mathbf{p}_2, u)$. Using (12) we obtain

$$e(\mathbf{p}_1, u) - e(\mathbf{p}_2, u) = \int_{p_{i2}}^{p_{i1}} \frac{\partial e(\mathbf{p}, u)}{\partial p_i}\, dp_i = \int_{p_{i2}}^{p_{i1}} x_i(\mathbf{p}, u)\, dp_i \qquad (13)$$

Referring back to figure 5.4, we see that if the demand curve is the graph of the *compensated* demand function for good i, then the area $B + C$ which represents the integral with respect to p_i of x_i from p_{i2} to p_{i1} does indeed measure the benefit to the consumer of the price reduction shown. Thus the consumer surplus measure can be rigorously justified if real income is unchanged along the demand curve being used. What can be said in defence of consumer surplus if real income or the prices of other goods change along with p_i is an issue we do not tackle here.

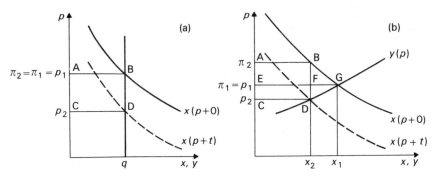

FIGURE 5.5   The effect of a sales tax

Persuaded therefore that the approach being adopted is not entirely arbitrary, we can now develop a partial equilibrium version of the argument of section 5.3 that taxes on transactions cause inefficiency. The effect of a sales tax in two different markets is illustrated in figure 5.5. (Look back at figure 1.3 and section 1.4 if you do not remember the details of the argument.) In market (a) supply is completely inelastic, and the no-tax equilibrium is at B. A tax shifts the demand curve downwards, so the suppliers' price falls to p_2 while the consumers' price remains at p_1. The government has raised tax revenue measured by the area ABDC, entirely from suppliers' rents. The quantity sold remains constant. Contrast market (b) where the shift of the demand curve moves suppliers' price down to p_2 while consumers' price rises to $\pi_2 = p_2 + t$. The quantity falls from x_1 to x_2, and the government raises tax revenue measured by the area ABDE. However, the rise in consumers' price reduces consumer surplus by the area ABFE plus the area BGF. Also producers' revenue falls from p_1x_1 to p_2x_2 while costs fall by the area under the supply curve between D and G so that profits fall by the area EFDC plus the area FGD. (Look back at section 3.6 and figure 3.12 if this is not clear to you.) Thus the losses suffered by consumers and producers *exceed* the revenue raised by the amount represented by the area BGD. This is the loss of consumer surplus and profits associated with the quantity $x_1 - x_2$ which is no longer traded as a result of the tax. There are consumers willing to pay more than the cost of producing this extra output, but the tax prevents them getting together with producers in mutually advantageous trade. Removal of the tax would reduce government revenue but improve consumers' and producers' welfare to such an extent that consumers and producers could pay the government its lost revenue and still be better off. This would be a Pareto improvement, so the tax has caused inefficiency, with the extent of the inefficiency represented by the area BGD.

We can compare different types of tax using this technique. Suppose that a government has decided to try to raise the incomes of farmers, who are suffering from competition from low-cost foreign suppliers. The

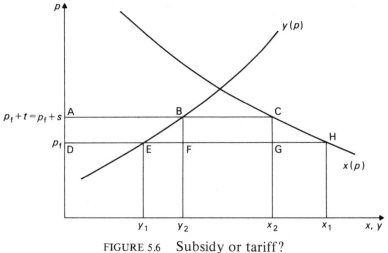

FIGURE 5.6   Subsidy or tariff?

obvious method of doing this is simply to hand money over to farmers, but governments seem to find this politically difficult to do; so let us suppose that the government has to choose between a *subsidy* to farm production and a *tax on imports* (often called a *tariff*). Let us suppose that supply from foreigners is infinitely elastic. Then the market is as illustrated in figure 5.6, where foreign supply is available at the fixed price p_f, $y(p)$ is this country's supply curve of farm produce and $x(p)$ is the demand curve for this country's consumers.

In the absence of government action the market price must be p_f. (It is left to you as exercise 5.6 to show that the price could be neither higher nor lower than p_f.) At this price, domestic production is y_1, and consumption is x_1, so that imports are $x_1 - y_1$. Suppose now that farmers received a subsidy s on each unit produced. The market price will stay at p_f, but farmers receive $p_f + s$ so that the quantity they supply rises to y_2, so imports fall to $x_1 - y_2$, and the government pays out sy_2 in subsidy, represented by the area ABFD in the diagram. Producers' profits rise by ABED, so that, of the revenue spent by the government, the amount measured by the area BEF is lost — this is the efficiency loss of the subsidy. On the other hand, if instead importers have to pay a tax t on each unit imported, the market price will rise to $p_f + t$, so domestic production will again rise to y_2 (if $t = s$), domestic consumption falls to x_2, imports fall to $x_2 - y_2$, and the government receives $t(x_2 - y_2)$ in tariff revenue, represented by the area BCGF. Again, producers' profits rise by ABED, but now there is a loss of consumer surplus of ACHD. If we subtract from this loss the gains made by the government and by the producers, we have a net loss represented by the two areas BEF and CGH, this being the efficiency loss of the tariff.

Again, the source of these losses is easily identified. Goods can be bought from foreigners at the price p_f, so BEF represents the extra cost of producing $y_2 - y_1$ at home instead of importing it, while CGH represents the loss of consumer surplus to those consumers who were willing to pay at least p_f to buy $x_1 - x_2$ from foreigners but are prevented from doing so by the tariff.

We see that the tariff is a less efficient method of redistributing income to the farmers than is the subsidy, because it imposes the extra loss CGH which the subsidy does not. On the other hand, the tariff saves the government the subsidy cost ABFD and raises revenue BCGF, so the government gains ACGD at the expense of consumers by switching from the subsidy to the tariff. The final point to note is that political discussion of import taxes frequently implies that they are taxes on foreigners to benefit domestic producers. This example shows that this is not the case: the tariff is a tax on domestic consumers which benefits producers (and raises government revenue).

5.6 Externalities

We now turn to problem (iii) raised in the introduction. Consider the case of an industry which in the process of production emits pollution into the environment. Those who are affected by this pollution then have to incur the costs of alleviating its effects. Thus we have the situation depicted in figure 5.7.

The supply curve does not now measure marginal cost. The producers have to pay the costs of inputs and those costs determine supply; but

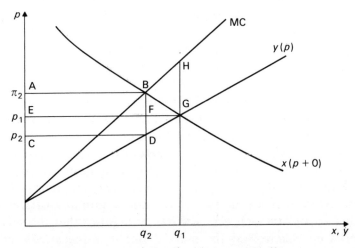

FIGURE 5.7   A production externality

producers do not have to take any account of the costs imposed on others by pollution. These costs mean that the true marginal cost curve lies above the supply curve. (One way of expressing this is to say that the supply curve shows the marginal *private* cost of production while the true marginal cost curve shows the marginal *social* cost of production.)

The market equilibrium is at point G where price is p_1 and output is q_1. This equilibrium is not efficient. Consider the effect of a sales tax which restricted output to q_2 raising consumer price to π_2 and reducing producer price to p_2. From our earlier analysis of the effect of a sales tax (see figure 5.3(b)) we know that the loss of consumer surplus, the loss of producer profit and the gain of government revenue add up to a net loss given by the area BGD. However, there is now an additional consideration: the difference between the supply curve and the true marginal cost curve is the marginal cost of pollution, so that the reduction in pollution cost, which is a gain to those who suffer from pollution, is given by the area BHGD. Thus there is a net *gain* to society from the reduction in output, represented by the area BHG. The original equilibrium was inefficient.

The logic should be clear: the consumers who were being supplied with the last $q_1 - q_2$ units of output are not willing to pay the true marginal cost of production, so the area between the marginal cost curve and the demand curve measures the loss caused by their being supplied.

The equilibrium at B is preferred to the equilibrium at G by all individuals only if those who lose from the change are compensated by those who gain. Consumers and producers of the good lose; the government and the polluted gain. The gainers could afford to pay enough money to the losers to compensate them for their loss, and still have positive gains for themselves. If compensation is not actually paid, we have an improvement in efficiency but also a change in the distribution of income as a result of correcting the externality by means of a tax.

An exactly analogous argument goes through in the case where the externality is beneficial, that is where social cost is less than private cost. Now a *subsidy* is needed to correct the externality, as you can very easily check.

There are many situations where externalities may exist in production or in consumption: on a congested road, an extra road-user will impose costs on other road-users by slowing them down; a factory which trains unskilled workers will benefit other factories in the neighbourhood as workers move from one factory to another; a beautiful garden gives enjoyment to passers-by as well as to the owner; immunization against infectious disease reduces the risk to the non-immunized of catching the disease; and so on. In each case, efficiency requires that the *social* costs and benefits be balanced at the margin, but it is the *private* costs and benefits which the market balances.

5.7 Public goods

An extreme form of externality in consumption is the case of a public good. A public good is a good of which it is the total availability that gives satisfaction to an individual, rather than the quantity which the individual owns. An example is radio and television signals: they cannot be provided to some consumers without at the same time being supplied to all consumers in the same area. (This statement obviously does not apply to television signals provided by cable.) Other examples are defence, roads, clean air, and police. Some public goods are subject to congestion – the more people use a given road the less effective the road is at serving road-users – but they are public goods none the less. (There are many other goods, such as education, health services, housing, and garbage collection, that are provided in many societies by government rather than through the market. They are *not public goods*, though there may be significant externalities involved in their consumption.)

The condition that describes how much of a public good ought to be produced is quite different from that for a private good. In (10) the function $B(x)$ is defined so as to measure the total benefit which consumers receive from consuming x units of a good. We could as easily define the benefit functions for each individual:

$$B^h(x^h) = \int_0^{x^h} p^h(x)\, dx \tag{14}$$

where $p^h(x)$ is individual h's inverse demand function. If we seek to maximize total benefit less cost for an ordinary 'private' good, whose cost function is $c(y)$, we have the problem

$$\underset{x^1,\ldots,x^H}{\text{maximize}} \sum_{h=1}^{H} B^h(x^h) - c(x^1 + \ldots + x^H) \tag{15}$$

which has H necessary conditions for maximization:

$$B^{h'}(x^h) = c'(y) \qquad h = 1, \ldots\ H \tag{16}$$

which can be written

$$p^h(x^h) = c'(y) \qquad h = 1, \ldots, H \tag{17}$$

the conditions that will be satisfied in a competitive market in which all consumers pay the same price and that price equals marginal cost. This is just another way of putting the simple argument of section 5.1, and you should note the importance of the assumption that the total benefit is the unweighted sum of the benefits to individuals, each individual's benefit being measured by his willingness to pay.

An individual's benefit from a public good, however, depends on total availability of the good, so that if we seek to maximize benefit less cost we have

$$\text{maximize}_{y} \sum_{h=1}^{H} B^h(y) - c(y) \tag{18}$$

with the single necessary condition

$$\sum_{h=1}^{H} B^{h'}(y) = c'(y) \tag{19}$$

that is

$$\sum_{h=1}^{H} p^h(y) = c'(y) \tag{20}$$

A unit of a public good should thus be supplied if all individuals *together* are willing to pay the cost of producing it, with each individual contributing the amount which measures the value that he attaches to the unit. These contributions will typically vary from individual to individual.

(For those of you who have worked through section 5.3 it is left as exercise 5.11 to extend the proof of the Pareto optimality of competitive general equilibrium to the case where there are public goods, of which different individuals must consume the same quantities but for which they may pay different prices.)

This seems to suggest how the supply of public goods could be arranged by the market. Those who want the good produced must join together, each paying an amount representing the value of the good to him, and they will then obtain the good if the total willingness to pay exceeds the cost of production.

Consider, however, the case of a public good whose marginal cost of production is constant at $1000. There are 100 identical consumers in the economy and each values access to one unit of the good at $15, two units at $27 and three units at $36, that is $p(1) = 15$, $p(2) = 12$ and $p(3) = 9$. Clearly it is optimal to produce 2 units of the good, and have each individual contribute $20 to cover the cost of production. Suppose, however, that people do not know each other's true preferences, and place yourself in the position of one of the 100 individuals. You could pretend that you have no desire to have the good produced. If the remaining 99 individuals are honest, they will agree to have 2 units of the good supplied, with the cost divided among them, and you will obtain the benefit at no cost. You have an incentive to be a *free rider*. Of course, other individuals may be dishonest and attempt to be free riders too, but it is not obvious that this should change your strategy. So long as the other 99 are willing together to contribute $2000 or more for 2 units of the good, you have no incentive to offer anything. If together they are willing to contribute less than $1973, the goods will not get produced even if you offer $27 so you may as well offer nothing. It is only if they contribute more than $1973 and less than $2000 that your offering a contribution will be in your interests. The chances of just enough people being dishonest for the total contributions to fall in this critical range may seem so small that it is best for you to offer nothing. And if everyone makes this calculation, all will offer nothing and none of the public good will get produced. The analysis is essentially unchanged if there are genuine differences in preferences between individuals.

The story is a little different if non-contributors can be excluded from the benefits of the public good, but there are still problems. Attempting to charge different amounts to different people would give an incentive to understate one's desire for the good; but a flat-rate contribution may not raise enough revenue to cover the cost of a good, and will exclude those who are willing to pay less than the flat-rate contribution. It is clearly inefficient to exclude such individuals, for the marginal cost of allowing an extra individual access of a public good is zero unless there is congestion.

These problems may be alleviated but are not entirely solved by handing provision of public goods over to the government. The government has to find out what peoples' needs and desires for public goods are and it has to raise money to pay for the goods which are produced. If taxes to pay for public goods are tied closely to individuals' stated desires, we are still left with the free-rider problem, the incentive to understate true desires. If, on the other hand, public goods are provided out of general tax revenue and access to them freely provided, we are more likely to have an efficient level of provision, but at the cost of a redistribution of income from those who pay taxes but benefit little from the public goods to those who enjoy great benefits, and also at whatever cost in terms of inefficiency is involved in raising the tax revenue.

Consider some examples. *Defence* is supplied free of charge, to an extent decided on by the government, and paid for by the taxpayer. A pacifist attaches no value to the 'good' he receives, but he has to pay taxes. *Roads and bridges* are usually free to the user, though the ownership of cars and the use of fuel are in many countries fairly heavily taxed. Fuel taxes may be a reasonable approximation to having the beneficiaries pay, though they do impose an inefficient charge on the use of uncongested roads. Taxes on car-ownership do not have this inefficient effect but they do inefficiently discourage the ownership of cars, and they also imply redistribution from the car-owner who uses his car very little to the heavy user. Tolls on the use of roads and bridges lead to inefficient underuse of uncongested facilities but they imply less redistribution. The *television* licence fee which in Britain finances the non-commercial BBC television and radio services ensures that a television owner is not discouraged from extra use of TV signals; but it does inefficiently discourage the marginal purchase of a TV set. The same could be said about cable TV services which have a fixed annual charge independent of use. Both systems imply redistribution from the occasional viewer to the frequent viewer. Those cable TV systems that charge by the programme avoid this redistribution but at the efficiency cost of discouraging marginal consumers of a good which can be supplied at zero marginal cost.

All of this discussion leaves aside two important issues: whether there are methods by which a government can find out peoples' true desires for public goods, and whether democratic governments are likely actually to attempt to satisfy optimally citizens desires' for public goods. To tackle these issues would be beyond the scope of this book.

5.8 Price controls

Suppose that a legal limit is placed on the price of a particular good. Obviously if the equilibrium price is below the limit, there is no effect, so we can confine our attention to the case where the maximum price is below the equilibrium price. This is illustrated in figure 5.8.

The equilibrium price is p but the price is fixed at p_{max}. At this price consumers wish to buy q_2 but producers wish to sell only q_1, so there is an excess demand of $q_2 - q_1$. Since not all consumers' demands can be fully met there will be a shortage of the good. We cannot proceed further with

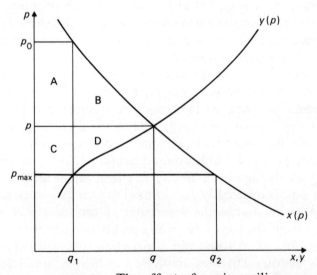

FIGURE 5.8   The effect of a price ceiling

the analysis of price controls without considering how goods actually get allocated between different consumers. There are various possibilities:

(i) The government can *sell ration coupons*. It prints q_1 coupons, announces that a unit of the good may be bought only if a ration coupon is handed over by the consumer along with the price. Clearly the price a consumer is willing to pay for a ration coupon is the difference between the price he is willing to pay for the good and the price p_{max} he actually pays for the good. In fact the demand curve for ration coupons is identical to the demand curve for the good, except that the horizontal axis is moved up by p_{max}. The market for ration coupons is illustrated in figure 5.9. There are consumers who are willing to pay at least p_0 for q_1 units of the good, so they will be willing to pay $p_0 - p_{max}$ for q_1 ration coupons, and this will be the equilibrium price that the government will be able to charge. The consumers are effectively paying p_0 for the good: p_{max} to the producers, $p_0 - p_{max}$ to the government, and q_1 is being consumed. The government is receiving revenue from the sale of ration coupons represented by the areas A and C in figure 5.8. The outcome is identical to the outcome if the government had imposed a tax equal to $p_0 - p_{max}$. There is an efficiency loss of consumer surplus and profits given by the areas B and D.

(ii) The government can *issue ration coupons free and allow their resale*. The difference between this and the previous case is that when the coupons come on the market they are owned by individuals rather than by the government. The market is still as illustrated in figures 5.8 and 5.9, except that the revenue A + C accrues to the initial recipients of coupons instead of the government.

(iii) The government can *issue ration coupons and ban their resale*. It is easily seen that this is worse for every consumer than possibility (ii). The consumer who would have been willing to pay more than p_0 for an extra unit of the good, that is to pay more than $p_0 - p_{max}$ for an extra ration

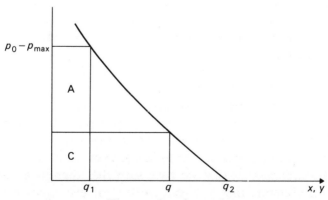

FIGURE 5.9   The market for ration coupons

coupon, is not allowed to undertake this transaction. On the other hand, the consumer who would have preferred $p_0 - p_{max}$ in cash to having a ration coupon, that is, the consumer who values a marginal unit of the good at less than p_0 is also barred from undertaking the transaction that would make him better off.

(iv) The goods can be allocated by *queueing, with resale of goods permitted*. Then the price p_0 would be the equilibrium, and since a profit of $p_0 - p_{max}$ could be made by queueing to buy a unit of the good at the controlled price, an individual who valued his time at w per hour (because that is his wage rate, or the marginal value he attaches to leisure) would be willing to queue for h hours to buy one unit, where $wh = p_0 - p_{max}$. In this case, we have the efficiency losses B and D as before, and the areas A and C now represent the value of time spent in queues, *which is a further loss* to society. This arrangement is unambiguously worse than arrangements (i) and (ii).

(v) Finally, there is the possibility of *allocation by queueing, with resale forbidden*. This case is not easy to compare directly with (iv). In (iv) consumers could effectively pay someone else to queue for them; now they must queue for themselves. Some consumers who value the good highly may value their time even more highly so they do not buy. Queueing time will be shorter than in the previous situation. There may therefore be some consumers who were unable to buy at the price p_0, but who are now able to queue and buy at the price p_{max}, since their value of time w' and the time spent in the queue h' satisfy $p_{max} + w'h' < p_0$. These consumers are better off than they were in (iv); but those who are driven out by the prospect of queueing are worse off. However, consumers are worse off than if they had simply been given a ration coupon, which they could not resell: for then they would have bought the good for p_{max} with no queueing cost. Thus there is a way of distributing ration coupons that makes arrangement (iii) better for some and not worse for everyone else than arrangement (v).

What do we conclude from all this about the case for price controls in a competitive market? The obvious argument for a price ceiling is that it benefits the consumer. However, we have seen that since a shortage of goods is created the price control cannot benefit all consumers. It is sometimes argued that when consumers have to queue for goods, a fairer allocation of resources will result since poorer people, who did not have enough money to buy goods when they were allocated only by price, are now able to obtain goods since time is more equally distributed than money; indeed poorer people with lower wages have lower opportunity cost for time, so can better afford to queue than richer people. The problem with this argument is that we have seen that there is a way of distributing ration coupons that makes it better for *everyone* to have goods allocated by ration coupons than by queues — because queues waste everyone's valuable time. So if we want to benefit the poor, perhaps we should simply give them more ration coupons than the rich? It was, however, shown above that it is better for everyone if ration coupons can be resold, so resale should be permitted. Further, when price is controlled, and excess demand is controlled by the issue of resellable ration coupons, the effect is the same as a tax, except that the government is giving away the tax revenue in the form of valuable coupons. Surely if the government really wanted to do something about the disadvantaged position of the poor in the market it would do better simply to tax the consumption of the good, and distribute the tax revenue *as cash* to the poor?

Exercises

5.1   Outline an argument for permitting employers to hire workers for dangerous occupations, unhindered by government regulations on safety. Identify any weak points you believe there are in the argument.

5.2   Outline an argument for permitting consumption of and trade in narcotic drugs. Are there any weak points in your argument?

5.3   Mr A goes into a shop and buys 10 lb of potatoes at 16p per lb and 3 lb of carrots at 10p per lb. Mrs B goes into another shop and buys 6 lb of potatoes at 13p per lb and 3 lb of carrots at 10p per lb. Assuming the vegetables are of the same quality, discuss the possibility of a mutually beneficial exchange between Mr A and Mrs B, should they meet.

5.4   Two consumers have stocks of goods (x_1^1, x_2^1) and (x_1^2, x_2^2) respectively. Their respective utility functions U^1 and U^2 satisfy

$$\frac{U_1^1(x_1^1, x_2^1)}{U_2^1(x_1^1, x_2^1)} > \frac{U_1^2(x_1^2, x_2^2)}{U_2^2(x_1^2, x_2^2)}$$

where the subscripts indicate partial differentiation. What sort of exchange would be a Pareto improvement?

5.5   If the inverse demand function for a good is $p = x^{-b}$, what is the elasticity of demand? Find the consumer surplus at price $p = 1$, (i) if $0 < b < 1$, (ii) if $b = 1$, (iii) if $b > 1$. Comment.

5.6   In the agricultural market discussed in section 5.5 explain carefully why the domestic equilibrium price would be p_f in the absence of government intervention, and why it rises to $p_f + t$ in the presence of a tariff.

5.7   (i) Suppose that a good is imported from abroad (and for simplicity assume that foreign supply is infinitely elastic) and the government wishes to discourage consumption of this good. Discuss the relative merits of a tax on consumption and a tax on imports.

(ii) If the government's aim instead was to reduce the quantity of imports, discuss the relative merits of a production subsidy, a consumption tax, and an import tax.

5.8   Many large cities suffer from road traffic congestion, which is particularly severe at rush-hours. In the light of this discuss whether any of the following policies are good or bad:

(i)   charging private vehicles tolls for driving in the city;
(ii) charging private vehicles heavily for the use of day-long parking facilities, but less for short-term parking;
(iii) reducing the availability of parking facilities;
(iv) setting aside 'bus lanes' from which private vehicles are excluded at rush-hours,
(v)   requiring public transport to operate profitably;
(vi) allowing old-age pensioners to travel free on public transport except at rush-hours.

*5.9   Here are some extracts from an article in the *New Statesman* of November 28, 1980

Today it costs 10p to travel 5 miles on South Yorkshire's bus service, compared with 50p to travel the same distance in West Yorkshire. Last year 64 per cent of South Yorkshire's income was in the form of subsidy compared with 21 per cent in West Yorkshire. Put another way, each passenger cost the ratepayers of West Yorkshire 5p compared with 10p in South Yorkshire.

The effect of the pricing policy has been to increase the number of passengers on South Yorkshire's buses ... and one of the effects of this increase in business is that South Yorkshire gives better value for money on every commonly accepted measure of efficiency (see table).

THE BEST-VALUE BUS SERVICE

	South Yorks.	West Yorks.
Cost of carrying each passenger	16p	23p
Number of passengers carried per member of staff	52,000	38,000
Average number of passengers per bus	18	13
Cost of running one bus one mile	£1.19	£1.33
Number of bus miles per member of staff	7,000	6,600
Number of miles travelled by each bus per year	34,000	29,000

Have you been given enough information to judge which bus serivce gives the 'best value'? If so, which is it? If not, what additional information would you want before coming to a conclusion?

5.10   What do you believe are the principal arguments for and against the following types of government intervention in the economy:

(i)   the provision of free medical care in place of a system of commercial provision of medical care and medical insurance;
(ii)   the subsidizing of declining industries like steel-making, ship-building and textile manufacture;
(iii)   direct investment and involvement by government in advanced technological projects like supersonic passenger aircraft, electronic components production, and space exploration.

*5.11   Extend the model of section 5.3 to include some public goods with each individual paying a price for each public good, these prices possibly varying between individuals. In a competitive equilibrium, individuals choose their private consumption and labour supply for given prices for public and private goods, quantities of public goods, and non-labour money income; and firms choose production plans given prices, where the price of a public good to a firm is the sum of the prices charged to individuals. Prove that a competitive general equilibrium is Pareto efficient.

5.12   Suppose there are 100 people willing to pay £1000 each to have a new road built in their community, while another 100 would pay £500 each. If the road would cost £125,000 discuss the desirability of having it built and any problems that might arise in raising the money to pay for it.

5.13   Should there be a charge for borrowing books from public libraries?

5.14   Suppose that the demand function for the use of a bridge is

$$p = 100 - 0.1x$$

where p is the price in cents that a bridge-user would pay, and x is the number of daily crossings. If the bridge costs $450 daily to keep open, should it be kept open, and if so how should it be paid for?

5.15   Consider an individual consumer in the market for the price-controlled good discussed in section 5.8. Draw a budget line between this good and all other goods, when the good has price p_{max} but the consumer is prevented by rationing from buying more than r units of the good. Now suppose that ration coupons can be bought or sold at the price $p_0 - p_{max}$. Draw the new budget line and show that the consumer is either better off than or as well off as with the first budget line.

What would his budget line be if the good could be bought in unlimited quantities at the price p_0? Or if ration coupons had to be bought from the government at the price $p_0 - p_{max}$ with the price of the good fixed at p_{max}. What assumptions about income effects must therefore underlie the partial equilibrium analysis of possibilities (i) and (ii) in section 5.8?

5.16   Assume that the government of a country maintains stores in which it sells bread at the subsidized price p. It limits the quantity of bread it will sell to any one person by giving each person non-transferable ration coupons. It does, however, permit the existence of a free market in unsubsidized bread, in which anyone who wants more bread than he has ration coupons can buy all he wants at the price $p_1 > p$.

Assume that consumers cannot resell bread they buy at subsidized prices, and also that the supply of unsubsidized bread is perfectly elastic.

Using indifference curves between bread and other goods, with the type of budget constraint implied above, show how a consumer will allocate his expenditure between bread and other goods. Do this for two consumers, one who at the equilibrium desires more bread than the number of available coupons, and one who desires less.

Assume that the total number of ration coupons issued is less than the total quantity of bread bought. Now suppose that the government, while still issuing coupons free, allows consumers to buy and sell ration coupons. If bread is not an inferior good, by deriving demand and supply curves for coupons, find what will be the equilibrium market price of a coupon.

5.17   In the light of the discussion in section 5.8, go back to exercise 1.32 and see if you wish to revise your answer.

CHAPTER 6

Theories of Non-competitive Behaviour

 6.1 Introduction

Both the descriptive theory of chapters 1 to 4 and the prescriptive theory of chapter 5 assume explicitly that all agents behave competitively, that is they take all prices as determined independently of their own actions. These theories also assume, explicitly or implicitly, that agents are fully informed of all relevant details of the economy in which they act. In this chapter, we will look at some cases where these assumptions are not true, and will see that many of the conclusions of earlier chapters are then very significantly modified. It should be clear that we are using the word 'competitive' in a way that is very different from everyday usage: the behaviour we study in this chapter is as aggressively self-interested as that studied in previous chapters – the difference is that agents are now not price-takers (or are not fully informed about the economy in which they participate).

6.2 *The monopolistic firm*

Perhaps the least plausible competitive assumption is the assumption that firms take the prices of their product as given. We start therefore with the simplest case of a firm which is a *price-maker* rather than a price-taker, the case of *monopoly*, where a market is supplied by one firm only.

The firm produces output y and has cost function $c(y)$. Its output price p is not a constant but a function of y: $p = p(y)$ is the inverse demand function in the market for the product since this firm's output is the total quantity available to consumers. Since $p'(y) < 0$, the firm faces a downward-sloping demand function.

The profit-maximization problem for such a firm is

$$\text{maximize } p(y) y - c(y) \qquad (1)$$
$$y$$

for which the first-order condition is

$$p(y) + p'(y) y - c'(y) = 0 \qquad (2)$$

while the second-order condition is

$$2p'(y) + p''(y) y - c''(y) < 0 \qquad (3)$$

(compare (2.49)–(2.51)). Thus the necessary condition is that marginal cost $c'(y)$ should be set equal not to price but to marginal revenue (MR), which is defined as

$$\text{MR} = R'(y) = p(y) + p'(y) y \qquad (4)$$

the firm's revenue being

$$R(y) = p(y) y \qquad (5)$$

Marginal revenue has a very simple interpretation. When a competitive firm sells an extra unit of output it gains p, but a monopoly has to reduce its price in order to sell more, if all output has to be sold at a single price, so that the gain is what it receives for the extra unit, $p(y)$, *less what it* loses by reducing the price at which its existing output is sold, $p'(y) y$. (Remember that $p'(y) < 0$.) Note that we can unite

$$\text{MR} = p \left(1 + \frac{y}{p} \frac{dp}{dy} \right) = p \left(1 + \frac{1}{e_{xp}} \right) \qquad (6)$$

where e_{xp} is the price elasticity of demand for the good, since the inverse demand function $p(y)$ is derived by inverting the demand function $x(p)$ and setting $x = y$. Hence MR is positive if and only if $e_{xp} < -1$, that is $|e_{xp}| > 1$.

From (4) we see that when $y = 0$, MR and $p(0)$ are equal, but otherwise MR $< p(y)$. Consider, for example, the linear function $p = a - by$. We have $R = ay - by^2$, so that MR $= a - 2by$. The marginal revenue curve is a straight line twice as steep as the demand curve when the demand curve is a straight line.

Figure 6.1 gives a graphical representation of a profit-maximizing monopolist. Profits are maximized at y_1 where MC $=$ MR, with MC cutting MR from below so that the second-order condition (which can be written $d(\text{MR} - \text{MC})/dy < 0$) is satisfied. The value of profits is

$$p(y_1) y_1 - c(y_1) = (p_1 - \text{AC}_1) y_1.$$

Just as in the theory of the competitive firm, it is possible that a monopolistic firm will prefer to produce nothing at all: if its maximum profits are negative. Also it is easy to produce examples of monopolistic firms which continue production in the short run even though losses are made — see exercise 6.1.

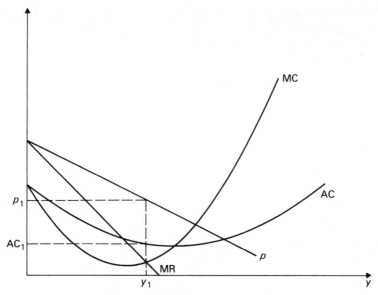

FIGURE 6.1   A profit-maximizing monopolist

Note that we cannot define a supply function or draw a supply curve for a monopoly. Equation (2) cannot be solved to give an expression for y as a function of p, because p is not exogenous. We cannot from knowledge of the firm's cost function and from the price actually charged deduce what quantity will be supplied: for the firm's decisions depend on its beliefs about the shape and position of the demand and marginal revenue curves.

Suppose, however, we compare two industries with identical demand and marginal cost functions, one being a competitive industry, the other consisting of a single monopolistic firm. We can easily show that output will be lower in the monopolistic case. In the competitive industry the supply curve is the industry's marginal cost curve which in turn is the sum of the firms' marginal cost (supply) curves. Output is chosen so that price is equal to marginal cost, because all firms are price-takers. The price-making monopoly, by contrast, chooses a price–output combination that makes marginal revenue equal to marginal cost. Figure 6.1 makes it clear that the monopoly's output is lower. The economic logic is simple: by restricting output, the monopoly can raise price and profit. In a competitive industry, the same would be true, but no firm has an incentive to reduce output, since a single firm's actions do not affect the price, and thus the larger quantity is produced. (This comparison, however, ignores the possibility that industries which become monopolized are those in which there are substantial economies of scale, in other words industries with increasing returns to scale. Case 6 of section 3.4 showed that competitive behaviour is unlikely to be maintained in an industry in this position.)

The logic of monopolistic behaviour throws light on the pricing of some forms of labour too. There are many occupations – principally the 'professions' such as medicine, law and accountancy, but also some 'less skilled' occupations such as newspaper printing and dock labour – where trade unions (sometimes disguised as 'professional associations') control the entry of new workers. The objectives of trade unions are probably too complex to be characterized as 'profit maximization' in any sense, but those unions which can control entry certainly do exercise this control, in the knowledge that restricted supply implies a higher price.

A monopolistic firm may have so little impact in any of the markets in which it buys inputs that it can behave as a price-taker in these markets. The theory of cost minimization set out in sections 2.4–2.8 then applies without qualification, so that the cost function written as $c(y)$ above is in fact $c(\mathbf{w}, y)$, where $\mathbf{w}$ is the vector of input prices. It is easy to show (see exercise 6.2) that if such a monopoly has production function $y = F(\mathbf{z})$ it will hire inputs in quantities which satisfy

$$\text{MR} \, \frac{\partial F}{\partial z_i} = w_i \qquad i = 1, \ldots, n \tag{7}$$

(compare (2.6)). The logic should be clear: the marginal cost of an input is equated to the marginal benefit, the input price being the marginal cost and the benefit being the increase in revenue obtained from the extra output. The term on the left-hand side of (7) is called the *marginal revenue product* of input i.

A large firm may, however, be so influential in the markets in which it buys its inputs that the input price depends on the quantity it buys, so that $w_i = w_i(z_i)$ with $w_i'(z_i) > 0$. For such a firm cost minimization as well as profit maximization are different from a competitive firm. Equation (2) describes optimal choice of output, and it is not difficult (see exercise 6.5) to show that optimal choice of inputs is described by the equations

$$(p(y) + p'(y) y) \, \frac{\partial F}{\partial z_i} = w_i(z_i) + w_i'(z_i) z_i \qquad i = 1, \ldots, n \tag{8}$$

which can alternatively be written as

$$p \left(1 + \frac{1}{e_{xp}} \right) \frac{\partial F}{\partial z_i} = w_i \left(1 + \frac{1}{e_{zi}} \right) \qquad i = 1, \ldots, n \tag{8a}$$

or

$$\text{MR} \, \frac{\partial F}{\partial z_i} = \text{MC}_i \qquad i = 1, \ldots, n \tag{8b}$$

where $e_{zi} = w_i/(w_i'(z_i) z_i) = (w_i/z_i)(dz_i/dw_i)$ is the elasticity of supply of input i to the firm, and MC_i stands for 'marginal cost of input i'. If $w_i'(z_i) > 0$, MC_i is greater than w_i for exactly the same sort of reason that MR is less than p: the cost of hiring an extra unit of input i is the price that must be paid *plus* the rise in the price paid to the existing units of input i necessary to attract the extra unit if the same price must be paid to all. A firm which in this way is a price-maker in an input market is called a *monopsony* or *monopsonist*.

6.3   The welfare economics of monopoly

We have seen that a monopoly produces a level of output at which output price *exceeds* the marginal cost of production. The argument in section 5.1 that in a competitive market the correct (or 'efficient') level of output is produced depends crucially on the fact that price *equals* marginal cost. (Also the formal argument in section 5.3 that a competitive equilibrium is Pareto efficient uses in its final step the fact that firms are price-takers.) So we should not be surprised to find that a monopolized market produces an inefficiently low level of output.

Figure 6.2 reproduces figure 6.1, with the AC and MR curves omitted for clarity. Suppose the price were reduced from p_1 to p_2 and the quantity sold raised from y_1 to y_2. Consumer surplus would increase by the amount

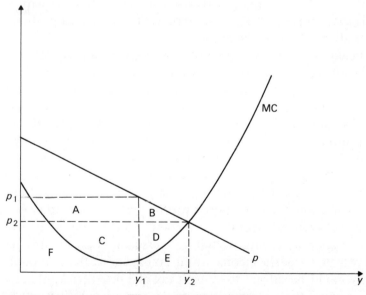

FIGURE 6.2   The inefficiency of monopoly

represented by areas A and B. Sales revenue would change from $A + C + F$ to $C + D + E + F$, so would rise by $D + E - A$. Costs would rise by E, so profits would fall by $A - D$. (We know that profits fall because y_1 was the monopolist's profit-maximizing output level.) Thus the gain in consumer surplus exceeds the loss of profit by the amount given by the area $B + D$.

How can output be raised from y_1 to y_2? Our analysis of externalities in competitive markets suggests that taxes and subsidies are a suitable way to shift the equilibrium. The monopoly takes into account the loss of revenue from its existing sales if it cuts price to raise sales, but this is not a true loss to society, merely a transfer from the monopoly to its existing customers. Thus the monopoly underestimates the true social value of output, so the appropriate policy is a subsidy. If a per-unit subsidy of s is paid, then (compare (1)) the firm's profits become $p(y)y + sy - c(y)$ where $p(y)$ is the price paid by consumers, so that the necessary condition for maximization is

$$p(y) + p'(y)y + s - c'(y) = 0 \tag{9}$$

that is

$$MR = c'(y) - s \tag{10}$$

The second-order condition is still (3). Equation (9) defines y as an implicit function of s and differentiating gives

$$(c''(y) - 2p'(y) - p''(y)y)\frac{dy}{ds} = 1 \tag{11}$$

so that $dy/ds > 0$ when (3) is satisfied. Clearly profits rise with s also: in fact, it is easy to show that if $\pi(s)$ represents maximized profits for given s, then $d\pi/ds = y$ (see exercise 6.6(a)).

Graphically, this can be represented by drawing a curve $MC - s$, s units below the MC curve, with the intersection between this new curve and the MR curve determining the new level of output. To attain the optimal level of output y_2 in the case shown in figures 6.1 and 6.2 it is necessary to introduce a subsidy equal to the vertical distance between MC and MR at y_2. Then into the welfare calculation in figure 6.2 we have to introduce an extra element: an amount sy_2 will be paid out by the government as subsidy and the monopoly's profits will be raised by $sy_2 - (A - D)$ compared with the original equilibrium. It may seem paradoxical to introduce a policy that raises the monopoly's profits, but this is another example of a conflict between efficiency and income distribution: it is efficient to raise the monopoly's output, but to persuade it to do this requires a method which transfers income from taxpayers to the monopoly. If the monopoly could be subject to a profit tax at a rate that would recover the subsidy revenue, this redistribution could be reversed. (It is left to you to consider why paying to the monopoly an amount of money as a subsidy which then has all to be repaid as a profit tax has any effect on the behaviour of the firm — see exercise 6.6(b).)

6.4 *Price discrimination*

The interpretation of marginal revenue given above shows why a monopoly does not supply up to the point where price equals marginal cost: to gain extra customers the monopoly would have to cut the price paid to existing customers. If the firm can charge different prices to different customers, the argument no longer holds. A necessary condition for such *price discrimination* is that the product is not resellable. Examples of price discrimination are found in rail and air fares, hotel prices, medical charges, and postal charges.

Perfect discrimination occurs when every consumer can be charged at a different rate for each part, however small, of total output he consumes. Obviously the rate which should be charged by a profit-maximizing firm is the maximum price any consumer is willing to pay, and this information is given by the inverse demand function. Total revenue is found by adding the revenue received on each part of sales, that is by integrating the inverse demand function, to give

$$R(y) = \int_0^y p(x)\, dx \qquad (12)$$

(Compare (5.10).) That this is the correct measure is confirmed by observing that $R(0) = 0$ and that $R'(y) = p(y)$ so the rate at which revenue is increased by extra sales is given by the price at which the extra sale is made. Profits are

$$\pi(y) = \int_0^y p(x)\, dx - c(y) \qquad (13)$$

and the necessary condition for profit maximization (recalling that $R'(y) = p(y)$) is

$$p(y) - c'(y) = 0 \qquad (14)$$

This is the same rule as would be satisfied by a competitive industry. The reason is simple: since the marginal sale can be made at the price the marginal consumer is willing to pay, without cutting the price paid on existing sales, the inverse demand function is the perfectly discriminating monopolist's marginal revenue function.

Thus perfect price discrimination gives rise to an efficient level of output. This gain in efficiency is accompanied by a redistribution of income compared with non-discriminatory monopoly: consumers receive no consumer surplus, it all accruing as revenue to the monopoly, as we see when we compare (5.10) and (12). (It is easy to produce examples in which a non-discriminating monopolist would make losses by producing and would therefore produce nothing; whereas the discriminating monopolist produces the positive efficient level of output.) When we compare perfect price discrimination with competition, we find no efficiency difference since output is the same in both cases, but discrimination implies redistribution of consumer surplus to the monopoly.

It is worth at this point looking back at the discussion of public goods in section 5.6, since the same issues are involved. Efficient provision of public goods is ensured if the supplier of public goods can act as a perfectly discriminating monopolist.

It is, however, virtually impossible that any firm can have enough information about its market to discriminate perfectly. In fact, therefore, only a few different prices can be charged. This we call *imperfect price discrimination*. Suppose the market can be split into two parts with respective inverse demand functions $p_1(x_1)$ and $p_2(x_2)$. Then the firm's profits are a function of x_1 and x_2:

$$\pi(x_1, x_2) = p_1(x_1) x_1 + p_2(x_2) x_2 - c(x_1 + x_2) \tag{15}$$

since output is $x_1 + x_2$. We have two necessary conditions for profit maximization.

$$p_i(x_i) + p_i'(x_i) x_i - c'(x_1 + x_2) \qquad i = 1, 2 \tag{16}$$

that is

$$c'(y) = MR_i = p_i \left(1 + \frac{1}{e_i}\right) \qquad i = 1, 2 \tag{17}$$

where MR_i is the marginal revenue in market i and e_i is the elasticity of demand.

Thus if $|e_1| > |e_2|$, $p_1 < p_2$: the discriminating monopolist charges a higher price in the market in which demand is less elastic.

Consider air fares as an example. Return fares for tickets subject to restrictions on advance booking and length of stay are much cheaper than unrestricted tickets. The objective is to split the market into two separate parts: tourists plan their trips in advance and can usually satisfy the restrictions; but the restrictions are specifically designed so that business travellers are forced to buy the expensive tickets. Business travellers can be expected to have less elastic demand for air travel than tourists, so the theory does seem to describe the practice. (Note that it is not accurate to say that it is because business travellers are richer than tourists that it is sensible to charge them more – it is differences in elasticity of demand rather than income differences that matter.)

This example is atypical in the sense that the good being provided to both sets of customers is essentially the same – restrictions on advance booking and length of stay do not significantly reduce the cost to an airline of providing service. Most forms of price discrimination, however, involve genuinely different service being produced to customers in order to split the market: first-class air travellers get better food and wider seats than second-class travellers, library editions of books are bound in more durable covers than paperback editions; and so on.

This can be incorporated into the theory by letting cost depend on both x_1 and x_2 rather than their sum, so that profits are

$$\pi(x_1, x_2) = p_1(x_1) x_1 + p_2(x_2) x_2 - c(x_1, x_2) \tag{18}$$

with first-order conditions

$$\frac{\partial c}{\partial x_i} = p_i(x_i) + p_i'(x_i) x_i \qquad i = 1, 2 \tag{19}$$

that is,

$$\mathrm{MC}_i = \mathrm{MR}_i = p_i \left(1 + \frac{1}{e_i} \right) \qquad i = 1, 2 \tag{20}$$

Thus though the marginal cost of supplying the separate markets may be different (because wider seats or hard covers do cost more) this will not be the full explanation of the price difference: the *gap* between price and marginal cost will be larger in the market with the lower elasticity.

Clearly, all of this generalizes immediately to the case of a market split into more than two parts.

Since imperfect price discrimination looks like an intermediate case between non-discrimination and perfect discrimination, it is tempting to conclude that it will result in a more efficient level of output than the non-discriminatory monopoly but not the fully efficient level of perfect discrimination. However, the first half of that conclusion is incorrect: it is *not* the case that imperfect discrimination necessarily raises the quantity sold. You are asked in exercise 6.12 to show this by example. The point is that since price discrimination allows separate prices to be established in each market one price will be lowered and the other raised from the non-discriminatory price. (Exercise 6.13 asks you to think about why both will not go in the same direction.) Thus in one market, consumers who were formerly excluded from consumption though they were willing to pay more than marginal cost are now permitted to consume; but in the other market, consumption is reduced, so inefficiency is increased. The efficiency gain in the first market need not outweigh the loss in the other. Contrast the case of perfect discrimination, where since all inefficiency is eliminated there must be an efficiency gain.

To sum up. From the viewpoint of efficiency, consumers who are willing to pay marginal cost should be supplied. Perfect price discrimination fulfils this aim, imperfect price discrimination *may* get closer to fulfilling it than non-discrimination. Both types of discrimination also have implications for income distribution which may or may not be thought desirable.

It is simple to extend the theory to the case of monopsony. A firm will wish to offer different prices for different sources of supply of the same input if the elasticity of supply if different from the two sources. The detailed derivation is left to you (as exercise 6.15).

6.5   Oligopoly and game theory

In one sense the monopolistic firm and the perfectly competitive firm are at opposite extremes: one has a whole market to itself, the other faces competition from so many other firms that the price at which it sells is outside its control. The two types of firms do, however, have one thing in common: they can make their plans without worrying about their competitors' reactions, the monopoly because it has no competitors, the competitive firm because its actions alone have an insignificant effect on the market as a whole. In fact, few firms are truly monopolies, and few industries consist of truly competitive firms, so we should consider intermediate possibilities between competition and monopoly. Such intermediate possibilities are collectively known as *imperfect competition*. In almost all such intermediate cases, a firm has to take explicit account of its rivals', and potential rivals', reactions. The study of how agents act in situations where their actions may influence other agents' reactions is the subject matter of the *theory of games*.

An industry in which there are a small number of firms is called an *oligopoly*. The simplest set of assumptions to make is that: (i) firms do not collude; (ii) each firm attempts to maximize profits on the assumption that other firms' outputs are fixed. Suppose that the market demand curve for a product is linear:

$$p = a - bx \tag{21}$$

and that there are n firms each of which has a linear cost function

$$c_f = cy_f \qquad f = 1, \ldots, n \tag{22}$$

a, b and c being constants. The quantity consumed, x, is equal to the sum of firms' outputs:

$$x = \sum_{f=1}^{n} y_f \tag{23}$$

Consider a typical firm, whose profits are

$$\pi_f(y_f, x) = (a - bx) y_f - cy_f \tag{24}$$

The firm seeks to maximize this with respect to y_f on the assumption that all the other firms' outputs are fixed, so that, from (23), $dx/dy_f = 1$. Thus we have the first-order condition

$$a - c - bx - by_f = 0 \tag{25}$$

(the second-order condition being clearly satisfied). Now (25) is satisfied for all f, so summing over all f and using (23) gives

$$n(a - c - bx) - bx = 0 \tag{26}$$

so that

$$x = \frac{n}{n+1} \frac{a-c}{b} \tag{27}$$

and

$$y_f = \frac{1}{n+1} \frac{a-c}{b} \tag{28}$$

The argument applies whatever the value of n. With $n = 1$ we have the monopoly outcome $x = (a - c)/2b$. As n increases, each firm's output falls but total supply rises, and as n approaches infinity, total output approaches $(a - c)/b$, the competitive output that would be produced if firms were price-takers. (No great significance should be attached to this last result, however. It has been derived in a very simple example. More important, there is no indication of how the actual value of n in any particular case might be determined.)

The equilibrium described by (27) and (28) was derived on the assumption that all firms are identical and each firm acts as if the output of other firms is given. This assumption is due to the 19th century French economist Cournot, and the equilibrium we have derived is called a *Cournot equilibrium*. (It is an example of a broader equilibrium concept in game theory called a Nash equilibrium.) In the Cournot equilibrium no firm has an incentive to change its output away from the equilibrium value so long as all other firms are choosing their equilibrium outputs.

Further consideration of this example is aided by confining our attention to the case $n = 2$. An oligopoly with two firms is called a *duopoly*. Equation (25) becomes for firm 1

$$a - c - by_2 - 2by_1 = 0 \tag{29}$$

so that

$$y_1 = \frac{a - c - by_2}{2b} \tag{30}$$

Similarly, firm 2 will choose y_2 to satisfy

$$y_2 = \frac{a - c - by_1}{2b} \qquad (31)$$

These functions describing y_1 as a function of y_2 and y_2 as a function of y_1 are called *reaction functions* and they are graphed as *reaction curves* in figure 6.3. The Cournot equilibrium is $y_1 = y_2 = (a - c)/3b$ and is shown in the figure at point C where the two curves cross.

It is natural to ask whether this equilibrium is stable. Suppose we start with $y_2 = 0$, so that firm 1 is a monopoly and chooses the monopoly output level $(a - c)/2b$. The market is at point P_1. Firm 2 will react by raising y_2 so that we shift to P_2. Given this value of y_2, firm 1 will wish to reduce output, so we go to P_3 and so on until the duopoly equilibrium point C is reached It is easy to see that the market will converge to C whatever the starting point, *if* at each step one firm believes the other's output is fixed. The problem with this argument is that such beliefs are immediately shown to be incorrect, and it is not very satisfactory to base a theory on the assumption that agents will act on the basis of beliefs

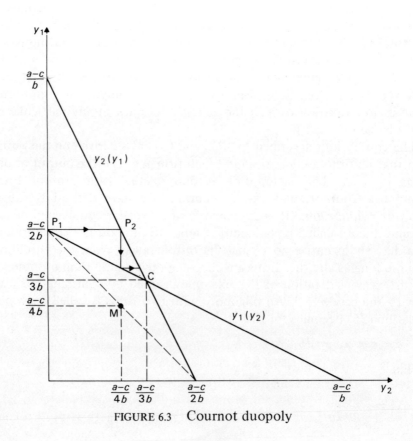

FIGURE 6.3   Cournot duopoly

which are systematically incorrect. Contrast the situation at the actual equilibrium: the first firm's belief that y_2 is fixed at $(a-c)/3b$ (so that the optimal value of y_1 is $(a-c)/3b$) is well-founded, because y_2 does indeed take this value (because, in turn, firm 2 has the correct expectation of y_1).

Suppose now that firm 1 becomes aware that firm 2 has a reaction function described by (31), and that firm 1 maximizes profits on the assumption that (31) is satisfied rather than on the assumption that y_2 is fixed. Thus firm 1's aim is

$$\text{maximize}_{y_1, y_2} (a - by_1 - by_2) y_1 - cy_1 \tag{32}$$

$$\text{subject to } y_2 = (a - c - by_1)/2b$$

which can be rewritten

$$\text{maximize}_{y_1} \tfrac{1}{2}(a - c) y_1 - \tfrac{1}{2}by_1^2 \tag{33}$$

whose solution is

$$y_1 = \frac{a - c}{2b} \tag{34}$$

so that

$$y_2 = \frac{a - c}{4b} \tag{35}$$

This is the *Stackelberg equilibrium*, where firm 1 is the *leader* and firm 2 the *follower*. It is shown as the point S_1 in figure 6.4.

To understand the difference between the two equilibria it may be helpful to look at the contours of firm 1's profit function. These contours are the curved lines in the diagram, with profits being lower the further away the contours get from the monopoly point $y_1 = (a - c)/2b$, $y_2 = 0$. The contours are vertical as they cross the $y_1(y_2)$ line – since that line is defined by maximizing profits given y_2. The Stackelberg leader chooses the point on the $y_2(y_1)$ line that is on the highest contour: hence the choice of S_1.

Clearly there is a symmetric Stackelberg equilibrium at S_2 with firm 2 the leader and firm 1 the follower. This raises the obvious difficulty that in a Stackelberg equilibrium there has to be an unexplained asymmetry of sophistication. If both firms try to be leaders each will discover that their hypothesis that the other firm would passively remain on its reaction curve is incorrect, so there is no equilibrium so long as both seek to lead.

So far we have assumed that firms behave non-cooperatively. However, as Adam Smith pointed out in his classic book *The Wealth of Nations* in 1776: 'People of the same trade seldom meet together, even for merri-

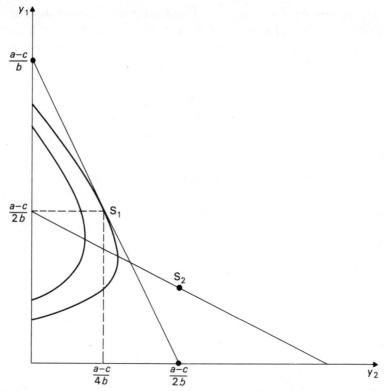

FIGURE 6.4   Stackelberg duopoly equilibrium

ment and diversion, but the conversation ends in a conspiracy against the publick, or in some contrivance to raise prices.' Staying with the duopoly example, let us consider the possibility that the firms *collude*. (In the language of game theory, we are considering the possibility of a *cooperative* solution to the game.) If the firms act together, and maximize joint profits, they have to choose a level of total output to satisfy

$$\text{maximize } (a - by) y - cy \tag{36}$$
$$y$$

which has, of course, as solution the monopoly equilibrium $y = (a-c)/2b$. They then have to decide how to allocate production and profits between them, but the obvious thing to do is for them to agree to set

$$y_1 = y_2 = \frac{a - c}{4b} \tag{37}$$

which point is indicated by M in figure 6.3.

There is, however, a serious problem with this cooperative solution: each firm has an incentive to break the agreement. Let us suppose that $a = 13$, $b = 1$ and $c = 1$, so the Cournot equilibrium is $y_1 = y_2 = 4$ while the cooperative solution is $y_1 = y_2 = 3$. Let us also for simplicity make the entirely arbitrary assumption that the firms, having agreed to produce 3 units each, in contemplating whether to break the agreement consider only the output level 4 as an alternative. It is easily calculated that profits are related to outputs as shown in the following table:

	$y_2 = 3$	$y_2 = 4$
$y_1 = 3$	$\pi_1 = 18$ $\pi_2 = 18$	$\pi_1 = 15$ $\pi_2 = 20$
$y_1 = 4$	$\pi_1 = 20$ $\pi_2 = 15$	$\pi_1 = 16$ $\pi_2 = 16$

The firms now find themselves in the situation known to game theorists as the *prisoner's dilemma*. Firm 1 can argue that if firm 2 sticks to the agreement to set $y_2 = 3$, it can increase its profits from 18 to 20 by breaking the agreement; while if firm 2 breaks the agreement and sets $y_2 = 4$, firm 1 can raise its profits from 15 to 16 by also breaking the agreement. Thus firm 1 has an unambiguous incentive to set $y_1 = 4$. (When one action is better than another action irrespective of the action of the opposing agent, game theorists call it a *dominant strategy*.) But symmetrically, firm 2 will set $y_2 = 4$ and *the firms are both worse off than if they had kept their agreement*. (If you are sufficiently stimulated by the issues raised in this section to study game theory further you will quickly find out why this problem is given the curious title of the 'prisoners' dilemma'.)

This illustrates why collusive agreements between firms (often called 'cartels') may be unstable arrangements. We should not, however, jump to the conclusion that the agreement *must* break down. It is plausible that the situation described above will be repeated period after period. Suppose that firm 1 makes the following threat to firm 2: 'if you set $y_2 = 4$ in any time period, then I will set $y_1 = 4$ for the following two periods'. If firm 2 now cheats, its profit will rise from 18 to 20 in the first period, but then fall to 16 for the next two periods. The gain of 2 in the first period is unlikely to outweigh the loss of 4 over the remaining two periods, and firm 2 calculates that it is best to maintain y_2 at 3. Meanwhile, of course, it makes a symmetrical threat to firm 1 to ensure that y_1 stays at 3.

In this simple example, therefore, we have succeeded in describing four different possible equilibria, not all equally plausible but all certainly possible. In the Cournot duopoly equilibrium total output is $2(a-c)/3b$ so the price is $c + (a-c)/3$; in the Stackelberg equilibria, output is $3(a-c)/4b$ so the price is $c + (a-c)/4$; and in the collusive equilibrium, output is $(a-c)/2b$ and price is $c + (a-c)/2$. These equilibria all have the property that output is lower than the competitive output $(a-c)/b$ and price higher than marginal cost c, but they differ in how far away from the competitive equilibrium they are.

6.6   Differentiated products and monopolistic competition

In the example discussed in the previous section the firms produced the same product, and the price of that product was whatever was required to sell all that was produced. A much more realistic model of oligopoly would assume that firms in the same industry produce goods which are very similar but not identical. The differences might be fairly trivial, such as the packaging of different soap powders, or they might be reasonably significant, such as the detailed technical specification of different cars. Then each firm can set the price for its own product.

Suppose there are two firms producing closely competing but differentiated products. Firm 1 faces a demand function $y_1 = y_1(p_1, p_2)$ for its product, where p_1 is the price of its product and p_2 is the rival's price, and where the partial derivatives of the demand function satisfy $y_{11} < 0$ and $y_{12} > 0$. Similarly, firm 2's demand function $y_2 = y_2(p_1, p_2)$ has the properties $y_{21} > 0$ and $y_{22} < 0$. The firms' cost functions are respectively $c_1(y_1)$ and $c_2(y_2)$. If firm 1 sets its price on the assumption that p_2 is given it will aim to solve the problem

$$\underset{p_1}{\text{maximize}}\, p_1 y_1(p_1, p_2) - c_1(y_1(p_1, p_2)) \tag{38}$$

and the solution $p_1 = p_1(p_2)$ is its reaction function. Similarly firm 2 can derive its reaction function $p_2 = p_2(p_1)$. A Cournot–Nash price equilibrium would be a pair of prices (p_1, p_2) with the property

$$p_1 = p_1(p_2(p_1)) \tag{39}$$

A Stackelberg price equilibrium with firm 2 as leader would be derived by supposing that firm 2 chooses p_2 to solve the problem

$$\underset{p_2}{\text{maximize}}\, p_2 y_2(p_1(p_2), p_2) - c_2(y_2(p_1(p_2), p_2)) \tag{40}$$

while (38) continues to describe firm 1's behaviour. A cooperative price equilibrium would be a pair (p_1, p_2) which solved

$$\underset{p_1, p_2}{\text{maximize}}\, p_1 y_1(p_1, p_2) + p_2 y_2(p_1, p_2) - c_1(y_1(p_1, p_2)) - c_2(y_2(p_1, p_2)) \tag{41}$$

(though such a solution might have to be supplemented by a profit-sharing agreement).

Again we proceed by example. Suppose that $y_1 = 7 - 2p_1 + p_2$, $y_2 = 7 + p_1 - 2p_2$, $c_1 = y_1$, $c_2 = y_2$. Firm 1's profits are therefore

$$\pi_1 = 9p_1 - 2p_1^2 + p_1 p_2 - 7 - p_2 \qquad (42)$$

and maximizing with respect to p_1 for given p_2 gives the reaction function

$$p_1 = \tfrac{9}{4} + \tfrac{1}{4}p_2 \qquad (43)$$

and, symmetrically, firm 2's reaction function is $p_2 = (9 + p_1)/4$. Thus we have the Cournot–Nash price equilibrium

$$p_1 = p_2 = 3 \qquad y_1 = y_2 = 4 \qquad (44)$$

The reaction functions are drawn in figure 6.5, and this equilibrium is at C where they intersect.

In the Stackelberg equilibrium with firm 2 as leader, (43) describes firm 1's behaviour, but firm 2 maximizes

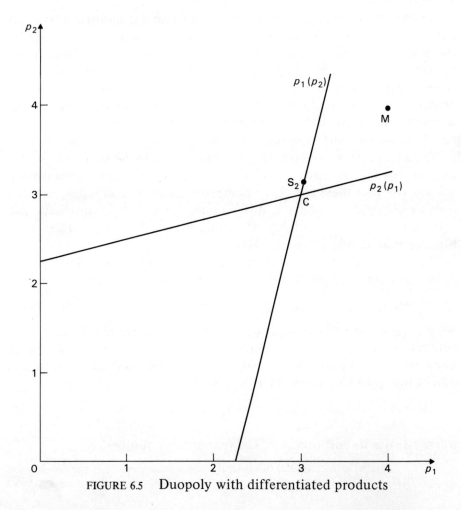

FIGURE 6.5   Duopoly with differentiated products

$$\pi_2 = 9p_2 - 2p_2^2 + p_2(\tfrac{9}{4} + \tfrac{1}{4}p_2) - 7 - \tfrac{9}{4} - \tfrac{1}{4}p_2$$
$$= 11p_2 - \tfrac{7}{4}p_2^2 - \tfrac{37}{4} \tag{45}$$

so that it chooses $p_2 = 22/7$ and firm 1 then sets $p_1 = 85/28$. This point is shown as S_2 in figure 6.5.

In the cooperative equilibrium, the two firms act together like a two-product monopoly to maximize

$$\pi_1 + \pi_2 = 8(p_1 + p_2) - 2(p_1^2 + p_2^2) + 2p_1 p_2 - 14 \tag{46}$$

with respect to p_1 and p_2. The solution is $p_1 = p_2 = 4$, $q_1 = q_2 = 3$, and it is shown as M in figure 6.5.

In short, this example is directly analogous to the example of the previous section, with the only real difference being that here firms are setting prices for differentiated products rather than quantities of a homogeneous product.

Like the the previous example, it shows that an oligopolistic market can have several types of equilibrium, and it is not obvious which would be the actual outcome in reality. Perhaps the most serious omission is the fact that we have assumed a fixed number of firms in the industry. In reality, entry of new firms, or the fear of such entry, would modify all the equilibria. It is plausible that the easier it is for other firms to enter an industry, the closer will be both the Cournot–Nash and the cooperative equilibria to the competitive equilibrium.

We cannot here investigate that proposition properly. We can, however, look at one market structure in which entry of new firms does matter. We suppose that there are a large number of firms in an industry, but each produces a product which is differentiated from others' products, and there is no barrier to the entry of further firms. This is the market structure called *monopolistic competition*.

The typical firm faces a demand curve for its product that is a function of the prices of all its rivals' products as well as its own price

$$y_i = y_i(p_1, p_2, \ldots, p_n) \tag{47}$$

with $\partial y_i / \partial p_i < 0$ and $\partial y_i / \partial p_j \geqslant 0$, $j \neq i$. Because the firm has many competitors, it assumes that its rivals do not react to its own individual decisions, so in setting its price it makes the Cournot–Nash assumption that other firms' prices are given. Thus its objective is

$$\underset{p_i}{\text{maximize}} \; p_i y_i(p_1, \ldots, p_n) - c_i(y_i(p_1, \ldots, p_n)) \tag{48}$$

where $c_i(y_i)$ is its cost function. The first-order condition is

$$y_i + p_i \frac{\partial y_i}{\partial p_i} - c_i'(y_i) \frac{\partial y_i}{\partial p_i} = 0 \tag{49}$$

and recalling that the elasticity of demand for y_i with respect to its own price p_i is given by

$$e_i = \frac{p_i}{y_i} \frac{\partial y_i}{\partial p_i} \qquad (50)$$

we can rewrite (49) as

$$c_i'(y_i) = p_i \left(1 + \frac{1}{e_i}\right) \qquad (51)$$

so that, just like a monopolist, the firm equates marginal cost to marginal revenue, but now marginal revenue has to be more carefully defined, as the value to the firm's revenue of an extra unit of output *if* all other firms keep their prices constant.

However, in equilibrium a further condition must be satisfied. If the typical firm is making positive profits, new firms would be attracted to this market by the prospect of also making profits by producing a similar product. Thus the market will be in equilibrium with the number of firms constant only if price is equal to average cost:

$$p_i = c_i(y_i)/y_i \qquad (52)$$

Equations (51) and (52) together imply, since $e_i < 0$, that marginal cost $c_i'(y_i)$ is less than average cost $c_i(y_i)/y_i$ so that, from equation (3.4) and the accompanying discussion, we know that average cost is a decreasing function of output.

The firm's equilibrium is illustrated in figure 6.6, in which the demand curve d_i indicates the combinations of p_i and y_i available to the firm if other firms' prices are constant, MR_i is drawn on the same assumption, and y_i^* is the output the firm chooses to produce. It should be obvious to you why the demand curve is *tangent* to the average cost curve at y_i^*, if (51) and (52) are satisfied (see exercise 6.24).

If the demand curve d_i had cut the average cost curve, then the firm would be making positive profits. New firms would have entered, and although the precise details of how d_i would change are complicated by the need to consider how all firms' prices would react to new entry it is fairly obvious that the d_i curve would be shifted leftwards until the tangency equilibrium was attained. Similarly, if d_i lay below $c(y_i)/y_i$ everywhere, exit from the industry would drive d_i rightwards.

At the equilibrium, price exceeds marginal cost, and also there is 'excess capacity' in the sense that the firm is producing at an output lower than the output at which average cost is lowest. We have to be wary of jumping to the conclusion that there is inefficiency. If in figure 6.6 the demand curve d_i intersected the minimum point on the average cost curve and the firm were persuaded (by taxation or subsidy) to produce at this point, then price would equal marginal cost and the average cost of production

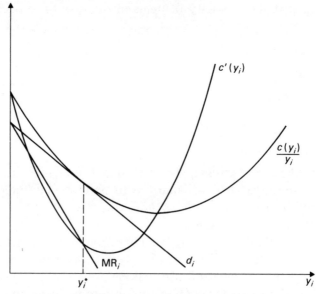

FIGURE 6.6   Monopolistic competition

would be as low as possible, but this could only be the case if the d_i curve lay to the right of the equilibrium d_i curve, that is if there were fewer firms in the market. The consumers are faced in this situation with a less wide range of choice of products, and if consumers genuinely value diversity of products in this market they may be worse off as a result of having a smaller range of products available even if prices are lower.

A further point to consider about monopolistic competition is that since there are many firms in the market, each individual firm may find that the demand elasticity e_i is very high, so that when (52) and (51) are satisfied price and average cost are very close to marginal cost, so that the outcome is not very different from perfect competition.

When, finally, we consider what sort of markets might be monopolistically competitive the obvious examples are branded goods such as consumer electronic goods, cars, or soap; or retail services like grocery shops. In each case the goods offered by different suppliers are very similar, but sufficiently different for each seller to have a demand for his good that is not infinitely elastic. When, however, we look at the markets for soap, television sets, cars we see markets in which in both Europe and America almost all the goods are supplied by a handful of firms in each case. Thus oligopolistic behaviour, in which each firm takes some account of competitors' reactions, seems more plausible than the behaviour assumed in the theory of monopolistic competition. When we look at grocery shops, petrol stations, hairdressers, massage parlours and so on, we see many suppliers, but *in any one locality* there are at most a handful, so that each supplier probably sees himself as really competing only with a small number of nearby rivals, and again oligopolistic behaviour is more plausible than monopolistic competition.

In summing up the discussion of the theory of oligopoly and of monopolistic competition, perhaps the most obvious thing to say is that the theory is much less 'cut-and-dried' than either the theory of competitive markets or the theory of monopoly. We have proceeded mainly by looking at a series of closely related examples, and these examples are sufficient to display a wide diversity of possible outcomes. The important issue of how oligopolistic behaviour is likely to be influenced by the entry of new competitors (or fear of such entry) has been looked at only in the extreme case of monopolistic competition, where we obtained the not very surprising result that since the assumptions are not very different from the assumptions of perfect competition, the outcome is not very different either.

6.7 Markets with imperfect information

We are now almost ready to draw together the several strands of theory developed in this and the previous chapter, but before we do that it should be pointed out that there is a set of issues which have been largely ignored in the theories we have developed here. We have assumed that firms and individuals make their decisions in an environment about which they know all relevant information: firms know the production functions available to them, consumers know the prices and qualities of all products on the market that may be of interest to them, and so on. In reality, however, agents are imperfectly informed about their economic environment, information is costly to acquire, and the environment is constantly changing as a result of random events (such as the weather, or accidents) and of other agents' unpredictable behaviour. Some of the most interesting and fundamental questions in economic theory are concerned with how institutions and individuals react to uncertainty and imperfect information. Here we cannot properly investigate these issues, but a few examples may help you be wary of applying the theories we have developed to situations where they are not applicable without modification.

Institutions and practices which at first sight may seem monopolistic, and therefore undesirable, may be more reasonably explained as responding to imperfect information. Consider patents, for example. A patent gives an inventor the right to exclusive use of his invention (or to charge other users) for a period of years. He has therefore a monopoly on the use of his invention and will earn monopoly profits. Efficient *use* of new inventions is possible only if all are granted access. The function of the patent, however, is to give potential inventors an incentive to search for useful knowledge. There is no simple answer to the question of how *much* patent protection inventors should receive so as to achieve the correct balance between efficient use of information and adequate incentive to make new discoveries.

Another apparently monopolistic practice is the common feature in professional team sports of employing players on long-term contracts with the player sometimes not being free to play for another team even after his formal contract has expired. Thus when one team wants another team's player, it has to pay a 'transfer fee' to persuade that team to release the player from his cotnract. At first sight the teams are together organizing a monopsony in the market for players by preventing the wages of good players being bid up as different teams tried to recruit them, but the abolition of long-term contracts would surely depress the wages of the less good players while raising the wages of the best. (The details of the argument are left to you to work through.) A player at the start of his career will be uncertain about how good he will turn out to be, so he may be happy to accept a system of employment that raises the wages he will get if he turns out to be a lower quality player, at the cost of reducing the wages he will receive if he turns out to be very good. In short, the teams are absorbing some of the risk that their players face. (Of course, there is another facet of this issue: a team that is very good at developing the talents of young players will receive high transfer fees, so the system also provides incentives to the teams to search out and nurture talent, rather like the patent system.) Again, there is no clear-cut answer to the question of what precise degree of freedom of contract gives the optimal balance between risk-sharing on the one hand and incentives to players to perform well on the other.

There are firms which specialize in taking on risks, the firms called insurance companies. In return for the payment of an insurance premium the company will compensate you if your house is burned down, or your car is stolen, or you fall ill. Problems arise in the operation of insurance contracts because of the insurance companies' imperfect information about their clients' circumstances and behaviour. Suppose that you know your health is a little less good than average but not so bad that a medical examination will identify you as a 'bad risk', then you will be rather keen to buy health insurance. If, on the other hand, you are extraordinarily healthy you may choose to take the risk of being uninsured. Thus the insurance company will tend to find that its customers are less healthy than average, so that it will face a higher level of claims than it would face if its customers were a representative cross-section of the population. There is a problem of *adverse selection*. This problem arises in other markets too. The market for used cars is an example: if you own a very reliable car you are less likely to sell it, so the used cars offered for sale are likely to be less reliable than average. The result of adverse selection may be that certain types of good, which consumers would be willing to pay for, will not in fact be offered.

A second problem that arises with insurance is that if your house is fully insured against fire you may be less careful about fire precautions. This is the problem of *moral hazard*. The obvious way to deal with this problem is for the insurer to refuse to insure the full value of the house, so that the owner still suffers some loss if the house is burned. An honest and careful individual who really wants full insurance may be unable to buy it.

Thus, in situations of uncertainty and imperfect information you need first to be careful of how you interpret the function of certain economic institutions, and secondly to be aware of the possibility that certain goods and services may not be available to consumers, even if the consumers are willing to pay the cost of supplying the goods and services.

6.8   *A summing-up on welfare economics*

The analysis presented in the last two chapters presents some strong arguments in favour of the market allocation of resources, but also raises some significant problems. What role is implied for government intervention in the allocation of resources? The following are a sample of the range of possible responses to that question.

(1) The government should do next to nothing, and leave the market to do its job. There should, perhaps, be some income redistribution to the poorest members of society (strictly in the form of cash, which they can spend as they see fit); and there should be collective provision of defence, legal and police services and of roads and bridges. There are problems of externalities, information, public goods and monopoly which mean the market functions imperfectly, but collective attempts to improve matters will function even less perfectly. Political decision-making confers power on a centralized bureaucracy, whereas the market decentralizes decision-taking.

(2) The market should be the primary method of allocating resources, but subject to a considerable degree of government intervention and control. The government should use the tax system to redistribute income and wealth, should supply public goods, should supply some private goods like education and health services (because of positive externalities, market imperfections, and income distributional effects), should prohibit the consumption of some goods where there are strong negative externalities (such as the burning of coal in domestic fires) or where consumers simply seem not to act in their own best interests (such as the consumption of narcotic drugs), should impose taxes and subsidies on some goods so as to bring market prices into line with social costs and benefits, and should

regulate or take over ownership of firms which have substantial monopoly power.

(3) The allocation of resources should be determined principally by government planning, with the market given a very minor role. Private ownership of the means of production should be largely forbidden, so that most land-holdings and all but the smallest firms should be collectively owned and controlled. In theory the competitive market may function efficiently, but in practice monopoly is so pervasive that the theory does not apply and the market concentrates power in the hands of a few monopoly capitalists, with profits not acting as a guide to the efficient re-allocation of resources but simply as the spoils of monopoly. The market gives rise to great inequality in the distribution of income, and the political power of the rich makes redistribution ineffective, so long as the market system is maintained. By rewarding individual effort, the market discourages co-operation and altruism.

(In this book we have not looked at the criteria that a government might use in actually planning an economy, and it is important to realize that simple rejection of the price system and announcement that the economy is to be planned does not answer the question of *how* it should be planned. In fact it turns out that a great deal of the theory which has been developed above is of use and relevance in the theory of economic planning. Many of the activities of economic planners can be interpreted as attempts to do by non-market methods what the theory of the competitive market says should happen if the market functions correctly.)

In all our analysis of the price system we have assumed that markets are in (or near) equilibrium. The apparent chronic existence of unemployment, both of men and resources, in market economies raises the question of whether the market does really attain equilibrium. This and related topics are the subject of the rest of the book, as we turn from *microeconomics* to *macroeconomics*.

Exercises

6.1   Draw a diagram to illustrate the case of a monopoly which in the short run will produce a positive level of output but in the long run will cease production. Is it necessarily the case that if the firm makes short-run losses it will choose to cease production in the long run?

6.2   A monopoly with production function $y = F(z)$ is a price-taker in the markets for inputs and its cost function is $c(w, y)$. By considering the relationship between marginal cost and marginal products show that, if it chooses y to maximize profits, equation (7) will be satisfied.

Alternatively, consider simply the choice of z to solve

$$\text{maximize } p(F(z)) F(z) - wz$$
$$\qquad z$$

and show that (7) must be satisfied.

6.3   A monopoly uses inputs z_1 and z_2 to produce output y, has the production function $y = z_1^{1/3} z_2^{2/3}$ and faces input prices $w_1 = 8$, $w_2 = 2$. It believes that the demand function for its product is $p = y^{-2}$.

(a) Write down its profit as a function of z_1 and z_2 and attempt to maximize this function.

(b) Derive the firm's cost function and draw a graph of its marginal cost and marginal revenue. Explain why your attempt to maximize profits failed.

(c) What should the firm actually produce if its belief about the demand function is correct? Do you find its belief credible?

(d) Suppose that the firm finds that its demand function is actually $p = 24y^{-1/2}$. What is its optimal policy?

6.4   A study of the taxi business in one American city reveals that only a limited number of taxi licences are issued by the city authorities, and most of them are held by company A, which has persuaded the city that it would be harmful to issue more licences. Licences may be bought and sold. Company A does not sell the licences it holds, but the market price for the licences which are traded is $30,000 per licence. There is evidence that company A does not actually use all the licences it holds.

Would you expect taxi fares in this city to be equal to, less than, or more than the marginal cost of providing the service? Do the facts above offer any evidence to support your belief? Why does company A not use all its licences or sell its unused licences? Is there a more efficient policy for the city to adopt than its present practice? Why might such a policy improvement not actually be implemented by the city?

6.5   Derive formally the cost-minimizing and profit-maximizing first-order conditions for a monopsonist.

6.6   (a) For the firm described in equations (9)–(11) let $\pi(s)$ be the maximized value of profits given s. Show that $d\pi/ds = y$.

(b) If, as discussed at the end of section 3.3, a monopoly is granted on output subsidy and simultaneously subjected to a profits tax which exactly recoups the subsidy revenue then the government ends up neither paying anything to nor receiving anything from the monopoly. How can such a policy, which seems to have no effect, change the firm's behaviour?

6.7   Suppose that the government of a country has control over an industry which is the only source of supply in the world of a particular product. If the government takes account only of the welfare of its own citizens, what policy should it adopt on: (a) foreign sales; (b) domestic sale of the product?

6.8   Construct an example in which a non-discriminating monopolist would make losses by producing, so would choose not to produce; while a perfectly discriminating monopolist will produce the positive efficient level of output.

6.9   Consider again the bridge described in exercise 5.12. Suppose it were privately owned. What is the owner's optimal policy: (a) if he must charge all users the same price; (b) if he can discriminate perfectly? Which case is preferable from society's point of view?

6.10   On the cover of a paperback book, you find in large print the statement: 'These are unabridged paperback reprints of established titles widely used by universities throughout the world. These lower priced editions are published for the benefit of students.' In small print you read: 'This edition may be sold only in those countries to which it is consigned by the publisher. It is not to be re-exported, and it is not for sale in the USA, Mexico or Canada.' Discuss these statements. Is it relevant that American students are commonly required to obtain course textbooks, whereas elsewhere texts are often 'recommended' rather than 'required'?

6.11   The market for a firm's product is split into two groups of consumers whose respective demand functions are

$$y_1 = p_1^{-2} \qquad y_2 = p_2^{-3}$$

The firm's cost function is $c(y_1 + y_2) = 0.6(y_1 + y_2)$. Find the firm's profit-maximizing policy: (a) if it must charge the same price in both market, (b) if it can charge different prices. Discuss what happens to $y_1 + y_2$, as well as to y_1 and y_2 separately. (This is easier to do if you formulate the problem as one of choosing optimal prices rather than optimal quantities.)

6.12   By considering a firm with constant marginal cost of production c which can set a price p_1 for one part of its market, in which the demand function is

$$y_1 = a_1 - b_1 p_1$$

and a different price p_2 in the rest of its market, where the demand function is

$$y_2 = a_2 - b_2 p_2$$

a_i, b_i being positive constants, show that imperfect price discrimination does not necessarily lead to output being higher than in the case of single price monopoly.

6.13 Why with price discrimination must at least one consumer face a lower price than in the absence of discrimination while at least one other must face a higher price?

6.14 A firm produces one good, the relationship between its total cost c and output y being given by the cost function $c(y)$. A part y_1 of the output is sold directly to the public at a price p_1 which is determined by the inverse demand function $p_1 = p_1(y_1)$. The rest of the output $y_2 = y - y_1$ is sold at a price p_3 to a subsidiary company which packages and sells the good at the price p_2 to another section of the public whose inverse demand function is $p_2 = p_2(y_2)$. The total cost of packaging and distribution by the subsidiary is $g(y_2)$.

Derive the conditions for maximizing the joint profits of the parent firm and its subsidiary. If the parent controls the subsidiary simply by fixing the price p_3 and instructing the subsidiary to maximize its own profits, find the subsidiary's profit-maximizing rule and hence prove that the price p_3 should be set equal to the parent firm's marginal production cost, if total profits are to be maximized.

6.15 Outline the theory of discriminating monopsony.

6.16 Suppose that there are two factories in a town. The work done in one of them is believed to be unsuitable for women, and no women are employed. The other factory employs both men and women, who are equally efficient at the required work. In the absence of laws prohibiting sex discrimination in wage rates, would you expect different wages to be paid to men and women in the second factory?

*6.17 A competitive industry is formed into a cartel. All of the firms agree to sell only to the cartel. The price received by the firms is fixed by the cartel management, who undertake to buy all the output the firms want to supply. The management will then sell the goods at some other price. What will the two prices be if the cartel aims to maximize the total profits made by the firms and the cartel management? If the cartel management instead maximizes only its own profits, what will be the effect on output and on total profits.

6.18   Suppose that in the duopoly analysed in section 6.5 the firm's cost functions were

$$c_f = cy_f + dy_f^2 \qquad f = 1, 2$$

How would this change their reaction functions and the different equilibria?

6.19   In the oligopoly analysed in section 6.5 suppose that the firm's cost functions were

$$c_f = cy_f + g \qquad f = 1, \ldots, n$$

where g is a constant. Suppose that there is an unlimited number of firms with access to the same technology and there is free entry into and exit from the industry. Find the number n of firms which will actually produce output in the long-run Cournot equilibrium.

6.20   In the n-firm oligopoly of section 6.5 suppose that one firm acts as a Stackelberg leader towards the remaining $n - 1$ firms. What will be the equilibrium?

6.21   Suppose that there are only two firms in the market described in exercise 6.19 and one acts as a Stackelberg leader. Derive the second firm's reaction function, paying particular attention to the circumstances in which it will choose to produce nothing. Are there values of g for which firm 1 will choose an output level which ensures that firm 2 does not enter the market?

6.22   Consider a collusive oligopoly in a market where advertising is effective at attracting existing consumers from one supplier to another but has no effect on total demand for the product. What rule should the firms adopt on advertising? Comment on the fact that professional associations such as the Law Society of England and the American Medical Association do not allow their members to advertise their services to the public.

6.23   In a monopolistically competitive industry each firm believes that the price it can obtain for its product is a function of the quantities supplied by all firms in the industry, so the typical firm has inverse demand function $p_i = p_i(y_1, y_2, \ldots, y_n)$. Suppose that each firm chooses an output level on the assumption that other firms' output levels are given. Will the outcome differ from that described in equations (49)–(52)?

6.24   Why is the demand curve in figure 6.6 tangent to the average cost curve?

6.25   Suppose that in a monopolistically competitive market there are n

firms, and the firms face the demand functions

$$y_i = p_i^{-2} \left(\sum_{\substack{j=1 \\ j \neq i}}^{n} p_j^{-1/2} \right)^{-2} \qquad i = 1, \ldots, n$$

and the cost functions

$$c(y_i) = cy_i + g$$

where c and g are constants, and each firm assumes that all other firms' prices are given when it sets its own price. What is the equilibrium number of firms in this market? Discuss the properties of the demand functions.

6.26   Assume that all the barbers in a city form an association. They set the price of haircuts so as to maximize their total profits. They do not have the power to stop new entry but they can force any new barber to charge the association's prices. How long will entry continue and what will happen to the price of haircuts? Has the existence of the association done any good or any harm?

6.27   Explain in detail why the abolition of long-term contracts for professional team sports players might be expected to lower the wages of poorer players while raising the wages of the best players.

6.28   If the organiser of a concert is uncertain about the level of demand for tickets, what should be his attitude to ticket touts? (Compare exercises 1.32 and 5.17.)

6.29   Why do commercial insurance companies not offer unemployment insurance?

6.30   It is believed that a high proportion of blank recording tape is used by its purchasers to copy music from records and pre-recorded tapes. The musicians whose music is thus copied do not receive royalties on the privately made copies. Discuss whether there should be a tax on the sales of blank tape, with the proceeds being distributed to musicians.

CHAPTER 7

Introduction to Macroeconomics

7.1 *Introduction*

Up to now we have dealt with issues concerning individual consumers and firms and the supply and demand of particular goods. This is the subject matter of microeconomics. In contrast with these issues, we now turn to the examination of *macroeconomic* issues such as the determination of 'total national income', 'the level of unemployment', 'the general price level', and so on.

It may not be obvious that such concepts deserve serious attention. The general price level and the level of national income are statistical artefacts whose values depend on the concepts and definitions of statisticians. Further, if one were to draw from microeconomic theory the message that there is a systematic tendency for markets to be in equilibrium, then one might doubt the very existence of a phenomenon that could meaningfully be called unemployment, for why should the supply of labour persistently exceed demand?

There is, however, evidence from the real world that the economic system is not always in equilibrium – the high worldwide unemployment levels of the 1930s and early 1980s and the high worldwide inflation rates of the 1970s, for example – and this evidence has been a major motivation to the development of macroeconomic theory.

It would be natural to take our microeconomic models as the starting point in our treatment of macroeconomics: using and adapting microeconomic analysis so as to explain the apparent existence of unemployment, or to answer the twin questions of why inflation occurs and whether it matters.

In fact, we start with models from which almost all microeconomic considerations seem to be deliberately excluded. The logic of consistent choice and of maximization which was central in our earlier discussion seems to have no place. Arbitrary assumptions are frequently made.

Perhaps most striking is the fact that prices, which play such an important role in microeconomic theory, have no role in much of the macro-economic theory we shall discuss.

Gradually, as our treatment of macroeconomic theory progresses, more microeconomic considerations creep in, but a synthesis of micro-economics and macroeconomics would require development of both bodies of theory to a level beyond the scope of this book.

7.2   *The simplest model*

We start with a model in which prices have absolutely no role. In an economy in a particular time period we might observe quantities y_1, $y_2, \ldots, y_n$ of various goods being produced and sold at prices $p_1, p_2, \ldots, p_n$. The value of total output is

$$Y = \sum_{i=1}^{n} p_i y_i$$

If factor quantities $z_1, z_2, \ldots, z_m$ are supplied by individuals at prices $w_1, w_2, \ldots, w_m$, then the total profits of firms are

$$\pi = \sum_{i=1}^{n} p_i y_i - \sum_{j=1}^{m} w_j z_j$$

The incomes of individuals consist of earnings from factor supplies and of profits so total income is

$$\boxed{\pi + \sum_{j=1}^{m} w_j z_j}$$

which also equals Y. Total income is equal to the value of total output.

In all of what follows, we pay no attention to how total output Y is divided between different goods, and how producers' and consumers' decisions might determine such a division. It is rather as if we supposed that only one good was being produced, with Y standing for the output level of this good.

We focus our attention on saving and investment as a plausible source of macroeconomic problems. Individuals' income is divided between consumption and saving, the objective of their saving being to provide extra consumption to them or their heirs at a future date. Output is divided between consumption and investment, where investment con-sists of addition to the stock of plant and equipment available to producers, and where the objective of investment is to increase future production. If the demand for particular goods for current consumption is different from the supply of such goods, the existence of this disequilibrium might be expected to cause changes, including relative price changes, which might move markets closer to equilibrium. It is not immediately obvious how the market might make mutually compatible the desire of individuals to save and of firms to invest.

We initially make two very simple assumptions about producers' behaviour: (i) their demand for goods for investment, which we write as I, is exogenously given; (ii) their total supply of goods, that is, total output Y, is always adjusted to equal demand. Clearly neither of these assumptions follows naturally from our previous discussion of producers' behaviour. The second assumption, in particular, implies the existence of unemployed inputs some of which, if demand increases, can be brought into employment to enable output to be increased in line with demand.

Now we have to consider how individuals, whose total income is Y, choose to divide that income between consumption C and saving $S(=Y-C)$. What guidance can the microeconomic theory of the consumer give? Effectively, in choosing their level of current consumption C individuals are choosing between current and future consumption.

Let us consider a very simplistic model of how such a choice might be made. Suppose a consumer lives for two time periods, having incomes y_1 and y_2 in the respective periods. At the end of the second period he wishes to leave no bequest to heirs. He can borrow or lend at the interest rate r. He chooses consumptions c_1 and c_2 in the respective periods. Since y_1-c_1 is the saving he does in the first period, in the second period he has available for consumption the sum of his second-period income and of his savings with interest. If y_1-c_1 is negative, it is the debt he must repay with interest from his second-period income. Thus

$$c_2 = y_2 + (1+r)(y_1 - c_1) \tag{1}$$

or equivalently

$$c_1 + \frac{c_2}{1+r} = y_1 + \frac{y_2}{1+r} \tag{1a}$$

is his budget constraint: he chooses c_1 and c_2 to maximize his utility $u(c_1, c_2)$ subject to this constraint. (See figure 7.1.)

The maximization problem is identical to the standard consumer maximization problem discussed in chapter 4, since the budget constraint (1a) is of the form $p_1 c_1 + p_2 c_2 = m$, where in this case $m = y_1 + y_2/(1+r)$, $p_1 = 1$ and $p_2 = 1/(1+r)$. The fact that the price of second-period consumption is $1/(1+r)$ of the price of first-period consumption reflects the fact that one can be exchanged for the other through borrowing or lending at the interest rate r. Clearly the optimal choice of consumption in each period will depend on y_1, y_2 and r. Returning to our previous notation, the implication is that current consumption C will depend on current income Y but also on future income and on the interest rate.

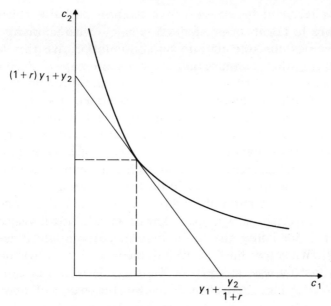

FIGURE 7.1   Intertemporal consumption choice

Is this a good theory of consumption and saving decisions? Obviously the two-period structure is not a good description of the real world where individuals have lives of uncertain length. In fact the model, as you can imagine, is easily extended to many time periods, and its conclusions remain that current consumption and saving depend on current and future incomes and on interest rates. One can also argue that for most people uncertainty about the length of their life does not dominate their decision-making. A more serious problem is that, as students should be painfully aware, it is not easy to borrow money for current consumption against a promise to repay the debt out of future income, and it is virtually impossible to obtain such loans at the same interest rate as is offered on savings. Ruling out borrowing, or having separate interest rates on borrowing and lending would complicate the model further.

But the most crucial problem with this as a theory of saving decisions is the fact that people usually do not know what their income will be in the future. Perhaps the best indication most people have of their likely future income is their current income. Then we should have c_1 dependent on y_1 and r, where the dependence on y_1 reflects a double role for y_1: a measure of currently available income *and* an estimate of future income.

To simplify matters, however, we shall ignore the effect of the rate of interest. Partly this reflects the fact that the direction of the effect of r on c_1 is ambiguous (as you are asked to show in exercise 7.3), partly it reflects the fact that introspection about how one makes one's own saving and consumption decisions does not suggest a major influence for the interest rate, but the decisive consideration is that it makes virtually no difference to the theories we develop below whether or not we ignore the influence of the interest rate on consumption. We therefore adopt the hypothesis that consumption depends on current income alone: $C = C(Y)$.

What form will the dependence on C on Y take? Clearly C will be an increasing function of Y: more income now, and more income expected in the future, means that more current consumption can be afforded. How much more? If an individual's income this year rises by $1000, and he is convinced that this increase in income will also be obtained in all future years, then his consumption expenditure would rise by an amount in the region of $1000. It is more likely, however, that he will be uncertain that the increase in income will be obtained in all future years (consider especially the possibility that there will be years in which he does not, because of old age or illness, earn any income) so that his consumption will rise in fact by less than $1000. Thus the derivative of $C(Y)$ satisfies $0 < C_Y(Y) < 1$. This derivative is called the *marginal propensity to consume*.

In arriving finally at our hypothesis about consumption and saving decisions, expressed mathematically in the *consumption function* $C = C(Y)$ we should recognize not only that we have made a series of simplifying assumptions but also that we have informally given much importance to individuals expectations of the uncertain future, but our formal hypothesis gives no role to uncertainty.

To the two assumptions made earlier about producers' behaviour, we now add our hypothesis about consumers' behaviour: (iii) consumption is a function of income, with a marginal propensity to consume between 0 and 1.

Formally, our model can be written

$$Y = C + I \tag{2}$$

$$C = C(Y) \qquad 0 < C_Y < 1 \tag{3}$$

where equation (2) incorporates our two assumptions (i) and (ii) about producers' behaviour, and (3) incorporates assumption (iii) about consumers' behaviour.

It is important to note that equation (2) is an *equilibrium condition* that states that supply is equal to demand, where as always 'supply' and 'demand' mean the quantities which the respective agents *desire* to trade. It is possible that the quantity which individuals and firms want to buy is different from the quantity that firms want to sell. If $Y > C + I$ or $Y < C + I$, some firms or individuals will not have their plans fulfilled, and we are not at an equilibrium.

Putting the two equations together by eliminating C gives

$$Y = C(Y) + I \tag{4}$$

which implicitly defines Y, the equilibrium level of output and income, as a function of I. In our microeconomic models, it is the price of the good which adjusts to bring about equilibrium. In this case, there are no prices to adjust, but, on the assumptions we have made, there is a unique level of output and income Y which satisfies (4).

The determination of the equilibrium value of Y is shown in figure 7.2, where the function $C(Y) + I$ whose slope is less than 1 intersects the function Y whose slope is 1. Without knowing the form of the function $C(Y)$ we cannot solve explicitly for Y, but we can, just as in the examples of chapter 1, derive comparative statics results by differentiation. Differentiating (4) with respect to I gives:

$$\frac{dY}{dI} = C_Y \frac{dY}{dI} + 1 \tag{5}$$

so that

$$\frac{dY}{dI} = \frac{1}{1 - C_Y} \tag{6}$$

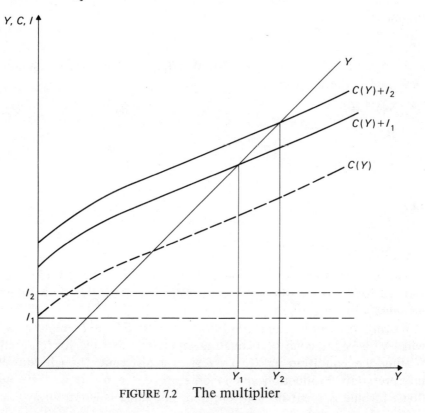

FIGURE 7.2　The multiplier

Since $0 < C_Y < 1$, $dY/dI > 1$. The value of dY/dI, which in this model is $1/(1 - C_Y)$, is called the *multiplier*. An exogenous increase in investment demand leads to a greater increase in the equilibrium level of output. This is seen in figure 7.2 when the rise in investment from I_1 to I_2 raises the equilibrium level of Y from Y_1 to Y_2.

At first, the idea that an exogenous increase in demand of one unit should lead to a much bigger increase in output, say of three units if C_Y takes the plausible value of 2/3, may seem paradoxical. The key is that as output expands to meet the increased demand for investment, income expands so consumption demand expands, and the multiplier measures the expansion in output which meets both the exogenous increase in investment demand and the endogenous increase in consumption demand generated by the output expansion itself.

(In analysing macroeconomic models we shall be doing much differentiation, and it is useful to follow the convention adopted above of using the derivative notation dy/dx — or the partial derivative notation $\partial y/\partial x$ where appropriate — to indicate the effect of a change in an exogenous variable on the equilibrium value of an endogenous variable, while using subscript notation to indicate differentiation or partial differentiation of a function which is part of the structure of the model.)

An alternative way to set out the model is to define saving S as $Y - C$, so that savings are a function of Y defined by

$$S(Y) \equiv Y - C(Y) \tag{7}$$

Since $S_Y = 1 - C_Y$, it follows that $0 < S_Y < 1$. The model can now be expressed in the single equation

$$S(Y) = I \tag{8}$$

so that

$$S_Y \frac{dY}{dI} = 1 \tag{9}$$

and

$$\frac{dY}{dI} = \frac{1}{S_Y} \tag{10}$$

Obviously (8), (9) and (10) are exactly equivalent to (4), (5) and (6), and we have derived the same multiplier. The derivative S_Y is called the *marginal propensity to save*.

Writing the equilibrium condition as $Y = C(Y) + I$ emphasizes that what we have is a condition equating supply and demand for total output. Writing the condition as $S(Y) = I$ gives a different, though equivalent, interpretation. Production and income are the same, as we have noted. Some income is spent on consumption, but some is *withdrawn* as saving.

Some of the demand for production is that same consumption demand, but some is the newly *injected* demand of firms for investment. In equilibrium, we require that withdrawals, $S(Y)$, equal injections I. Generally, we shall use the 'supply equals demand' form of the equation.

Consider now the example where we know that the consumption function is linear: $C(Y) = a + cY$. In this case the equilibrium condition is

$$Y = a + cY + I \tag{11}$$

which can be solved explicitly to give

$$Y = \frac{a + I}{1 - c} \tag{12}$$

so that the multiplier is $1/(1 - c)$. We can also solve for C and derive $C = (a + bI)/(1 - c)$.

If we wish to consider in this model the effect of an exogenous change in consumers' desire to consume, we introduce a 'dummy variable' e, representing this desire, into the consumption function so that

$$C = C(Y, e) \qquad C_e > 0 \tag{13}$$

(Look back at the end of section 1.7 for an earlier application of dummy variables.) Thus the equilibrium condition is

$$Y = C(Y, e) + I \tag{14}$$

and differentiating with respect to e gives

$$\frac{\mathrm{d}Y}{\mathrm{d}e} = C_Y \frac{\mathrm{d}Y}{\mathrm{d}e} + C_e \tag{15}$$

so that

$$\frac{\partial Y}{\partial e} = \frac{C_e}{1 - C_Y} > 0 \tag{16}$$

Thus a reduction in thrift, an increase in the desire to consume, raises income. Consider now the effect on actual saving, which is

$$S = Y - C(Y, e) \tag{17}$$

so that

$$\frac{\partial S}{\partial e} = (1 - C_Y) \frac{\partial Y}{\partial e} - C_e = 0 \tag{18}$$

A reduced *desire* to save leads to no change in actual saving, as the effect is exactly cancelled out by the effect of the fall in the equilibrium level of income. This is known as the *paradox of thrift*. (If you look at the model in 'withdrawals equals injections' form, the source of the result should be immediately apparent.)

7.3   *Introducing foreign trade and the government*

Consider two extra variables: exports X and imports M. Let X be exogenous and let $M = M(Y)$ with $0 < M_Y < 1$. (M_Y is the 'marginal propensity to import'.) Exports are an extra source of demand for output, but part of demand is met by imports, so the equilibrium requires that supply of domestically produced goods equals total demand less imports:

$$Y = C(Y) + I + X - M(Y) \qquad (19)$$

(Alternatively, the equilibrium condition can be written

$$S(Y) + M(Y) = I + X \qquad (19a)$$

Foreign demand for goods is an injection, while income spent abroad is a withdrawal; but this is intuitively much less obvious than the supply–demand argument that gives us (19).)

To derive, for example, the effect of X on Y we differentiate (19) to get

$$(1 + M_Y - C_Y) \frac{\partial Y}{\partial X} = 1 \qquad (20)$$

and, in fact,

$$\frac{\partial Y}{\partial X} = \frac{\partial Y}{\partial I} = \frac{1}{1 + M_Y - C_Y} \left(= \frac{1}{S_Y + M_Y} \right) \qquad (21)$$

This multiplier is smaller than the multiplier derived in (6) for the model without foreign trade. The intuition behind this result is that some of the extra demand generated in the expansion flows abroad so the expansion is less.

In certain circumstances, exports should not be an exogenous variable since one country's exports are another country's imports. If our country is sufficiently large relative to our trading partners, the amount we import from them will have a significant multiplier effect (caused by the increase in their exports) on their income, which in turn will raise their imports from us, and raise our income. Consider the case of two countries, indexed by superscripts 1 and 2. We have two equilibrium conditions

$$Y^1 = C^1(Y^1) + I^1 + X^1 - M^1(Y^1)$$
$$Y^2 = C^2(Y^2) + I^2 + X^2 - M^2(Y^2) \qquad (22)$$

but since $X^1 = M^2(Y^2)$ and $X^2 = M^1(Y^1)$ these become

$$Y^1 = C^1(Y^1) + I^1 + M^2(Y^2) - M^1(Y^1)$$
$$Y^2 = C^2(Y^2) + I^2 + M^1(Y^1) - M^2(Y^2) \qquad (22a)$$

These are two equations in the two unknowns Y^1 and Y^2 and the effects of a change in I^1 are found by differentiating both equations with respect to I^1 to give,

$$(1 + M_Y^1 - C_Y^1) \frac{\partial Y^1}{\partial I^1} - M_Y^2 \frac{\partial Y^2}{\partial I^1} = 1$$

$$- M_Y^1 \frac{\partial Y^1}{\partial I^1} + (1 + M_Y^2 - C_Y^2) \frac{\partial Y^2}{\partial I^1} = 0$$

(23)

whence

$$\frac{\partial Y^1}{\partial I^1} = \frac{1 + M_Y^2 - C_Y^2}{(1 + M_Y^1 - C_Y^1)(1 + M_Y^2 - C_Y^2) - M_Y^1 M_Y^2} > 0 \qquad (24)$$

$$\frac{\partial Y^2}{\partial I^1} = \frac{M_Y^1}{(1 + M_Y^1 - C_Y^1)(1 + M_Y^2 - C_Y^2) - M_Y^1 M_Y^2} > 0 \qquad (25)$$

It is easily seen from (24) that $\partial Y^1/\partial I^1 > 1/(1 + M_Y^1 - C_Y^1)$, so that the multiplier is larger than in the previous case where we assumed the country's exports were exogenous. Again the intuition is simple: the demand which is met by foreign supplies itself generates some extra demand for our goods, and this feedback raises the equilibrium level of output.

It is equally important to introduce the role of the government into this model. For simplicity, let us initially assume there is no foreign trade.

Governments can demand goods, and can also raise taxes. Denote government expenditure on goods by G and taxation by T. There is no *necessity* for the government to make $G = T$ – it can run a deficit, with $G > T$, and raise money in various ways other than taxation in order to pay its bills. In due course we shall see that how the government raises money to cover a deficit is a matter of some importance.

Government expenditure is an additional source of demand; but taxation does not *directly* affect demand or supply. It is a *transfer* from individuals to the government, which affects demand by reducing the income available to households for consumption and saving. We define *disposable income* as $Y - T$ and suppose that

$$C = C(Y - T) \qquad (26)$$

(and we shall now write C_Y to mean the derivative of C with respect to $Y - T$). Now the equilibrium equation is

$$Y = C(Y - T) + I + G \qquad (27)$$

and we have three multipliers:

$$\frac{\partial Y}{\partial G} = \frac{\partial Y}{\partial I} = \frac{1}{1 - C_Y} > 0 \qquad (28)$$

$$\frac{\partial Y}{\partial T} = \frac{-C_Y}{1 - C_Y} < 0 \tag{29}$$

Increased government expenditure raises output in exactly the same way as increased investment; a rise in taxation reduces consumption and causes a contraction in output.

A *balanced budget* expansion of government expenditure is a rise in G accompanied by an equal change in T, so that $dT/dG = 1$. The effect of such a change is

$$\frac{\partial Y}{\partial G} + \frac{\partial Y}{\partial T} \frac{dT}{dG} = \frac{\partial Y}{\partial G} + \frac{\partial Y}{\partial T} = 1 \tag{30}$$

There is a balanced budget multiplier of 1. Why this multiplier should be positive is easy to understand: a rise in G by one unit raises demand for goods by one unit, whereas a one unit increase in T does not reduce demand by one unit because only some of it would have been consumed. Thus, an equal rise in G and T does raise demand. The explanation of why the final effect is an output expansion of exactly one unit is postponed to the next section.

It is straightforward to extend the model to include both foreign trade and government activity. The equilibrium equation becomes

$$Y = C(Y - T) + I + G + X - M(Y) \tag{31}$$

(Note the assumption that M is a function of Y rather than $Y - T$. It is left to you in exercise 7.9 to justify this.) In this model, there are four multipliers to derive: the effects on Y of changes in I, X, G and T. The derivation of these multipliers, and of the balanced-budget multiplier, is left to you.

Of course, these models could equally well be handled using the 'withdrawals equals injections' version of the equilibrium condition. Defining saving as disposable income less consumption:

$$S(Y - T) \equiv Y - T - C(Y - T) \tag{32}$$

we obtain the condition equivalent to (31):

$$S(Y - T) + T + M(Y) = I + G + X \tag{33}$$

Saving, taxation and imports are all withdrawals from income; investment, government expenditure and exports are all injections into demand.

These models all assume the existence of unemployed resources but also imply that the government has tools of *fiscal policy* – changes in expenditure and taxation – which should be powerful weapons in dealing with unemployment. If, for some reason, the equilibrium of the economy is at a level of output such that there is substantial unemployment, the government can, it seems, remedy this by increases in G or reductions in T or both.

There are, however, several reasons why matters cannot be so simply dealt with. In the first place, the government's information about the economy is always imperfect, so that the size of required policy changes is always in doubt. This problem is somewhat alleviated by the existence of 'automatic fiscal stabilizers' – the fact that tax receipts are higher when income is higher because of the way taxes are levied, and the fact that unemployment compensation payments tend to be lower when income is higher – but such stabilizers cannot wholly eliminate the problem. (Note that government payments, like unemployment compensation and social security payments, should be treated as negative elements in T *not* as part of G, which represents direct government expenditure on goods.)

Further the above models assume that the market always adjusts immediately to any new equilibrium. In the next section we consider a model with time lags and see that such lags have significant implications for fiscal policy.

Even more fundamentally: (i) these models do not consider how the government's financing of differences between G and T might affect the economy; (ii) there is no theory of investment, which is assumed to be exogenously fixed, though it is easy to think of reasons why in reality investment might be affected by government policy; (iii) there is no role whatsoever for prices in these models. This last point is particularly important because, although supply and demand for goods are equated, there are unemployed resources in the economy. In particular, unemployment of labour implies that supply of labour exceeds demand. We should consider the possibility that there may be mechanisms in the economy which could tend to correct unemployment without government intervention.

7.4   *Simple dynamic models*

It is, perhaps, not entirely plausible that consumption should depend on strictly *current* income. How can people plan their consumption on the basis of an income level which is itself partly determined by actual consumption? The multiplier models describe the equilibrium, but to understand how equilibrium might be reached, we make the more plausible assumption that consumption is planned on the basis of the *previous* period's income.

Suppose that the consumption function is linear. Then we replace (2) and (3) by

$$Y_t = C_t + I_t \tag{34}$$

$$C_t = a + cY_{t-1} \qquad 0 < c < 1 \tag{35}$$

Suppose now that the level of investment is the same from period to period, so $I_t = I$. Then supply equals demand when

$$Y_t = a + cY_{t-1} + I \tag{36}$$

but the economy is in equilibrium only when the level of income Y_{t-1} on which consumers base their plans is the same as the actual level Y_t. Thus equilibrium income Y_e is determined by

$$Y_e = a + cY_e + I \tag{37}$$

and is the equilibrium described by (11). Formally, the model is very similar to the cobweb cycle model of section 1.3; indeed the point there made that equilibrium requires the fulfilment of expectations as well as the equation of supply and demand has reappeared here.

Subtracting (37) from (36) gives

$$Y_t - Y_e = c(Y_{t-1} - Y_e) \tag{38}$$

and since $0 < c < 1$ it follows that if the economy starts away from equilibrium, then each period it gets closer and closer to equilibrium. Indeed, successive application of (38) for $t = 1, 2, 3, \ldots$ gives

$$Y_t = c^t Y_0 + (1 - c^t) Y_e \tag{39}$$

which shows clearly that $Y_t \to Y_e$ as $t \to \infty$.

Suppose that in time period 0 investment is at the level I and income Y_0 is at the equilibrium level $(a + I)/(1 - c)$. Now from time period 1 onwards investment is at the new level $I + \Delta I$. From (37) it follows that the new equilibrium level of income is $Y_e = (a + I + \Delta I)/(1 - c) = Y_0 + \Delta I/(1 - c)$. Since we are starting away from that equilibrium, it will not be attained at once. In fact, (39) implies that

$$Y_t = Y_0 + \Delta I \frac{1 - c^t}{1 - c} \tag{40}$$

$$= Y_0 + \Delta I(1 + c + c^2 + \ldots + c^{t-1}) \tag{41}$$

(where (41) follows from the well-known method of summing a geometric progression).

Equation (41) not only shows how the new equilibrium is gradually approached, but also helps us understand why the multiplier is greater than 1. The initial injection of extra demand ΔI raises Y_1 by this amount. Next period we have the extra demand ΔI but also extra consumption demand of $c\Delta I$ arising from the previous period's increased income so that Y_2 is $(1 + c) \Delta I$ above Y_0. Each successive period, income is higher, but each successive increase is smaller because only a part of the extra income is injected as extra consumption demand in the next period.

Applying the same technique to more complex linear models helps us similarly to understand other multipliers. Thus in the model with foreign trade let $C_t = a - cY_{t-1}$ and $M_t = mY_{t-1}$ so that with I and X constant the behaviour of the economy is described by

$$Y_t = a + cY_{t-1} + I + X - mY_{t-1} \tag{42}$$

a straightforward generalization of (36), so that analogously to (41) we have, in the event of a permanent change in investment from $I + \Delta I$ starting from the old equilibrium $Y_0 = (a + I + X)/(1 - c + m)$,

$$Y_t = Y_0 + \Delta I[1 + (c - m) + (c - m)^2 + \ldots + (c - m)^{t-1}] \tag{43}$$

The final equilibrium is $Y_e = Y_0 + \Delta I/(1 - c - m)$ and from (43) we see that the multiplier is less than in (41) because an initial injection of demand of 1 unit gives rise next period to c units of extra consumption demand but m units of extra import demand so the increase in demand in this economy is $c - m$. In turn, in the third period there is a further increase of $(c - m)(c - m)$, and so on.

Now consider a lagged model with government fiscal policy but no trade. The economy is described by the equation

$$Y_t = C_t + I_t + G_t \tag{44}$$

$$C_t = a + c(Y_{t-1} - T_{t-1}) \tag{45}$$

It is left to you as exercise 7.11 to show that if the economy starts at time 0 with G_t at G, and output Y_0 at its equilibrium level and if G_t then rises to $G + \Delta G$ in time 1 and subsequently, then

$$Y_t = Y_0 + \Delta G(1 + c + c^2 + \ldots + c^{t-1}) \qquad t \geqslant 1 \tag{46}$$

with final equilibrium

$$Y_e = \frac{a - cT + I + G + \Delta G}{1 - c} = Y_0 + \frac{\Delta G}{1 - c}$$

However, consider an economy starting at time 0 with T_t at T and output Y_0 in equilibrium. By paying careful attention to the consumption function (45) you can show that if T_t rises to $T + \Delta T$ in time periods $t = 1$ onwards,

$$Y_1 = Y_0$$
$$Y_t = Y_0 - \Delta T(c + c^2 + \ldots + c^{t-1}) \qquad t \geqslant 2 \tag{47}$$

with final equilibrium

$$Y_e = \frac{a - cT - c\Delta T + I + G}{1 - c} = Y_0 - \frac{c\Delta T}{1 - c}$$

It is now easy to put (46) and (47) together to derive the effect of a balanced budget expansion of G and T to $G + \Delta G$, $T + \Delta G$ from periods

$t = 1$ onwards:

$$Y_t = Y_0 + \Delta G = Y_e \qquad t \geqslant 1 \tag{48}$$

so that the final equilibrium is achieved immediately!

These results are easy to understand. A rise in government expenditure of one unit has exactly the effect of a rise in investment so (46) is exactly like (41). A rise in taxation of one unit is different. It has no direct effect on demand, and its effect on consumption is delayed one time period. The first effect then is a reduction of c units in consumption in the second period, and this in turn feeds through into later periods. Comparing (46) and (47) we see that the difference between the effect of ΔG and of ΔT is simply that the first term of the series is missing in (47), because a change in government expenditure has a direct unit for unit effect on demand which a taxation change does not have. The fact that the balanced budget multiplier is 1 and has its full impact immediately, as shown in (48), follows at once.

These simple dynamic models serve the function of clarifying the forces underlying the multiplier. They are also more realistic than the unlagged models and have an important message for policy-makers. Suppose that the time period in the model of (44) and (45) is one year and that $c = 0.75$ so that the multiplier is 4. A government that raised expenditure by £1 billion expecting an instantaneous increase of £4 billion in income would be disappointed, for (46) shows that the income changes measured in £billion are $Y_1 - Y_0 = 1$, $Y_2 - Y_0 = 1.75$, $Y_3 - Y_0 = 2.3125$, $Y_4 - Y_0 = 2.7343$, $Y_5 - Y_0 = 3.0508$, and so on. The fact that a government's policies may act fairly slowly can cause substantial problems: a government faced by an imminent election may take measures, the long-run effect of which is disastrously large, in order to be sure of a short-run effect, a government losing patience with a wise policy because its effects are slow to appear may switch to an unwise policy.

For a modification of this dynamic multiplier model to take more fully into account the role of investment, see the appendix.

7.5　Investment and the rate of interest

Consider an investment project which requires expenditure of x_0 in period 0 and will yield profits of $x_1, x_2, \ldots, x_T$ in subsequent time periods. How should a potential investor judge such a project?

All of the x_i are measured in monetary units, such as pounds or dollars, but it would be a mistake to judge the value of the project simply as $x_1 + x_2 + \ldots + x_T - x_0$, for one would then be adding up sums of money which are received in different time periods, and $1 now is not the same as $1 in a year's time.

Suppose that banks and other financial institutions offer an interest rate of r per time period. This means that if \$1 is deposited in time period 0, $\$(1 + r)$ can be withdrawn in time period 1. Alternatively, if \$1 is borrowed from a bank at interest rate r in period 0, $\$(1 + r)$ has to be repaid in period 1. Thus \$1 in period 0 can be exchanged in the market for $\$(1 + r)$ in period 1. They have the same value. How much money in period 0 can be exchanged for x_1 in period 1? Clearly the answer is $x_1/(1 + r)$. We say that $x_1/(1 + r)$ is the *present value* in period 0 of x_1 in period 1. Effectively, $1/(1 + r)$ is the price at which period 1 money can be exchanged for period 0 money. (Compare the discussion in section 7.2 above of consumer lending and borrowing.)

More generally, \$1 deposited for t periods generates $\$(1 + r)^t$; so the present value in period 0 of x_t in period t is $x_t/(1 + r)^t$. The price at which period t money can be exchanged for period 0 money is $1/(1 + r)^t$.

The present value (PV) at time 0 of the whole stream of profits from the investment is therefore

$$PV_0 = \frac{x_1}{1 + r} + \frac{x_2}{(1 + r)^2} + \ldots + \frac{x_T}{(1 + r)^T} \tag{49}$$

The *net present value* (NPV) of the whole investment is found by subtracting from the present value the initial expenditure:

$$NPV_0 = -x_0 + \frac{x_1}{1 + r} + \frac{x_2}{(1 + r)^2} + \ldots + \frac{x_T}{(1 + r)^T} \tag{50}$$

The operation of multiplying x_t by $(1 + r)^{-t}$ is sometimes called *discounting*, and $(1 + r)^{-t}$ is called the *discount factor*. What we have done is to value each year's profit in terms of period 0 money by multiplying each sum of money by its price, exactly as we compute the money value of a bundle of ordinary goods $x_1, x_2, \ldots, x_n$ as $p_1 x_1 + p_2 x_2 + \ldots + p_n x_n$; or for an individual with income m who buys such a bundle we compute net expenditure as $-m + p_1 x_1 + \ldots + p_n x_n$.

If the interest rate varies from one time period to the next, being r_1 in period 1, r_2 in period 2 and so on, then it is fairly easy to show that the present value calculation becomes

$$PV_0 = \frac{x_1}{1 + r_1} + \frac{x_2}{(1 + r_1)(1 + r_2)} + \ldots + \frac{x_T}{(1 + r_1)(1 + r_2)\ldots(1 + r_T)}$$

$$\tag{49a}$$

with the same modification made to (50).

In the present value of the profit stream is greater than x_0, the project should be undertaken because the value of the returns is higher than the value of the returns that financial institutions would offer on a deposit of x_0. Equivalently, we can say that the project should be undertaken if the net present value is positive. (This argument assumes there is no risk involved: the investor is certain of the returns that the project offers and that the banks offer.)

If all the x_t are positive for $t \geqslant 1$, then PV_0 is a decreasing function of r, and as r rises it becomes less and less likely that any given project will pass the present-value test. The potential investor with money to spend finds it preferable simply to lend his money to a bank at the going interest rate rather than invest in a project; the potential investor who needs to borrow money to finance his investment project finds that the expected returns will not fully repay his debt with interest.

Even if some of the x_t are negative, it is likely that negative x_t appear in the early periods as the project is getting under way, in which case PV_0 will almost surely still be a decreasing function of r because $1/(1+r)^t$ is reduced more by a given rise in r the larger is t.

Thus the level of investment in the economy need no longer be taken to be exogenous. We can assume that

$$I = I(r) \qquad I_r < 0 \tag{51}$$

Note that, although the discussion of present value calculations was concerned with working out the money value of investment projects, what we are interested in ultimately is investors' willingness to buy plant, machinery and raw materials, for I is investors' demand for *goods*. (If there is any danger of confusing investment in this sense with a 'financial investment' such as depositing money in a bank we refer to I as 'real investment'.)

This is still a very incomplete theory of investment, for it treats the x_t describing the individual project as exogenously fixed. In fact the returns expected in the future from any one project depend on what other projects have been or will be undertaken, and they also depend on the future behaviour of the economy as a whole. For the present, however, leave such issues aside.

*7.6 Discounting in continuous time

The model of the previous section was formulated in discrete time. An alternative approach, which in some cases may be more useful, is to adopt a continuous time formulation.

Compound interest is growth at a fixed rate. In continuous time therefore, compound interest is represented by the exponential function. Only a function of the form

$$y(t) = y(0)\, e^{rt} \tag{52}$$

has the property of continuous growth at the rate r:

$$\frac{dy(t)}{dt} = ry(t) \tag{53}$$

This property of the exponential function can be understood by considering what happens to compound interest in discrete time when time is subdivided into finer and finer divisions. A unit of money invested for t time periods at an interest rate of r per time period becomes $(1+r)^t$ at the end of the process. If instead we were to compound the interest twice per time period and pay interest at the rate $r/2$ per half-period, then over the $2t$ half-periods the unit of money would grow to $(1+r/2)^{2t}$. Dividing each period more finely, into n subdivisions, gives the result $(1+r/n)^{nt}$. As n gets larger, we are getting closer to continuous compounding, that is, continuous growth, and since

$$\lim_{n \to \infty} \left(1 + \frac{r}{n}\right)^{nt} = e^{rt} \tag{54}$$

the exponential function becomes the appropriate measure of interest.

A sum of money $y(0)$ invested at continuously compounded interest rate r for time 0 to time t becomes $y(0)\,e^{rt}$ at time t. Thus the present value at time 0 of $x(t)$ received at time t is $x(t)\,e^{-rt}$. Hence an investment which produces a stream $x(t)$ $(0 \leqslant t \leqslant T)$ of earnings will have present value at time 0 of

$$PV_0 = \int_0^T x(t)\,e^{-rt}\,dt \tag{55}$$

since we integrate in order to sum a continuous flow. The rest of the argument of section 7.5 now follows in an essentially unchanged fashion.

7.7 Bonds and the rate of interest

A *bond* is a promise to pay fixed sums of money at fixed times: for example, a piece of paper that states that the British Government will pay £10 to the holder on March 31 each year up to and including March 31, 1993 and on March 31, 1993 will pay an additional £100 to 'redeem' the bond.

On April 1, 1983 this bond has the present value in £:

$$PV = \frac{10}{1+r} + \frac{10}{(1+r)^2} + \ldots + \frac{10}{(1+r)^{10}} + \frac{100}{(1+r)^{10}} \tag{56}$$

In general, a bond paying the sum a annually and b at the end of its life has present value:

$$PV = \frac{a}{1+r} + \frac{a}{(1+r)^2} + \ldots + \frac{a}{(1+r)^T} + \frac{b}{(1+r)^T} \tag{57}$$

$$= \frac{a}{r}\left(1 - \frac{1}{(1+r)^T}\right) + \frac{b}{(1+r)^T} \tag{58}$$

(where (58) is derived from (57) by using the standard method of summing a geometric series).

Some bonds last for ever (the British Government bonds called 'consols' are an example) and the value of such a bond can be found, by letting $T \to \infty$ in (58), to be a/r. A justification for this in terms of opportunity cost is easily seen, and is left to you to give in exercise 7.16.

From (58) it follows immediately that if $a/r = b$ then $PV = b$. Thus in exchange for the bond whose present value is given by (56) one should be willing to pay £100 if the market interest rate is 10%, that is if $r = 0.1$. However, what is important for the development of our theory is the fact that if the market interest rate r changes, since the sums a and b are constant, the value of the bond must change. From (57) we see that the present value of each annual payment is a decreasing function of r, so the present value of the bond will be a decreasing function of r. There are active and well-established markets in many types of bonds, and the price at which a bond can be bought or sold should equal its present value, so *there will be an inverse relationship between the price of bonds and the rate of interest.*

If the interest rate is expected to vary in the future then (57) has to be modified just as (49) was modified to give (49a):

$$PV = \frac{a}{1+r_1} + \frac{a}{(1+r_1)(1+r_2)} + \ldots + \frac{a+b}{(1+r_1)(1+r_2)\ldots(1+r_T)}$$

$$\tag{57a}$$

and no simplification like (58) is now available. Now the value of the bond depends on present and expected future market interest rates, and if *any* of these rates rise the value of a bond will fall.

(Do not be confused by the fact that a bond such as the one described above might be called something like '10% Treasury Stock 1993'. This is simply a shorthand description of a bond that pays the stream of future payments described above. It may well be that the bond was originally issued when the market interest rate was 10% so that the government was able to sell the bond for £100, but what matters now is the fixed pattern of payments on the one hand and on the other hand the current and expected future interest rates which may vary considerably and be very different from 10%.)

7.8   *The demand for money*

We now turn to discussion of the demand for money in the economy. Here it is of the utmost importance to understand the distinction between *stocks* and *flows*. When we were looking at multiplier models earlier, all the quantities discussed were flows: national income, investment, consumption, exports and so on are all measured in terms of dollars or pounds *per year*. However, the available supply of money, and the demand for money at any particular time are stocks, measured simply as so many dollars. Thus a statement such as 'an increase by the government in the money supply by $1 million must inevitably lead to an increase in expenditure of the same amount because people have more money to spend' should be viewed with great scepticism, because it asserts a direct relationship between two quantities which are not directly comparable: is it asserted that expenditure will rise by $1 million per week (that is $52 million per year), or by $1 million per month ($12 million per year), or by $1 million per year, or that expenditure will simply rise temporarily until $1 million extra is spent so that the rise in the equilibrium flow of expenditure is zero?

There is likely to be a relationship between the stock of money and the flow of economic activity, but it is a more subtle relationship than that implied in the above statement, and the key to the relationship is in the demand for money.

Let the level of national income be Y, measured in £million per year. This is the total value of *transactions* in goods taking place annually between consumers and producers in the economy. Since almost all transactions involve the use of money, it is reasonable to suppose that the amount of money which people wish to hold, that is the average level of their bank balances and cash holdings, will be a function of the level of transactions in which they anticipate being involved. Of course there are other types of transactions: such as transactions in financial assets, or transactions between firms in intermediate goods; but it is reasonable to suppose that the total value of transactions will be closely related to total income. Thus the amount of money which individuals and firms wish to hold will depend on the level of income and output. The simplest relationship to assume is that the demand for money is proportional to the level of income:

$$M_d = kY \tag{59}$$

$1/k$ is called the 'velocity of circulation', because it measures the average frequency with which money changes hands: if only transactions in goods between individuals and firms are considered so that Y *is* the level of transactions, and if $k = 1/4$ so that the level of annual transactions is four times the value of the stock of money held, then the average £1 changes hands four times per year.

But there is no particular reason for the velocity of circulation to be constant. It might be, for example, that as national income rises financial institutions develop in a way that allows people to hold proportionately lower average money stocks (the use of credit cards is an example). Money demand would still be an increasing function of Y but no longer a linear function:

$$M_\mathrm{d} = L(Y) \qquad L_Y > 0 \tag{60}$$

This *transactions* demand for money will be supplemented by other factors. Households and firms are never certain what transactions will be required in the immediate future, and should normally be expected to have a *precautionary* demand for money: a stock held against the possibility of the unexpected. We should expect this demand too to be a function of the actual level of transactions.

An individual's stock of money is one part of his stock of wealth, which consists in addition of his ownership of durable goods and of financial assets like bonds and shares. Why should anyone hold money at all when the holding of bonds would give rise to interest income? We have seen part of the answer to this question above: the overwhelming convenience of money as a means of facilitating transactions, expected and unexpected. The fact that money has an opportunity cost, the foregone interest on bonds (or dividends on shares) might lead one to expect that the transactions and precautionary demand for money should be affected by the rate of interest. It is possible to reduce one's stock of money even if the level of transactions is unchanged. Suppose an individual is paid £280 every fourth week and spends £10 daily. If he pays the £280 into a current account or holds it as cash, then his average stock of money will be £140. If the rate of interest on bonds is high he may be tempted to buy £140 worth of bonds at the start of the month and sell them after two weeks. This will reduce his average stock of money to £70. Similarly, for the precautionary demand for money: high interest on bonds will tempt the individual to take the risk of being occasionally caught short of money.

Therefore, it begins to look as if our demand for money function should be

$$M_\mathrm{d} = L(Y, r) \qquad L_Y > 0, \, L_r < 0 \tag{61}$$

This is reinforced when we realize that an individual (or firm) might actually *want* to hold some of his wealth in the form of money, quite apart from the need to finance transactions. In the absence of inflation, money is a safe asset: £100 kept as cash will still be £100 next year. Bonds vary in price, as we saw in the previous section, so that bonds bought for £100 may later become worth much less if the market rate of interest rises. The benefits of holding wealth in the form of bonds, the fixed annual payments and the chance of capital gains, must be balanced against the cost, the risk of capital losses. It seems likely therefore that an individual who does not wish to expose his wealth too much to the risk of loss will hold some of its as money. Since a rise in national income will normally be associated with a rise in wealth, the *asset* demand for money should be an increasing function of Y. A rise in r reduces the value of bonds so reduces total wealth as well as increasing the relative attractiveness of bonds and one might therefore expect that an asset demand for money is a decreasing function of r. We have therefore an additional reason to believe that $L_Y > 0$ and $L_r < 0$.

Finally, the fact that capital gains and losses can be made on bonds leads to the *speculative* demand for money. If interest rates are expected to fall, bonds are expected to rise in price so that one ought to hold as many bonds as possible. If interest rates are expected to rise, one should hold money rather than bonds. The case of a bond which lasts for ever serves to show why the speculative motive for holding money might be fairly strong. A bond which pays £10 for ever is worth £500 if the interest rate is 2%. Keeping £500 in bonds rather than in money for a year involves therefore an interest gain of £10. If, however, the interest rate were to rise to 3%, the price of the bond would fall to £333.33 and the capital loss of £166.67 clearly swamps the interest gain. On the other hand a fall in the rate of interest to 1% would double the value of the bond.

Thus the demand for money should be an increasing function of the difference between the expected interest rate r_e and the actual interest rate r. Thus we have

$$M_d = L(Y, r, r_e) \qquad L_Y > 0, \ L_r < 0, \ L_{r_e} > 0 \qquad (62)$$

since the speculative demand strengthens the negative effect of r (for given r_e) and implies a positive effect from r_e (given r).

All this discussion has assumed that bonds are the only alternative financial asset to money. In reality there are other types of asset, of which the most significant is shares (stocks) in companies. A share promises an annual dividend payment related to the company's profits, so that in contrast with a bond the amount which will be paid each year is uncertain and can vary from year to year. The same principle is applied, however, to valuing shares as to valuing bonds: the expected future returns are discounted. The assumption that bonds and money are the only financial assets serves to keep the theory simple, by excluding the complications that would be caused by the uncertainty of future returns on shares.

7.9 *Equilibrium in goods and money markets*

Combining equations (27) and (51) gives a new equation describing equality of supply and demand for goods in a closed economy:

$$Y = C(Y - T) + I(r) + G \qquad (63)$$

It is more convenient now to write this in the alternative form:

$$S(Y - T) + T = I(r) + G \qquad (64)$$

For given, exogenous, r these are essentially the same as (27) and (33). However, by considering equilibrium in the money market we can make the rate of interest endogenous, and develop a more complex, realistic and useful theory than the multiplier analysis of sections 7.2 and 7.3.

The determination of the *supply* of money is a complicated affair. The supply of banknotes available to individuals is directly controlled by the government, supply of money in the form of bank accounts depends on the behaviour of the banking system which may be quite difficult for the government to control. We circumvent these complications simply by assuming that the government does have sufficient control over the banking system to be able to regulate perfectly the supply of money. Then equilibrium in the money market is described by the equation

$$M = L(Y, r, r_e) \qquad (65)$$

where M is the supply of money.

Equations (64) and (65) are two equations in the two endogenous variables Y and r, with T, G, M and r_e being exogenous. Diagrammatically they are represented by the curves labelled IS and LM in figure 7.3. The downward slowing IS curve is the locus of points (Y, r) satisfying (64). As

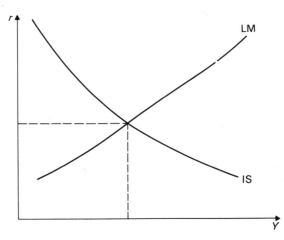

FIGURE 7.3   The IS–LM diagram

r falls, I rises so that Y must rise in order to raise S and preserve the equality. More formally, differentiating (64) with respect of r, treating Y as an implicit function of r shows that the implicit function has derivative

$$\frac{\mathrm{d}Y}{\mathrm{d}r} = \frac{I_r}{S_Y} < 0 \tag{66}$$

which is the negative slope of the IS curve. The upward-sloping LM curve is the locus of (Y, r) satisfying (65). As r rises, L falls and Y must rise to keep L equal to M. The implicit function $Y(r)$ defined by (64) has derivative

$$\frac{\mathrm{d}Y}{\mathrm{d}r} = -\frac{L_r}{L_Y} > 0 \tag{67}$$

which is the positive slope of the LM curve.

The point at which the IS and LM curves intersect in figure 7.3 gives the unique pair of values (Y, r) which satisfies both (64) and (65). It is the point at which both the 'goods market' and the 'money market' are in equilibrium.

However, the justification for the demand for money being sensitive to the interest rate was the existence of bonds. Should we not be concerned about supply and demand for bonds being equal? Consider a time period labelled t and suppose that at the start of the period individuals and firms ('the public') find themselves with stocks M_{t-1} and B_{t-1} of money and bonds respectively so that the public's stock of financial wealth is $M_{t-1} + B_{t-1}$. During the period there are flows of saving S_t and investment I_t and the difference $S_t - I_t$ represents that part of saving which is not invested in real capital assets, so it is the growth in the public's stock of financial wealth, and at the end of the period financial wealth is $M_{t-1} + B_{t-1} + S_t - I_t$. The public wish to hold the amount L_t in money at the end of the period so that the amount which they wish to hold as bonds, that is, the *demand for bonds*, is

$$B_t^{\mathrm{d}} = M_{t-1} + B_{t-1} + S_t - I_t - L_t \tag{68}$$

If the goods market is in equilibrium $S_t - I_t = G_t - T_t$. But $G_t - T_t$ is the government deficit, which can be met either by borrowing, that is by the government selling bonds, or by creating money, that is by the government paying some of its bills by printing extra banknotes or getting the banking system to expand the credit available to the government. Thus

$$S_t - I_t = G_t - T_t = M_t - M_{t-1} + B_t - B_{t-1} \tag{69}$$

where M_t and B_t are the money and bond supplies at the end of period t. Equations (68) and (69) together imply that

$$B_t^{\mathrm{d}} = M_t + B_t - L_t \tag{70}$$

but $M_t = L_t$ if the money market is in equilibrium. Thus if both goods and money markets are in equilibrium, $B_t^d = B_t$ which means that the bond market too is in equilibrium. (This is a particular case of a more general result known as *Walras' law*.) It is therefore sufficient to use the two equations (64) and (65) to describe equilibrium in all three markets.

7.10 Comparative statics in the IS–LM model

It is now a straightforward matter to analyse the effects of various exogenous changes. To find the effect of change in G on Y and r we differentiate (64) and (65) to get

$$S_Y \frac{\partial Y}{\partial G} - I_r \frac{\partial r}{\partial G} = 1$$

$$L_Y \frac{\partial Y}{\partial G} + L_r \frac{dr}{dG} = 0 \tag{71}$$

which solve to give

$$\left| \frac{\partial Y}{\partial G} = \frac{L_r}{S_Y L_r + I_r L_Y} > 0 \right. \tag{72}$$

$$\left. \frac{\partial r}{\partial G} = \frac{-L_Y}{S_Y L_r + I_r L_Y} > 0 \right| \tag{73}$$

since $S_Y > 0$, $L_Y > 0$, $I_r < 0$, $L_r < 0$. Note further that

$$\frac{\partial Y}{\partial G} = \frac{1}{S_Y + I_r L_Y / L_r} < \frac{1}{S_Y} \tag{74}$$

so that the effect of a change in government expenditure is to raise income, but by less than in the simple multiplier model, and also to raise the interest rate.

It is easy to see in figure 7.4 what is going on. Initially the equilibrium is at (Y_A, r_A). A rise in G with r constant has a multiplier effect in the goods market, for (64) with r (and therefore I) constant is the simple multiplier model. Thus a rise in G shifts the IS curve to the right at the rate $1/S_Y$. In particular, if r remained at r_A, a rise ΔG in G would increase income to $Y_A + \Delta G/S_Y$. The increased income, however, raises the demand for money (reduces the demand for bonds) which pushes up the rate of interest (pushes down the price of bonds), and the higher interest rate required to bring the money market (and the bond market) back into equilibrium reduces the level of investment, and this dampens the multiplier effect of the increased government expenditure. (This is sometimes

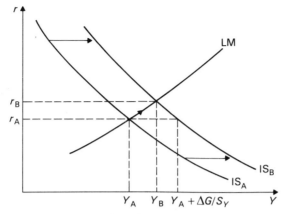

FIGURE 7.4   The effect of a rise in G

described as government expenditure 'crowding out' private investment.) We end up at the new equilibrium (Y_B, r_B).

It is easy to see similarly that a reduction in taxation, or a balanced-budget expansion will have qualitatively similar, though quantitatively different, effects.

Note that it is not correct to say that a fiscal expansion causes interest rates to rise (bond prices to fall) because the government must sell more bonds to cover its deficit. What is actually going on is that the rise in income caused by the fiscal expansion leads the public to try to sell some of its *stock* of existing bonds because its demand for money has risen, and it is this supply of bonds from the existing stock which is the cause of the fall in bond prices. The increased government deficit changes the *flow* of new bonds on to the market, but this is of a different order of magnitude. Also the flow continues, but once the interest rate has reached its new level, r_B in the case shown in figure 7.4, the interest rate does not rise any further. It is left to you as exercise 7.23 to explain carefully how the continuous supply of extra government bonds is absorbed in the new equilibrium without causing further rises in the interest rate.

The effects of a change in M can be analysed similarly, by differentiating (64) and (65) with respect to M:

$$S_Y \frac{\partial Y}{\partial M} - I_r \frac{\partial r}{\partial M} = 0$$

$$L_Y \frac{\partial Y}{\partial M} + L_r \frac{\partial r}{\partial M} = 1$$

(75)

which give

$$\frac{\partial Y}{\partial M} = \frac{I_r}{S_Y L_r + I_r L_Y}$$

(76)

$$\frac{\partial r}{\partial M} = \frac{S_Y}{S_Y L_r + I_r L_Y} \qquad (77)$$

This case is illustrated in figure 7.5. Initially the equilibrium is (Y_A, r_A).
A rise in the supply of money with G and T unchanged requires the
government to find some method of getting the new money into the
hands of the public. The obvious method is to buy bonds from the public
in exchange for money (or refrain from the bond sales that would be
required to cover an existing deficit). Such a policy reduces the rate of
interest, as the public will be willing to switch some of their financial
wealth from bonds to money only if bond prices rise. The fall in the
interest rate, from r_A to r_C in figure 7.5, leads to a rise in investment and
thus (by the usual multiplier process) a rise in income until equilibrium
in the goods market is restored and full equilibrium is reached at (Y_B, r_B).

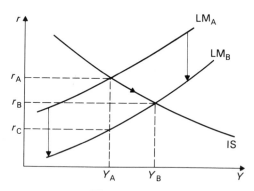

FIGURE 7.5   The effect of a rise in M

Alternative exogenous changes can be similarly considered. The
expected interest rate is already in the model. Variables such as the 'desire
to save' or the 'desire to invest' and so on can be inserted in the respective
functions, and their effects analysed.

7.11   Fiscal and monetary policy

We now have two apparently simple tools available to a government which
wishes to change the level of national income and thereby the level of
unemployment. It can adopt *fiscal policy*: changes in government
expenditure and in taxation. Alternatively it can adopt a *monetary
policy*: changing the supply of money in the economy. As we have seen,
the two sets of policies are connected because of the government's need to
finance the difference between government expenditure and taxation.
Conceptually, however, the two can be kept quite distinct: a change in
government expenditure or taxation with the resulting effects on govern-

ment finance entirely absorbed by sales or purchases of government bonds so that the money supply is unchanged is a pure fiscal policy; a change in the money supply with no change in government expenditure or taxation is a pure monetary policy; while a change in government expenditure or taxation not completely financed by bond sales or purchases is a mixture of monetary and fiscal policy. Why should a government choose one policy rather than the other?

(i) The *relative efficacy* of the different policies depends on the size of the four derivatives S_Y, I_r, L_Y, L_r. If $L_r = 0$, $\partial Y/\partial G = 0$ and $\partial Y/\partial M = 1/L_Y$; while if $L_r = -\infty$, $\partial Y/\partial G = 1/S_Y$ and $\partial Y/\partial M = 0$. Thus if one believes the demand for money to be very interest-inelastic, one should believe that monetary policy is effective and fiscal policy ineffective; while if the demand for money is very interest-elastic, monetary policy is ineffective and fiscal policy effective.

Conversely, if I_r is small, $\partial Y/\partial G$ is close to $1/S_Y$ and $\partial Y/\partial M$ is small so fiscal policy is effective and monetary policy ineffective; while a high value of $-I_r$ implies that fiscal policy is ineffective and monetary policy effective.

It is fairly easy to see what the different beliefs about L_r and I_r imply about the shapes of the IS and LM curves and then to give a diagrammatic analysis of the relative effectiveness of the two policies in different circumstances.

Another dimension to the relative efficacy of the different policies is the speed with which they have their effect. Since comparative statics only shows how the equilibrium changes and says nothing about the process by which the economy gets from one equilibrium to another, the model as developed here tells us nothing about the speed with which the new equilibrium is attained.

(ii) Some policies may be politically easier to implement than others. In the British parliamentary system, for example, changes in fiscal policy decided by the Treasury can be almost guaranteed to be implemented by parliament (even, sometimes, if some members of the government oppose the changes!). By contrast, the separation of powers in the United States between the executive and legislative branches of the government often means that fiscal changes considered essential by the President are rejected or delayed by Congress. In monetary policy, similarly, the extent to which the central bank is under the government's control may determine whether policy changes desired by the government are actually implemented.

(iii) The different policies have different effects on the *balance of payments*. It is fairly easy to extend the IS–LM model to an open economy. The equations are

$$S(Y - T) + T + IM(Y) = I(r) + G + X \tag{78}$$

$$M = L(Y, r) \tag{79}$$

where $IM(Y)$ is the level of imports and X is the level of exports. Clearly any policy which increases Y will make the *balance of trade X-IM* deteriorate. However, the *balance of payments* consists of the balance of trade plus net capital inflows (because a foreigner buying investment goods or a share in the ownership of investment goods in your country has the same effect on your receipts of foreign currency as if he bought some goods as imports). Monetary expansion reduces the rate of interest and so will make foreigners less willing to invest here and our residents more eager to invest abroad. There will be a reduction in capital inflow and an increase in capital outflow and the balance of payments will deteriorate if the exchange rate, the price of this country's currency relative to foreign currency, is constant. On the other hand, a rise in interest rate induced by fiscal expansion will set a favourable change in capital flows against the deterioration in the balance of trade, and the balance of payments may improve.

(iv) The different policies affect the *level of investment* differently. A fiscal expansion raises interest rates and the effect of the expansion is dampened by the consequent reduction in investment. A monetary expansion, by contrast, raises income precisely because the fall in the interest rate raises investment. The level of investment affects the size and shape of the capital stock of the economy in the future, and the government's view about what is a desirable level of investment on these grounds may influence its macroeconomic policy.

Although the models we have developed in this chapter are extremely useful for understanding a range of important issues in macroeconomic theory and macroeconomic policy, they suffer from some rather serious deficiencies. Many of the behavioural assumptions, as I have emphasized, are rather *ad hoc*. The links with our microeconomic theories are somewhat tenuous. There is no discussion of the phenomenon of inflation: though the problem of inflation has occupied the attention of policy-makers in recent years at least as much as the problem of unemployment. Indeed, prices (apart from the interest rate) seem to play no role in these models, and this takes us back to the theoretical issue raised at the start of the chapter: if prices are given a proper role to play, will the economy not simply attain an equilibrium in which unemployment does not exist? These are the issues to which the next chapter is addressed.

Exercises

7.1   Show how figure 7.1 should be modified if: (a) borrowing is impossible; (b) the interest rate on borrowing is higher than on lending.

7.2   Why do you think banks are reluctant to give loans to students to be repaid out of the students' future earnings?

7.3   In the model illustrated in figure 7.1, show how the budget line is shifted by a change in r and show therefore that the effect of r on c_1 depends on whether c_1 exceeds y_1.

7.4   Why is it in the 'paradox of thrift' model of section 7.2 that an increased desire to save leads to a fall in the equilibrium level of income that is just enough to cause there to be no change in the actual amount saved?

7.5   Discuss the effect on saving of a change in the desire to consume in an open economy.

7.6   In an economy with exogenous investment and no foreign trade, in which taxation is levied as a fixed proportion of total income, so that $T = tY$, and in which consumption is a fixed proportion of disposable income, so that $C = c(Y - T)$, find the effect on total savings of a change in c, the marginal propensity to consume.

7.7   In a closed economy with $T = tY$, consumption function $C = C(Y - T)$, and I and G determined exogenously, determine the effects on national income and on the government deficit of: (i) a change in G; (ii) a change in t.
   If the economy were an open economy with imports $M = M(Y)$ and exogenously determined exports X, find the effects of a change in G on national income, the government deficit and the balance of trade deficit.

7.8   Prove from equation (24) that $\partial Y^1/\partial I^1 > 1/(1 + M_Y^1 - C_Y^1)$.

7.9   Analyse the balanced-budget multiplier in the open economy whose equilibrium is described by (31). Explain carefully the difference between this result and the result for the closed economy. Justify the assumption that M depends on Y rather than $Y - T$. What would be the balanced-budget multiplier if M were a function of $Y - T$ rather than Y?

7.10   Suppose that, in the model described by equations (34) and (35), the economy is in equilibrium at time 0 with investment level I. In time period 1, investment rises to $I + \Delta I$, but in all subsequent periods it returns to level I. Trace the effects on income over time, show that Y_t tends to return to the original equilibrium level, and contrast with the result of a permanent increase in I described in (41).

7.11   In the model described in equation (44) and (45) prove that the effects over time of a permanent change in G, of a permanent change in T and of a permanent balanced-budget change in both G and T are respectively described by (46), (47) and (48).

7.12   Justify the present-value calculation (49a) when future interest rates differ from period to period.

7.13   Suppose that an individual lives for two periods. In the first period he can choose to spend a proportion T of his time in training and will receive a net income $Y(1 - T)$. In the second period his income is given by $(1 + 2\alpha T^{1/2}) Y$ where α is an index of 'ability'. If r is the rate of interest, find the value of T which maximizes the present value in the first period of his lifetime income, discuss the relationship between the optimal T and the values of r and α, and state the conditions under which $T = 1$.

*7.14   A machine lasts for T years and at age t produes a stream of net earnings $q(t)$ for its owner, where $q'(t) < 0$. The market interest rate is r, so that the value of a machine at age t is

$$P(t) = \int_t^T q(s)\, e^{-r(s-t)}\, ds$$

(i)   Suppose that lifetime T is not physically determined but is decided by the owner of the machine. How will T be chosen? How will T be changed by a change in r or a change in wage rates?

(ii)   What price would a rational investor be willing to pay for a new machine?

(iii)   Prove that

$$q(t) = rP(t) - \frac{dP(t)}{dt}$$

and interpret this equation as showing equality between the benefit and the opportunity cost of using a machine of age t.

(iv)   If, in fact, $q(t) = q\, e^{-\delta t}$, what will T be? Derive explicit expressions for $P(t)$ and $dP(t)/dt$.

7.15   The government wishes to borrow £100 and is willing to issue a bond in return. The market interest rate is 5%, and the government wishes to make the bond redeemable for £100 in 10 years' time. What annual payment on the bond will be required in order to make a rational saver willing to buy it? What would be the effect on an expectation of rising interest rates in the future?

7.16   Explain in terms of opportunity cost why a bond which lasts for ever has the value a/r where a is the annual payment and r the rate of interest.
    Prove that if a bond is sold for b and will be redeemed for b in T years' time, and if the annual payment is a and the market interest rate is r, then it must be that $b = a/r$. Explain this in terms of opportunity cost.

7.17   What is the present value on January 1, 1983 of a bond that lasts for ever and pays £100 on December 31 in even-numbered years only? And of one that pays £100 in odd-numbered years only? What is the sum of the two present values?

7.18   Other things being equal, what effect would you expect a rise in the interest rate to have on the price of company shares? Why is it necessary to say 'other things being equal'?

*7.19   Find the present value of a continuous cash flow at the rate of a per year for T years if the interest rate is r. Compare your answer with the value derived in (58) for a series of discrete annual payments. What happens to the present value as $T \to \infty$?

7.20   Discuss the effect on the velocity of circulation of money and the demand for money of the following institutional changes:

(i)   a shift towards monthly rather than weekly wage payment;
(ii)   the establishment of large numbers of institutions (such as British building society branch offices) where it is easy and costless to exchange money for interest-bearing assets and vice versa;
(iii)   a large increase in the number of bankruptcies (think about the effect on firms' willingness to do business on credit as well as the effect on wealth-holders);
(iv)   widespread use of credit cards.

7.21   What would be the consequences for the demand for money of a statement by the British Prime Minister that 'the Government are actively considering ways of reducing the rate of interest'?

7.22   Suppose that the demand for money is given by

$$L = 1375 + 0.25Y - 50r$$

where Y is national income, r% is the rate of interest, and $r > 2$, and that the demand for money becomes infinitely interest-elastic when $r = 2$, and that the supply of money M is 2500.
   Sketch the LM curve. What is the rate of interest: (i) when $Y < 4900$; (ii) when $Y = 6500$? What happens to the LM curve if M rises to 2600?

7.23   Suppose that the IS–LM system is in equilibrium and that at that equilibrium $G > T$, so that the government is running a deficit. Since M is constant, that deficit must be financed by the sale of bonds. Therefore there is a steady increase in the supply of bonds in the bond market. It is asserted in section 7.9 that the bond market is necessarily in equilibrium, which can only be the case if there is a steady increase in the demand for bonds. Whence comes this increase?

7.24   Analyse mathematically in the IS–LM model the effects of: (i) a change in T; (ii) a balanced-budget change in G and T; (iii) a change in the expected rate of interest; and (iv) an exogenous increase in the desire to save. Give a verbal and diagrammatic explanation of what happens.

7.25   Analyse the effects on the economy of the changes listed in exercise 7.20 and the statement quoted in exercise 7.21.

7.26   Analyse diagrammatically the effects of fiscal and monetary policy in the IS–LM system for different values of L_r and I_r. Justify carefully how the curves shift in the various cases.

7.27   Is it possible for the government to control both the money supply and the rate of interest?

7.28   Analyse the effect of a change in G on the balance of trade in the IS–LM model with foreign trade.

CHAPTER 8

Further Macroeconomics

8.1 *Aggregate demand and aggregate supply*

In the IS–LM model developed in the last chapter an important assumption is that the supply of goods is equal to whatever is the demand. This can only be true if there are unemployed resources. Another feature of the model is that prices play no role.

What role could prices play? If P is the money price of goods, then equations (7.64) and (7.65) become

$$S(Y - T) + T = I(r) + G \tag{1}$$

$$L(Y, r) = M/P \tag{2}$$

(The expected interest rate, r_e, plays no role in the argument here, so it is not explicitly included in the demand for money function.) To understand the meaning of this modified equation system you need to be clear about the distinction between *real* and *nominal* quantities.

Think of output as consisting of only one type of good, whose output is Y and whose price is P. The value of output is PY and that is the value of income too. However it is *nominal* income, for a rise in PY which was caused by a rise in P would not represent an increase in the purchasing power of income recipients. It is Y which measures the quantity of goods which can be bought with the income PY, so Y is *real* income. In equation (1) all variables are measured in real terms: S and T are those parts of real income Y which are saved by individuals, or received as taxes by the government, I and G are those parts of output Y which are invested, or used by the government.

M is the *nominal* stock of money, measuring in, say, billions of dollars the money held by the public as cash or in bank accounts. A change in P, the price of goods, with M unchanged, would change the purchasing power of the money stock. It is M/P, the *real* value of the money stock, which measures the purchasing power of the money stock. Clearly therefore equation (2) equates the real supply of money with the real demand, and states that the real demand for money is a function of real income (and the rate of interest).

That this is a natural assumption to make is most easily seen by supposing that the only demand for money is the transactions demand (see section 7.8): if real income doubles, the demand for money will increase, but since individuals' lifestyles, hours of work, and so on will be changing too, there is no presumption that the demand for money will exactly double; by contrast, if nominal income doubles because the price level has doubled with real income unchanged, the only essential change in individuals' situations is that $2 is worth what $1 used to be worth (and $2 is exactly as easy to earn or to save as $1 used to be) so it is plausible that exactly twice as much nominal money is demanded; hence equation (2).

It is not so easy to justify (2) when we consider the asset demand for money. Indeed if you followed carefully the argument of section 7.9 that the bond market must be in equilibrium if the goods and money markets are in equilibrium you would have grounds for being sceptical about (7.65) as a description of the demand for money. A reason for scepticism (see exercise 7.23) is that (7.65) implies that at an equilibrium in which the government is running a deficit with a constant money supply, individuals are steadily accumulating financial wealth, *all* of it in the form of the bonds being issued by the government to finance its deficit. It is not very plausible that *none* of the extra financial wealth would flow into extra demand for money. It is, in other words, not very plausible to exclude the value of wealth from the demand for money function.

This is even more the case when we consider changes in the price level, for such a change will generally change the real value of the stock of bonds held by individuals, since bonds entitle their owners to sums of nominal money. Surely such a change would affect the real demand for money? Equation (2) says not: if the price level doubles, the demand for real money is unchanged.

In spite of these problems, we still stick to the hypothesis embodied in (2). To introduce the 'wealth effects' hinted at in the preceding paragraphs would make life too difficult for us.

Equations (1) and (2) determine Y and r as implicit functions of G, T and M/P. Here we are particularly interested in the effects of changes in P. Differentiating (1) and (2) gives

$$S_Y \frac{\partial Y}{\partial P} - I_r \frac{dr}{dP} = 0$$

$$L_Y \frac{\partial Y}{\partial P} + L_r \frac{dr}{dP} = -\frac{M}{P^2}$$

(3)

which solve to give

$$\frac{\partial Y}{\partial P} = \frac{-I_r M/P^2}{S_Y L_r + I_r L_Y} < 0 \tag{4}$$

$$\frac{\partial r}{\partial P} = \frac{-S_Y M/P^2}{S_Y L_r + I_r L_Y} > 0 \tag{5}$$

These results correspond exactly to equations (7.76) and (7.77): an increase in P must have the opposite effect to an increase in M, since an increase in P affects Y and r simply by reducing the real value of the money supply. Diagrammatically it can be represented as a leftward shift of the LM curve.

The function $Y(G, T, M/P)$ defined by (1) and (2) is called the *aggregate demand* function. Diagrammatically it is shown in figure 8.1 which graphs Y against P. The downward slope of the graph follows from (4). The effect of changes in G, T and M have already been derived in the IS–LM model of chapter 7. Thus, for example, the fact that $\partial Y/\partial G > 0$ means that an increase in government expenditure from G to G' shifts the aggregate demand curve in figure 8.1 rightwards. Similar rightward shifts would result from a reduction in T or an increase in M.

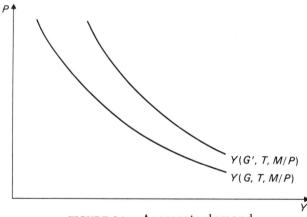

FIGURE 8.1 Aggregate demand

Let us suppose that the economy's ability to supply output depends on the quantities of available inputs in a way that can be described by a production function

$$Y = f(L, K) \tag{6}$$

where L is the quantity of labour used, and K is quantity of other inputs. In fact we shall assume throughout that K is constant. (We do not investigate the question of when it is legitimate to aggregate together all individual firms' production functions into a single function like (6) describing production possibilities in the economy as a whole.) The theory of chapters 2 and 3 shows that if producers behave competitively the quantity of labour they wish to hire will be that which makes the value of the marginal product of labour equal to the wage rate:

$$W/P = f_L(L, K) \tag{7}$$

Here W is the wage rate, so W/P can be called the real wage and equation (7) states that the marginal product of labour is equated to the real wage. Finally, the theory of section 4.7 shows that the quantity of labour which individuals are willing to supply will be a function of the real wage:

$$L = L(W/P) \tag{8}$$

We now have three equations, (6)–(8), in the variables L, Y and W/P. Let us assume that the labour supply function (8) is an increasing function of W/P. Diminishing returns to labour ensures that the labour demand function defined by (7) has the property that the quantity of labour demanded is a decreasing function of W/P. The labour market is then illustrated in figure 8.2 where (7) defines the downward-sloping labour demand curve and (8) defines the upward-sloping labour supply curve. Equations (7) and (8) are both satisfied only at the equilibrium point where labour demanded and supplied is L^* and the real wage is $(W/P)^*$. Then equation (6) fixes the level of output at $Y^* = f(L^*, K)$.

Thus the labour supply of individuals and the profit-maximizing behaviour of producers determine the fixed level of output Y^* which is independent of prices and which is called aggregate supply. Figure 8.3 shows both aggregate demand and aggregate supply in the same diagram, so that for example if G, T and M take values such that the aggregate demand curve is AD, then the price level must be P_1 if aggregate demand is

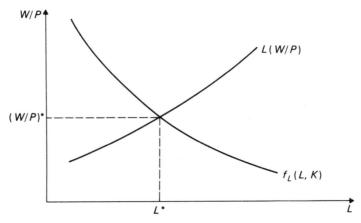

FIGURE 8.2   Labour market equilibrium

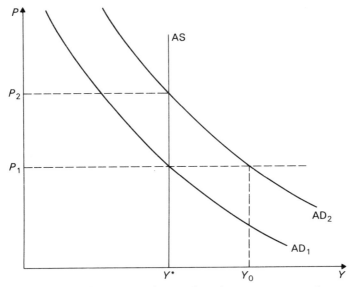

FIGURE 8.3   Aggregate demand and aggregate supply

to equal aggregate supply. For the sake of brevity let us call this the AD–AS model.

(There is a technical point to be made about the aggregate demand function. When we used equations like (1) and (2) to describe the IS–LM model, we explicitly assumed that producers supplied whatever output is demanded. Now we are using these equations to derive a curve at only one point of which do producers supply what is demanded. Effectively individuals base their saving and their demand for money on the expectation of having the level of income which satisfies (1) and (2), but this will not necessarily be the actual level of income. At, for example, the price level P_1 in figure 8.3, when AD is at AD_2, Y_0 is the income level which satisfies (1) and (2) so it is the income level on which saving and money demand are planned, but producers are only willing to supply Y^*. All of this means that we should be very wary of any statement about what might happen out of equilibrium in this model. We should confine our attention strictly to equilibrium points, at which individuals' income expectations are realized since producers do supply exactly the output demanded.)

Returning to the model, we see that it gives very different conclusions from the IS–LM model. Consider the effects in the two models of a rise in G, for example. The IS–LM model is equations (1) and (2) with P constant. (In the previous chapter, P was fixed at 1 but it was the fact that it was constant that mattered, not the value of the constant.) Then a change in G changes Y at the rate

$$\frac{\partial Y}{\partial G} = \frac{L_r}{S_Y L_r + I_r L_Y} > 0 \qquad (9)$$

This is represented in an IS–LM diagram by a rightward shift of the IS curve, and in figure 8.3 by a rightward shift of the aggregate demand curve from AD_1 to AD_2 and a change in the level of income from Y^* to Y_0 with P constant at P_1. The assumptions in the IS–LM model that producers are willing to supply whatever is demanded and that the price level is fixed together mean that the supply of output is infinitely elastic at the fixed price level. The horizontal line at P_1 in figure 8.3 shows the aggregate supply curve of the IS–LM model.

The AD–AS model is described by equations (1), (2), (6), (7) and (8); but (6), (7) and (8) fix Y at Y^*, so effectively the model is described by equations (1) and (2) with Y fixed at Y^* and P (as well as r) variable. Differentiating (1) and (2) with respect to G with Y, M and T fixed gives

$$-I_r \frac{\partial r}{\partial G} = 1 \qquad (10)$$

$$\frac{M}{P^2} \frac{\partial P}{\partial G} + L_r \frac{dr}{dG} = 0 \qquad (11)$$

so that

$$\frac{\partial P}{\partial G} = \frac{L_r}{I_r M/P^2} > 0 \qquad (12)$$

In figure 8.3 we have the same shift of the aggregate demand curve as before, but instead of a change in Y with P constant, we now have an increase in P from P_1 to P_2 with Y constant at Y^*. Instead, in other words, of a horizontal supply curve, we have a vertical supply curve.

When in the previous chapter we compared the IS–LM model with the multiplier model we noted the phenomenon of 'crowding out'. As government expenditure is raised in the IS–LM model we do not get the full multiplier effect because the rise in interest rates reduces investment. In the AD–AS model there is *complete* crowding-out. Consider equation (1) with Y and T fixed. The left-hand side is constant so the right-hand side must be constant too. This indeed is what (10) states: the rate of interest must rise sufficiently to cause a reduction in investment equal to the increase in government expenditure. It is left to you, in exercise 8.1, to look at the effect of taxation changes on investment.

Now contrast the effects of an increase in nominal money supply in the two models. In the IS–LM model the level of income increases at the rate

$$\frac{\partial Y}{\partial M} = \frac{I_r/P}{S_Y L_r + I_r L_Y} > 0 \qquad (13)$$

In the IS–LM diagram this appears as a rightward shift of the LM curve, and in figure 8.3 as a rightward shift in the aggregate demand curve and an increase in the level of Y with P constant. Thus in figure 8.3 the effect is essentially the same as the effect of a rise in G (although from the full IS–LM analysis we know that the effects on r are different). In the AD–AS model, again Y is fixed at Y^* and differentiating (1) and (2) with respect to M with Y, G and T fixed gives

$$I_r \frac{\partial r}{\partial M} = 0 \tag{14}$$

$$L_r \frac{\partial r}{\partial M} = \frac{1}{P} - \frac{M}{P^2} \frac{\partial P}{\partial M} \tag{15}$$

Hence $\partial r / \partial M = 0$ and

$$\frac{M}{P} \frac{\partial P}{\partial M} = 1 \tag{16}$$

Equation (16) states that the elasticity of P with respect to M is 1 so that a change in M brings about an equal percentage change in P. This has the effect of keeping M/P constant for the change in M/P is simply the right-hand side of (15) which must be zero. Indeed this could be deduced without any differentiation. Equation (1) shows that if Y, T and G are constant, I must be constant so r must be constant. Then in equation (2) since Y and r are constant, L and therefore M/P must be constant. A change in the nominal money supply changes only the price level: the real value of the money supply and all other variables are completely unchanged.

Next we consider the effect of a shift in the economy's production possibilities. Suppose that a change in the resources available to the economy or technical progress changes equations (6), (7) and (8) so that Y^* increases. In the IS–LM model nothing changes. If the old equilibrium was at P_1, Y^* on AD in figure 8.4, that is still the equilibrium. The

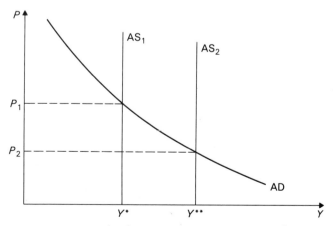

FIGURE 8.4   An increase in aggregate supply

economy could produce more if extra demand were forthcoming but the extra resources are left idle. By contrast, in the AD–AS model, the shift of the aggregate supply from the vertical curve AS_1 at Y^* to AS_2 at Y^{**} increases income from Y^* to Y^{**} as the price level falls from P_1 to P_2.

All of this raises two questions. How would the AD–AS model actually get from one equilibrium to another, in particular how would the required price changes take place? Is the AD–AS model a better description than the IS–LM model of what actually happens in the real world? It will be easier to answer these questions after the analysis of the next section.

8.2   Aggregate supply with a fixed nominal wage

Equations (7) and (8) and figure 8.2 describe a world in which competitive behaviour by individuals and firms changes the wage rate and the price level so as to ensure full employment of labour. In the real world, however, people seem reluctant to let their wages fall, even in the presence of substantial unemployment.

Let us therefore modify the aggregate supply model by assuming that W in equation (7) is a constant and by dropping equation (8). (Note why (8) must be dropped: if labour supply is dependent on the fixed nominal wage W being offered it cannot also be dependent on the level of the real wage W/P.) Equation (7) now determines L as a function of P, while (6) determines Y as a function of L. Since $f_{LL} < 0$, it follows from (7) that higher values of P (lower values of W/P) are associated with higher values of L; and, in turn, from (6) this implies that higher values of P are associated with higher values of Y. Thus if we were to graph the function $Y(K, W/P)$ defined by (6) and (7) against P we would obtain a curve such as the one depicted in figure 8.5 as SRAS. This function we call the *short-run aggregate supply* function because it is plausible that nominal wages might be fixed independently of the level of prices or of the level of unemployment only in the short run. Note that the fact that (7) is satisfied implies that competitive producers are hiring the quantity of labour and producing the quantity of output that is required for profit maximization. Note also that writing (7) as $P = W/f_L$ and recalling that W/f_L is equal to marginal cost shows that the short-run aggregate supply curve is the marginal cost curve of producers who face the fixed nominal wage W, just as we would expect from the microeconomic theory of chapters 2 and 3.

Consider then the consequences of, say, a rise in government expenditure, starting from a position of equilibrium in the AD–AS model such as point A in figure 8.5. The IS–LM analysis tells us that the effect is to raise income with the price level constant – that is, we move from A on the original AD curve to B on a new AD curve, income rises from Y^* to Y_0

and the price level remains at P_0. Now, however, we can bring the short-run aggregate supply analysis into play. Firms facing the fixed nominal wage rate W will produce the extra output only if a fall in the real wage rate W/P persuades them to hire more labour, or equivalently if a rise in the price P of output persuades them to expand output along their rising marginal cost curve. The excess demand $Y_0 - Y^*$ at the price P_0 drives price up to P_1, demand down to Y_1 and supply up to Y_1 so we have an equilibrium at C.

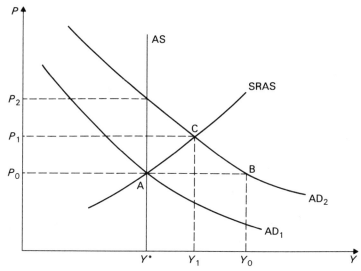

FIGURE 8.5   Short-run and long-run aggregate supply

Mathematically, the shift from A to C can be analysed by differentiating equations (1), (2), (6) and (7) with respect to G keeping T, M, K and W constant. We have

$$S_Y \frac{\partial Y}{\partial G} - I_r \frac{\partial r}{\partial G} = 1 \tag{17}$$

$$L_Y \frac{\partial Y}{\partial G} + L_r \frac{\partial r}{\partial G} + \frac{M}{P^2} \frac{\partial P}{\partial G} = 0 \tag{18}$$

$$\frac{\partial Y}{\partial G} - f_L \frac{\partial L}{\partial G} = 0 \tag{19}$$

$$\frac{W}{P^2} \frac{\partial P}{\partial G} + f_{LL} \frac{\partial L}{\partial G} = 0 \tag{20}$$

Eliminating $\partial r/\partial G$ from (17) and (18) and $\partial L/\partial G$ from (19) and (20) gives a pair of equations in $\partial Y/\partial G$ and $\partial P/\partial G$ which can be solved to give

$$\frac{\partial Y}{\partial G} = \frac{L_r f_L W}{(S_Y L_r + L_Y I_r) f_L W - f_{LL} I_r M} > 0 \qquad (21)$$

$$\frac{\partial P}{\partial G} = \frac{-L_r f_{LL} P^2}{(S_Y L_r + L_Y I_r) f_L W - f_{LL} I_r M} > 0 \qquad (22)$$

It is easy to see from (21) that $\partial Y/\partial G$ is smaller than in the IS–LM model and smaller still than in the simple multiplier model.

However, when we look at the labour market, illustrated in figure 8.6, we see why (Y_1, P_1) might not be a long-run equilibrium. As output expanded to Y_1 employment rose to L_1 and the real wage fell to W_0/P_1 where W_0 was the fixed level of W. Workers, however, do not really wish to supply this increased amount of labour at this real wage rate as we can see from the supply curve $L(W/P)$. Labour unions and individual workers would gradually realize their power to demand higher nominal wages in a situation where firms were seeking to expand output and employment. As W rises the SRAS curve in figure 8.5, which is defined by $P = W/f_L$ would shift upwards: P would rise, though more slowly than W, L would contract from L_1 to L^* and Y from Y_1 to Y^* until the economy arrives at the new long-run equilibrium at P_2, Y^* with a nominal wage W_2 satisfying $W_2/P_2 = W_0/P_0$.

Conversely, if G fell, the story we could tell is one of output contracting first, leading to a fall in the price level, unemployment of labour and a fall in the wage rate which restores long-run equilibrium at a lower price level and an unchanged income level. The story to be told when it is a monetary change which alters aggregate demand is essentially the same.

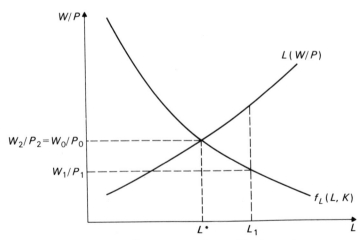

FIGURE 8.6   Labour market adjustments

It is important to stress that what has been done in this section is the development of one simple model that tells us a story about how the economy could move from one long-run equilibrium to another. There are arbitrary elements in this model, notably the assumptions that, in the short run, competitive firms can hire as much labour as they wish and the output price is flexible, while workers require a fixed nominal wage but are willing to supply as much labour as is demanded at this wage. Perhaps the most serious deficiency of the model is that it has implications which are at variance with the facts: when output is high, according to the model the marginal product of labour (which equals the real wage) is low, while when output is low, the marginal product of labour is high. The observed relationship between unemployment and labour productivity is rather different. There are alternative models of short-run behaviour which are more plausible, but also more complicated.

8.3   Which macroeconomic model?

We now have four macroeconomic models: the simple multiplier model, the IS–LM model, the short-run AD–AS model, and the long-run AD–AS model. They differ in the extent to which markets are assumed to adjust, from the multiplier model where essentially no market adjustment takes place through to the long-run AD–AS model in which all markets adjust fully to equilibrium. As a result they differ in the extent to which macro-economic disturbances appear as output and employment changes or as price, wage and interest rate changes.

The long-run AD–AS model is the one which is closest in spirit to the microeconomic theory developed in earlier chapters. The others make seemingly more arbitrary assumptions about agents' behaviour. Yet justifications can be offered for markets not adjusting instantaneously or even speedily to apparent disequilibrium. For example, if a worker loses his job, it may be more rational for him to look for another similar job at his old wage rate than immediately to accept a job at a lower wage. To develop microeconomic justifications for the many apparently arbitrary assumptions built into our macroeconomic models is, however, far beyond the scope of this book.

The crucial test of an economic theory is its ability accurately to describe and predict events in the real world. It is as difficult in the 1980s to accept as the final word on macroeconomics a theory in which price changes play no role as to accept a theory in which there is no unemploy-ment. There is no consensus among economists on which theory gives the best description of the real world: and to discuss how economists go about judging whether one theory is a better description or prediction of what happens in the real world is also beyond the scope of this book.

All of the models have the disadvantage of being comparative static: a market or set of markets moves from one equilibrium to another in response to an exogenous change. The fact that in the real world we observe systematic patterns of movement in employment, output and prices over time suggests the desirability of developing *dynamic* models capable of explaining these movements. In section 7.4 and the appendix to chapter 7 we developed dynamic versions of the simple multiplier model. The remainder of this chapter is devoted to dynamic versions of the AD–AS models. At last we shall have models in which inflation is possible, in which, that is to say, we model continuous change in the price level as opposed to the once-for-all changes of our present models.

8.4   The Phillips curve

In section 8.2 we analysed the short-run AD–AS model in which income could be different from the long-run AD–AS equilibrium. If, however, unemployment or overemployment in the labour market caused the nominal wage rate to change, income would move back to its equilibrium value. Now we look at how the actual movement of the wage rate in response to labour market disequilibrium can be explicitly modelled. As in the model of section 8.2 we assume that the goods price is always adjusted to keep the goods market in equilibrium, that is to persuade competitive producers to produce exactly what is demanded.

Suppose then that income were different from the long-run equilibrium Y^*, and that the nominal wage reacts gradually to the divergence between the desired supply of labour and the actual quantity of labour demanded. Since labour demand and output are linked by equation (6) we can model this as a relationship between the rate of change of wages and the divergence between Y and Y^*:

$$\hat{W}_t = f(Y_t - Y^*) \tag{23}$$

where $\hat{W}_t$ means $(W_{t+1} - W_t)/W_t$, the proportionate rate of change of wages over time, and where f has the properties $f(0) = 0$ and $f' > 0$. Such a relationship is illustrated in figure 8.7(a). It is usually called the *Phillips curve*.

Frequently the Phillips curve is presented in the alternative form of a relationship between the rate of change of wages (or of prices) and the level of unemployment. In our model, employment and income must move together so unemployment and income must move inversely. Thus we could equivalently show the Phillips curve as in figure 8.7(b) where U is the level of unemployment. The only extra question that this raises is that figure 8.7(b) shows $\hat{W} = 0$ at a positive level U^* of unemployment whereas figure 8.6 shows the corresponding level L^* of employment as

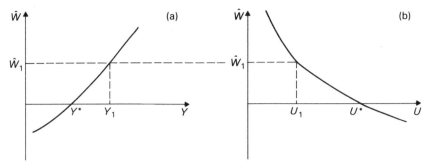

FIGURE 8.7   The Phillips curve

being the level at which supply and demand for labour are equal. The explanation is simply that in reality there are many different types of jobs and many different types of worker. At any given times there will be people *counted* as unemployed who are actually changing jobs, temporarily ill and incapable of work, or permanently unemployable. In none of these cases does the measured existence of 'unemployment' correspond to an economically meaningful excess of supply over demand in the labour market. Thus U^* is the level of such unemployment which will be measured even when demand and supply of labour are equal. It is commonly called the *natural rate of unemployment.*

Now it seems that macroeconomic policy has the power to raise income above the equilibrium level and reduce unemployment below the natural rate. Suppose that fiscal or monetary expansion shifts the economy to the income level Y_1. Equation (23) shows that wages start to rise and in section 8.2 we saw how this would cause short-run aggregate supply to shift back and income to fall. Suppose, however, that the government were to undertake persistent fiscal or monetary expansion so as to keep the income level at Y_1. Then we would have the situation illustrated in figure 8.8.

The real wage must be constant at the level required to persuade firms to produce Y_1. Therefore $\hat{P}$, the rate of growth of prices, must be constant and equal to $\hat{W}$, which, from (23) is equal to $f(Y_1 - Y^*)$. Obviously the larger is $Y_1 - Y^*$ the higher will be the rate of change of prices and wages; and conversely if the government holds Y below Y^* there will be a steady and equal decline in the price level and the wage rate, greater the further Y is below Y^*.

Mathematically, observe that if the output level Y_1, and the consequent inflation rate $\hat{W}_1$, is the target, the government can, having shifted the economy to Y_1, maintain it at this level by expansion of the nominal money supply at the rate $\hat{W}_1$. Then M/P is constant at the level required by the IS–LM equations (1) and (2) to hold aggregate demand at Y_1. The

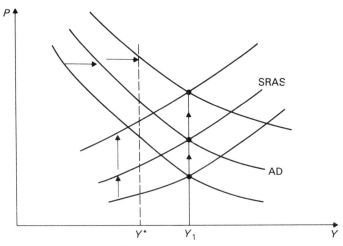

FIGURE 8.8   Permanent overemployment

price level changes at the same rate as nominal wages so W/P is constant at the level required by (7) and (6) to induce competitive firms to fix employment at L_1 and aggregate supply at Y_1. Thus equations (1), (2), (6), (7) and (23) are all satisfied and the government seems to have attained its objective.

Note that the argument above clearly shows that a single expansionary change in fiscal or monetary policy has only temporary effects. The government needs to make fiscal or monetary policy ever more expansionary to maintain output at a target level above Y^*. Clearly government expenditure cannot be raised indefinitely, for it cannot exceed national income, nor can taxation be reduced indefinitely. Inflation at the rate $\hat{P}_1 = \hat{W}_1$ tends to restore income back to the level Y^* because it reduces the real value of the money supply, so eventually to maintain income at Y_1 the nominal money supply will have to be expanded at the rate $\hat{W}_1$. In this sense one can readily understand statements like 'inflation is inherently a monetary phenomenon': our analysis suggests that inflation cannot persist for long unless it is accompanied by a continual increase in the money supply.

It seems therefore that government policy-makers have a choice between inflation and unemployment. Income can apparently be raised above the long-run equilibrium level, and unemployment reduced below the natural rate, at the cost of having inflation, the 'trade-off' between inflation and unemployment being the Phillips curve of figure 8.7(b).

How should governments make this choice? Most of us take for granted the undesirability of unemployment, but should we feel the same about inflation? If inflation is not undesirable, then why not have very low levels of unemployment, even if very rapid inflation is caused?

The common complaint against inflation is that it hurts people whose incomes are fixed in nominal terms: old people, for example, who had planned their savings so as to produce an adequate income for retirement. More generally, inflation hurts creditors and benefits debtors by reducing the real value of their assets and debts respectively. But surely if people know that there is inflation at a significant rate they will take this into account: saving in forms which maintain the real value of wealth (in property rather than in financial assets, for example), demanding pensions that keep pace with rising prices, making loans or going into debt on terms that take account of inflation? However, if we believe that people anticipate continuing inflation, we should modify our model, as we see in the remaining sections of this chapter.

*8.5 Inflationary expectations

If inflation were taking place continuously and if it were known to be government policy that inflation should continue so as to keep up employment and output, people would surely come to expect inflation in the future. This will affect the analysis considerably.

The first change is one which affects the rate of interest. It becomes important to distinguish between the real and nominal interest rate. Suppose a bank offers interest at the rate i per time period. One dollar deposited at time 0 will become $(1 + i)^t$ dollars by time t. However if prices are expected to rise at the rate π per year, then goods which one dollar would buy at time 0 will cost $(1 + \pi)^t$ dollars at time t. Thus the purchasing power of the $(1 + i)^t$ at time t is actually $(1 + i)^t/(1 + \pi)^t = (1 + r)^t$ where

$$1 + r = \frac{1 + i}{1 + \pi} \simeq 1 + i - \pi \qquad (24)$$

The approximate equality in (24) is derived by writing $(1 + \pi)^{-1}$ as $1 - \pi + \pi^2 - \pi^3 + \ldots$ and ignoring all terms involving products of i and π as being insignificantly small if i and π are small. The *real* interest rate is the rate at which the purchasing power of the deposit grows and is given by r, where (24) shows that

$$r \simeq i - \pi \qquad (25)$$

i being the *nominal* interest rate at which the nominal value of the deposit rises, and π being the expected inflation rate.

(It is easily checked that the error in the approximation in (24) and (25) really is small for 'normal' values of i and π. Also if interest and inflation were measured continuously using exponential functions, the equality of r and $i - \pi$ would be exact — see exercise 8.4.)

Interest rates enter our models in the investment function and the demand for money function. Which of the two interest rates should appear in these functions?

If you review the discussion of the demand for money in section 7.8 you will easily see that it is the nominal interest rate which enters the demand for money function. Individuals have to divide their financial wealth between money and interest-bearing assets like bonds. The difference between the returns on the two types of asset is the nominal interest rate, or, to put it another way, the nominal interest rate is the opportunity cost of holding money. Thus the demand for money function should be written $L(Y, i)$.

Now, however, consider the decision of whether to undertake the type of real investment discussed in section 7.5. Suppose there is no inflation expected. Then (7.50) applies and we calculate net present value as

$$NPV_0 = -x_0 + \frac{x_1}{1+r} + \frac{x_2}{(1+r)^2} + \ldots + \frac{x_T}{(1+r)^T} \tag{26}$$

If however inflation were expected at the rate π then the money value of future expected revenue should rise at this rate so x_t is replaced by $x_t(1+\pi)^t$. To calculate the net present value of these money returns we discount using the nominal interest rate i to obtain

$$NPV_0 = -y_0 + x_1 \frac{1+\pi}{1+i} + x_2 \left(\frac{1+\pi}{1+i}\right)^2 + \ldots + x_T \left(\frac{1+\pi}{1+i}\right)^T \tag{27}$$

and using (24) shows that (26) still holds. Therefore we can compute present values *either* using the nominal expected returns $x_t(1+\pi)^t$ and the nominal interest rate i, *or* using the real values of the expected returns x_t and the real interest rate r. Suppose π changed with r constant, so that i must have changed also. A change which is purely a change in expected future prices should have no effect on the real returns x_t so that (26) is unaffected: an investment project which previously had $NPV_0 > 0$ will still satisfy this, and conversely. By contrast, if π changes with i constant so that r will change, but the real returns x_t are unchanged then either (26) or (27) shows that NPV will in general change. Thus it is the real interest rate r on which real investment depends, and we should write the investment function as $I = I(r)$.

Hence, using (25), we can now write the IS–LM system (1) and (2) as

$$S(Y - T) + T = I(r) + G \tag{28}$$

$$L(Y, r + \pi) = M/P \tag{29}$$

Now recall the justification for the Phillips-curve equation (23): when employment exceeds desired labour supply, wages will be pushed up. If, however, workers expect the price level to rise over the next year at the rate π, they will believe that it is only in so far as W exceeds π that their *real* wage is responding to the shortage of labour. (It is left to you as exercise 8.5 to show rigorously that the rate of change of W/P is, in discrete time, approximately equal to $\hat{W} - \hat{P}$, and in continuous time exactly equal to $\hat{W} - \hat{P}$.) Thus in the presence of inflationary (or defla-tionary) expectations the Phillips-curve equation becomes

$$\hat{W}_t = f(Y_t - Y^*) + \pi_t \tag{30}$$

where $\pi_t = (P_{t+1}^e - P_t)/P_t$ the rate at which next year's price level is expected to be higher than the current price level. This is the *expectations-augmented Phillips curve*.

As in section 8.2, equations (6) and (7) can be combined to give a short-run aggregate supply function

$$Y_t = Y(K, W_t/P_t) \tag{31}$$

and, as before, the IS–LM equations combine to give the aggregate demand function

$$Y_t = Y(G, T, M_t/P_t, \pi_t) \tag{32}$$

This last function has the expected inflation rate in it because it appears in (29). A rise in π_t, other things being equal, reduces the demand for money and, as you can easily confirm formally, must therefore increase aggregate demand for goods – see exercise 8.6.

Now we need an explanation of how people form their expectations of inflation. One hypothesis is that of *adaptive expectations*

$$\pi_t = \alpha \hat{P}_{t-1} + (1 - \alpha) \pi_{t-1} \qquad 0 < \alpha \leqslant 1 \tag{33}$$

Expected inflation is a weighted average of the inflation rate which has just been observed and of the previously expected rate. The larger is α, the faster do expectations adapt to observed inflation. We will analyse the special case where $\alpha = 1$ so that people are assumed simply to expect the inflation rate they have just experienced to persist:

$$\pi_t = \hat{P}_{t-1} \tag{33a}$$

Our model of the economy is therefore described by equations (30), (31), (32) and (33a). Rather than attempt to give a complete account of the outcomes of all possible policies, we will analyse two policies: (a) monetary policy which keeps income at a level above the long-run equilibrium; and (b) expansion of the money supply at a fixed rate. Recall that in the absence of inflationary expectations, these two policies were equivalent: output was held high and there was inflation at a rate equal to the growth of the money supply.

There is one further problem to deal with. We shall need to derive the effect on income of a change in the money supply. Using (33a), (31) and

(32) we have

$$Y(K, W_t/P_t) - Y(G, T, M_t/P_t, P_t/P_{t-1} - 1) = 0 \tag{34}$$

which *for given* W_t *and* P_{t-1} implicitly defines P_t as a function of M_t. Differentiating (34) with respect to M_t gives

$$\left(-Y_w \frac{W_t}{P_t} + Y_m \frac{M_t}{P_t} - Y_\pi \frac{P_t}{P_{t-1}}\right) \frac{1}{P_t} \frac{\partial P_t}{\partial M_t} = \frac{Y_m}{P_t} \tag{35}$$

and then differentiating (31) we obtain

$$\frac{\partial Y_t}{\partial M_t} = \left(-Y_w \frac{W_t}{P_t}\right) \frac{1}{P_t} \frac{\partial P_t}{\partial M_t} \tag{36}$$

The sign of the left-hand side of (35) is ambiguous: $-Y_w$ is positive and Y_m is positive but $-Y_\pi$ is negative. To obtain the results $\partial P_t/\partial M_t > 0$ and $\partial Y_t/\partial M_t > 0$, which were the results derived in section 8.2 from the same model but without inflationary expectations, we require to *assume* that $-Y_w W_t/P_t + Y_m M_t/P_t - Y_\pi P_t/P_{t-1} > 0$. This amounts to assuming that the effect of inflationary expectations on the demand for money is not too large.

With this extra assumption, let us start at the position $Y_0 = Y^*, \hat{W}_0 = \pi_0 = 0$ with W_0/P_0 and M_0/P_0 at the levels required to satisfy (31) and (32). Since $\hat{W}_0 = 0$, $W_1 = W_0$ and we can use (35) and (36). If we want $Y_1 > Y_0 = Y^*$, (35) and (36) show that we must raise M_1 above M_0, and that P_1 will rise above P_0. (31) is now satisfied with $W_1/P_1 < W_0/P_0$. (30) shows that $\hat{W}_1 = f(Y_1 - Y^*) + \pi_1 = f(Y_1 - Y^*) + \hat{P}_0 > \hat{P}_0$. In figure 8.9, the economy has moved from the initial equilibrium at A on the original Phillips curve to the point B.

Now we want to have $Y_2 = Y_1$, so from (31) we must have $W_2/P_2 = W_1/P_1$, so $\hat{P}_1 = \hat{W}_1 > \hat{P}_0$ and $\pi_2 > \pi_1$. Thus, from (32), $M_2/P_2 < M_1/P_1$ so $\hat{M}_1 < \hat{P}_1$. Finally, from (30), $W_2 = f(Y_1 - Y^*) + \pi_2 = f(Y_1 - Y^*) + \hat{P}_1$. The economy has now moved from B to C in figure 8.9. In this and all subsequent time periods, the real wage has to be constant so (30), (31) and (33a) combine to give

$$\hat{P}_t = \hat{W}_t = f(Y_1 - Y^*) + \hat{P}_{t-1} > \hat{P}_{t-1} = \hat{W}_{t-1} \tag{37}$$

(while (32) shows the required rate of monetary expansion to maintain aggregate demand at this level) and we see that income can be maintained at Y_1 only at the cost of continually *accelerating inflation*, as the Phillips curve keeps rising as a result of rising expectations of inflation and the economy follows the path shown in figure 8.9 as B → C → D → ....

At any time the government has the option of abandoning the target of holding income above Y^*. Suppose that in time period 3 the government aims to reduce income to the level Y^*. The argument of equations (34) to (36) shows that to shift the economy back to the income level Y^* in period 3 the government must increase the money supply by less than the increase that would take the economy to D. The fall in income from $Y_2 = Y_1$ to $Y_3 = Y^*$ means that $W_3/P_3 > W_2/P_2$ so that $\hat{P}_2 < \hat{W}_2$. Then (30) shows that if Y_t is held at Y^*, for all $t \geqslant 3$, we will have $\hat{W}_t = \pi_t = \hat{P}_t = \hat{P}_2$, and (32) shows that the money supply will have to be increased steadily at this rate. This is shown in figure 8.9 as a shift from C to D^* where the value of $\hat{P}_2$ under this policy is indicated by $\hat{P}^*$. The position D^* is now a new equilibrium: output may be maintained indefinitely at Y^*, with inflation at the constant rate $\hat{P}^*$. Thus a *temporary* reduction in unemployment below the natural rate has been achieved at a cost of a *permanent* rise in the inflation rate.

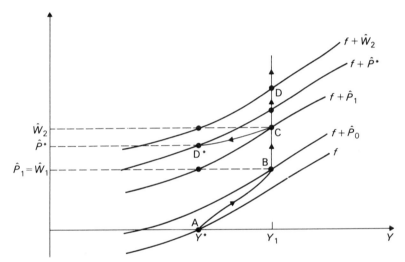

FIGURE 8.9   The expectations-augmented Phillips curve

It is left to you as exercise 8.7 to trace out in detail the path that would have to be followed in order to achieve a reduction in the inflation rate. It is fairly obvious that an increase in unemployment above the natural rate for some time will be required.

The alternative policy of steady money supply growth is better analysed in the slightly different model of the next section.

*8.6   A continuous time model

In some respects the model of the previous section is easier to analyse in a continuous time setting. Rates of change are now measured using time derivatives so that

$$\hat{W}_t = \frac{1}{W_t}\frac{dW_t}{dt} \qquad \hat{P}_t = \frac{1}{P_t}\frac{dP_t}{dt}$$

and π_t is the expected value of $\hat{P}_t$.

The adaptive expectations hypothesis is now formulated as π_t being a weighted average of past values of $\hat{P}_t$:

$$\pi_t = \int_{-\infty}^{t} \alpha\, e^{-\alpha(t-\tau)}\hat{P}_\tau\, d\tau \tag{38}$$

which implies that

$$\frac{d\pi_t}{dt} = \alpha\hat{P}_t - \alpha\pi_t \tag{39}$$

which is the continuous time version of (33). Now (30), (31) and (32) are unchanged except for the definitions of $\hat{W}_t$ and π_t.

Equations (31) and (32) together imply that

$$\frac{dY_t}{dt} = Y_w\frac{W_t}{P_t}(\hat{W}_t - \hat{P}_t) = Y_m\frac{M_t}{P_t}(\hat{M}_t - \hat{P}_t) + Y_\pi\frac{d\pi_t}{dt} \tag{40}$$

and with (39) this implies

$$\left(-Y_w\frac{W_t}{P_t} + Y_m\frac{M_t}{P_t} - \alpha Y_\pi\right)\hat{P}_t$$

$$= -Y_w\frac{W_t}{P_t}\hat{W}_t + Y_m\frac{M_t}{P_t}\hat{M}_t - \alpha Y_\pi\pi_t \tag{41}$$

For simplicity of notation let us write $-Y_w W_t/P_t$ as A, $Y_m M_t/P_t$ as B and αY_π as C. In general A, B and C are not constants, and they are all positive. We can use (30) to eliminate $\hat{W}_t$ from the equations so that (41) becomes

$$(A + B - C)\hat{P}_t = Af(Y_t - Y^*) + B\hat{M}_t + (A - C)\pi_t \tag{42}$$

and from (40) we have

$$\frac{dY_t}{dt} = -A\,[f(Y_t - Y^*) + \pi_t - \hat{P}_t] \tag{43}$$

Using (42) to eliminate $\hat{P}_t$ reduces our model to the two equations derived from (39) and (43):

$$\frac{1}{\alpha}\frac{d\pi_t}{dt} = \frac{1}{A + B - C}[Af(Y_t - Y^*) + B(\hat{M}_t - \pi_t)] \tag{44}$$

$$\frac{dY_t}{dt} = -\frac{A}{A+B-C}\,[(B-C)f(Y_t-Y^*)-B(\hat{M}_t-\pi_t)] \qquad (45)$$

As in the discrete time model of the previous section we need to make the further assumption that the effect of inflation on the demand for money is not too large. Specifically we assume that $A + B - C > 0$, which is almost identical to the assumption made in the discrete time model.

Now let us analyse the effects of the policy of letting the money supply expand at the fixed rate $\hat{M}_t = m$ in all time periods.

Equation (44) shows that π_t is constant when Y_t and π_t satisfy

$$\pi_t = \frac{A}{B}\,f(Y_t-Y^*)+m \qquad (46)$$

and this set of values is denoted by $\dot{\pi}_t = 0$ in figure 8.10. If π_t exceeds the value given by (46) for any given Y_t, (44) shows that $d\pi_t/dt < 0$, and vice versa. Equation (45) shows that Y_t is constant when Y_t and π_t satisfy

$$\pi_t = m - \frac{B-C}{B}\,f(Y_t-Y^*) \qquad (47)$$

If $B - C > 0$ we obtain a set of values as denoted by $\dot{Y}_t = 0$ in figure 8.10. When π_t lies above this line, (45) shows that $dY_t/dt < 0$, and vice versa. The arrows in figure 8.10 show the direction in which π_t and Y_t will move when (46) and (47) are not satisfied. Clearly when $\pi_t = m$ and $Y_t = Y_e$, both (46) and (47) are satisfied and π_t and Y_t are constant over time.

A typical path is traced out by the bold arrowed curve in figure 8.10. The economy starts with inflationary expectations at zero and output at the 'natural' level Y^*. The money supply is growing and this raises output above Y^* but also raises inflationary expectations. After some time output starts to fall back as the effects of inflation overtake the monetary expansion, and eventually inflationary expectations fall also. Then output starts rising again, and so on. The economy follows a cyclical path with inflation and output alternately rising and falling as they approach the long-run equilibrium $\pi = m$, $Y = Y^*$.

Although the policy analysed here is slightly different from that of the previous section, the basic message is the same: extra output can be attained only temporarily and at the expense of a permanent increase in inflation.

The path shown in figure 8.10 converges towards the long-run equilibrium. There seems to be nothing in the formal model that would rule out the possibility that the path actually gets further and further away (in a cyclical fashion) from the equilibrium point. You can confirm this by redrawing the diagram with a steep $\dot{\pi}_t = 0$ line and a shallow $\dot{Y}_t = 0$ curve (that is, with A/B large and $(B-C)/B$ small). This sort of instability seems

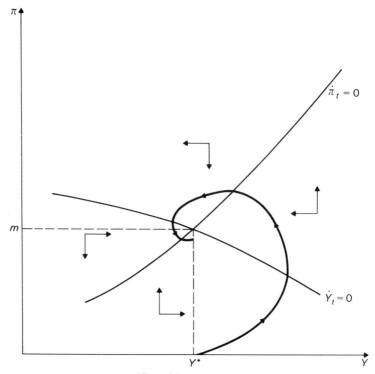

FIGURE 8.10   Continuous monetary growth

even more of a possibility if $B - C$ is negative, as you are asked to show in exercise 8.9. Let us not at this late stage ask whether, with further mathematical tools or further behavioural assumptions, we could rule out this possibility. Instead, observe simply that instability seems intuitively implausible – in exercise 8.9 you are asked to describe verbally how output and inflation change along an unstable path.

Finally in this model we can consider briefly the consequences of an alternative expectations hypothesis, that of *rational expectations*. Suppose that individuals believe that the economy converges to a long-run equilibrium in which inflation is equal to the rate of monetary expansion. Therefore if the government is known to be expanding the money supply at the rate m, inflationary expectations reflect this and

$$\pi_t = m \tag{48}$$

This is substituted in (30), (41), (42) and (43) so that (45) becomes simply

$$\frac{dY_t}{dt} = -\frac{A(B-C)}{A+B-C} f(Y_t - Y^*) \tag{49}$$

Then if we start in equilibrium with $Y_0 = Y^*$, equation (49) shows that the economy must remain in that equilibrium, because Y_t must be constant independently of the rate of monetary growth chosen by the government. From (42) we see that $P_t = m$ so the hypothesis in (48) could equally well be called 'self-fulfilling' expectations. The rate of inflation which individuals expect is always exactly equal to the true rate of inflation.

In this case the government has *no* scope for changing the level of output: any change in the monetary expansion rate is instantly absorbed as a change in inflationary expectations and in inflation itself. This model gives a conclusion that is the polar opposite of that of the simple multiplier model with which we started: in that model, government policy affected income, but not prices; in this model policy changes only prices and cannot affect income.

8.7 A concluding remark

One could characterize the adaptive expectations model of the previous two sections as a dynamic version of the short-run AD–AS model of section 8.2, while the rational expectations hypothesis gives a dynamic version of the long-run AD–AS model. It is therefore worth recalling the remark made in section 8.3 that there is no consensus among economists about which of these models is the best description of the real world. The relative merits of different macroeconomic models are the subject of much current research and controversy.

Exercises

8.1 Analyse the effects of a change in taxation in the long-run and the short-run AD–AS models. Compare the 'crowding out' effects on private investment of a rise in the government deficit if that rise is brought about by: (i) a rise in government expenditure, (ii) a fall in taxation.

*8.2 Consider an economy in which the production function is

$$Z = f(L, K, M)$$

where Z is the quantity of output produced, L is labour used, K is the quantity of other domestically-owned inputs used, and M is the quantity used of an output which must be bought from foreigners at the price q relative to output. Thus the net output available to the economy is

$$Y = f(L, K, M) - qM$$

Analyse the macroeconomic effects of a rise in q. Does this model give a good account of the effects of the oil price rises of the 1970's on oil-importing economies?

8.3   Prove that (21) gives a smaller value of $\partial Y/\partial G$ than the IS–LM model and the simple multiplier model.

8.4   Show that the approximate equality in (24) and (25) is exact when interest and inflation are measured continuously using exponential functions.

8.5   Show that the rate of change of the real wage is approximately equal to $\hat{W} - \hat{P}$ when rates of change are measured discretely as in section 8.5, and exactly equal to $\hat{W} - \hat{P}$ when rates of change are measured continuously as in section 8.6.

8.6   Prove that the aggregate demand function (32) has the property $Y_\pi > 0$.

8.7   Trace out in detail the path that the economy modelled in section 8.5 would have to follow in order to bring about a reduction in the rate of inflation.

8.8   In the continuous time model of equations (38)–(45) find the monetary policy that will keep Y_t constant at a level higher than Y^* and show that the inflationary consequences are qualitatively the same as in the discrete time model. (Assume that $B - C > 0$.)

*8.9   Draw the diagram corresponding to figure 8.10 for the case $B - C < 0$, paying careful attention to the relative slopes of the $\dot{\pi} = 0$ and $\dot{Y} = 0$ lines. Draw a path which does not converge to long-run equilibrium. Give a verbal account of what is happening to the economy along a path which is not converging to equilibrium.

8.10   In the models of sections 8.5 and 8.6, discuss the effects of fiscal policy changes. (It may be helpful to recall the effects of fiscal policy changes in the long-run AD–AS model.)

8.11   'We used to think that you could just spend your way out of a recession and increase employment by cutting taxes and boosting government spending. I tell you, in all candour, that that option no longer exists; and that insofar as it ever did exist, it only worked by injecting bigger doses of inflation into the economy followed by higher levels of unemployment as the next step. That is the history of the past twenty years.' (Mr James Callaghan, British Prime Minister, September, 1976.)

'The truth is that we cannot conquer unemployment if we are prepared to accept inflation . . . . Reflation, so far from conquering unemployment, leads to accelerating inflation and rising unemployment.' (Sir Geoffrey Howe, British Chancellor of the Exchequer, March 16, 1981.)

Comment on these statements in the light of any of the theories developed in this chapter.

The Profit Function

Several results stated in chapters 2 and 3 were not proved, because their proofs require the introduction of a further device, which is discussed in this appendix.

When we discussed the cost-minimizing firm solving the problem (2.13) by choosing $z(w, y)$, we defined the cost function $c(w, y)$ as the *minimized* value of cost, so $c(w, y) = wz(w, y)$. Similarly when we look at the profit-maximizing firm solving the problem (2.48) by choosing $y(p, w)$ and $z(p, w)$ it is natural to define the *profit function* $\pi(p, w)$ as the *maximized* value of profits, $\pi(p, w) = py(p, w) - wz(p, w)$.

The profit function has remarkable properties. Consider its derivative with respect to p:

$$\frac{\partial \pi(p, w)}{\partial p} = y(p, w) + p\frac{\partial y(p, w)}{\partial p} - \sum_{i=1}^{n} w_i \frac{\partial z_i(p, w)}{\partial p} \tag{1}$$

The first-order conditions for the solution of the profit-maximization problem are, however, given by equations (2.6) as $p(\partial F/\partial z_i) = w_i$ so that (1) becomes

$$\frac{\partial \pi(p, w)}{\partial p} = y(p, w) + p\left(\frac{\partial y(p, w)}{\partial p} - \sum_{i=1}^{n} \frac{\partial F}{\partial z_i}\frac{\partial z_i(p, w)}{\partial p}\right) \tag{2}$$

Further, the fact that the $y(p, w)$ and $z(p, w)$ must satisfy the equation $y = F(z)$ implies that

$$\frac{\partial y(p, w)}{\partial p} = \sum_{i=1}^{n} \frac{\partial F}{\partial z_i}\frac{\partial z_i(p, w)}{\partial p} \tag{3}$$

so that

$$\frac{\partial \pi(p, w)}{\partial p} = y(p, w) \tag{4}$$

Essentially the same argument shows that

$$\frac{\partial \pi(p, \mathbf{w})}{\partial w_i} = -z_i(p, \mathbf{w}) \tag{5}$$

(There is a result for the cost function $c(\mathbf{w}, y)$ which corresponds to (4) and (5):

$$\frac{\partial c(\mathbf{w}, y)}{\partial w_i} = z_i(\mathbf{w}, y) \tag{6}$$

You are asked to prove this result in exercise 4.7. Also in chapter 4, we introduce a function $e(\mathbf{p}, u)$, called the consumer's expenditure function, which has identical properties to the cost function, and the corresponding result for this function is

$$\frac{\partial e(\mathbf{p}, u)}{\partial p_i} = x_i(\mathbf{p}, u) \tag{7}$$

which is proved as (4.29).)

Results (4) and (5) (and (6) and (7)) are remarkable: when we differentiate $py(p, \mathbf{w}) - \mathbf{w}z(p, \mathbf{w})$ with respect to any price, the result we obtain is the same as we would obtain if y and $\mathbf{z}$ were constants. They are not constants, they are functions of prices, but the additional effects of a price change on profits which come through changes in y and $\mathbf{z}$ must sum to exactly zero! We see above that this happens because y and $\mathbf{z}$ are not arbitrary functions of p and $\mathbf{w}$: they reflect optimal profit-maximizing choices.

It is worth noting that (3.15) is the same sort of result: when z_2 takes its optimal cost-minimizing value $z_2(w_1, w_2, y)$, the derivative of cost with respect to output taking account of the change in the value of $z_2(w_1, w_2, y)$ (that is, long-run marginal cost) is the same as the derivative of cost with respect to output treating z_2 as constant (that is, short-run marginal cost).

Results of this type are known as *envelope theorems*. The long-run average cost curve consists of the lowest points traced out by the whole family of short-run average cost curves and is said therefore to be an envelope curve. Its slope at any point is the same as the slope of whichever short-run average cost curve touches it at that point.

Differentiating (4) with respect to w_i and (5) with respect to p gives

$$\frac{\partial y(p, \mathbf{w})}{\partial w_i} = \frac{\partial^2 \pi(p, \mathbf{w})}{\partial w_i \, \partial p} \tag{8}$$

$$\frac{\partial z_i(p, \mathbf{w})}{\partial p} = -\frac{\partial^2 \pi(p, \mathbf{w})}{\partial p \, \partial w_i} \tag{9}$$

Using the well-known result that the order of differentiation of a function of two variables can be reversed we have

$$\frac{\partial y(p, \mathbf{w})}{\partial w_i} = -\frac{\partial z_i(p, \mathbf{w})}{\partial p} \tag{10}$$

the result stated but not proved as (2.69). Similarly, we obtain (2.70):

$$\frac{\partial z_i(p, \mathbf{w})}{\partial w_j} = -\frac{\partial^2 \pi(p, \mathbf{w})}{\partial w_j \partial w_i} = -\frac{\partial^2 \pi(p, \mathbf{w})}{\partial w_i \partial w_j} = \frac{\partial z_j(p, \mathbf{w})}{\partial w_i} \tag{11}$$

Note now that cost minimization is simply profit maximization subject to the additional restriction that y is constant, while short-run profit maximization is simply (long-run) profit maximization subject to the constraint that some inputs are fixed.

Therefore the solutions to the cost-minimizing problem satisfy

$$\mathbf{z}(p, \mathbf{w}) = \mathbf{z}(\mathbf{w}, y(p, \mathbf{w})) \tag{12}$$

(which is (2.52)) and we have

$$\frac{\partial z_i(p, \mathbf{w})}{\partial w_i} = \frac{\partial z_i(\mathbf{w}, y)}{\partial w_i} + \frac{\partial z_i(\mathbf{w}, y)}{\partial y} \frac{\partial y(p, \mathbf{w})}{\partial w_i} \tag{13}$$

and also

$$\frac{\partial z_i(p, \mathbf{w})}{\partial p} = \frac{\partial z_i(\mathbf{w}, y)}{\partial y} \frac{\partial y(p, \mathbf{w})}{\partial p} \tag{14}$$

(which are (2.71) and (2.68) respectively). Substituting (10) and (14) in (13) gives

$$\frac{\partial z_i(p, \mathbf{w})}{\partial w_i} = \frac{\partial z_i(\mathbf{w}, y)}{\partial w_i} - \left(\frac{\partial z_i(\mathbf{w}, y)}{\partial y}\right)^2 \frac{\partial y(p, \mathbf{w})}{\partial p} \tag{15}$$

From (2.61) we have that $\partial z_i(\mathbf{w}, y)/\partial w_i \leqslant 0$, while (2.66) implies the second term is non-positive also, so we now have a proof of the fact stated as (2.72):

$$\frac{\partial z_i(p, \mathbf{w})}{\partial w_i} \leqslant \frac{\partial z_i(\mathbf{w}, y)}{\partial w_i} \leqslant 0 \tag{16}$$

Now consider the short-run profit maximization problem in which z_n is fixed in the short run and $\mathbf{z}^v$ denotes the vector of the remaining (variable) inputs. The problem then is

$$\underset{\mathbf{z}^v}{\text{maximize}} \quad py - \mathbf{wz} \tag{17}$$

$$\text{subject to} \quad y = F(\mathbf{z})$$

which is a standard profit-maximization problem except that the constant z_n appears in the production function and the constant $-w_n z_n$ appears in profits. The solution is a set of function $y(p, \mathbf{w}^v, z_n)$, $\mathbf{z}^v(p, \mathbf{w}^v, z_n)$ where $\mathbf{w}^v$ is the vector of prices of variable inputs, and we have the short-run profit function $\pi(p, \mathbf{w}, z_n)$. In exact analogy with (4), (5), (10) and (11) we have respectively (for $i, j \neq n$)

$$y(p, \mathbf{w}^v, z_n) = \frac{\partial \pi(p, \mathbf{w}, z_n)}{\partial p} \tag{18}$$

$$z_i(p, \mathbf{w}^v, z_n) = -\frac{\partial \pi(p, \mathbf{w}, z_n)}{\partial w_i} \tag{19}$$

$$\frac{\partial y(p, \mathbf{w}^v, z_n)}{\partial w_i} = -\frac{\partial z_i(p, \mathbf{w}^v, z_n)}{\partial p} \tag{20}$$

$$\frac{\partial z_i(p, \mathbf{w}^v, z_n)}{\partial w_j} = \frac{\partial z_j(p, \mathbf{w}^v, z_n)}{\partial w_i} \tag{21}$$

and analogously to (2.66) and (2.67) we have

$$\frac{\partial y(p, \mathbf{w}^v, z_n)}{\partial p} \geqslant 0 \tag{22}$$

$$\frac{\partial z_i(p, \mathbf{w}^v, z_n)}{\partial w_i} \leqslant 0 \tag{23}$$

Now these functions must satisfy

$$y(p, \mathbf{w}) = y(p, \mathbf{w}^v, z_n(p, \mathbf{w})) \tag{24}$$

$$\mathbf{z}^v(p, \mathbf{w}) = \mathbf{z}^v(p, \mathbf{w}^v, z_n(p, \mathbf{w})) \tag{25}$$

that is the short-run and long-run solutions coincide if the fixed factor is at its optimal long-run level. (Compare (12).) Thus

$$\frac{\partial y(p, \mathbf{w})}{\partial p} = \frac{\partial y(p, \mathbf{w}^v, z_n)}{\partial p} + \frac{\partial y(p, \mathbf{w}^v, z_n)}{\partial z_n} \frac{\partial z_n(p, \mathbf{w})}{\partial p} \tag{26}$$

and

$$\frac{\partial y(p, \mathbf{w})}{\partial w_n} = \frac{\partial y(p, \mathbf{w}^v, z_n)}{\partial z_n} \frac{\partial z_n(p, \mathbf{w})}{\partial w_n} \tag{27}$$

but substituting (10) (for $i = n$) and (27) in (26) gives

$$\frac{\partial y(p, \mathbf{w})}{\partial p} = \frac{\partial y(p, \mathbf{w}^v, z_n)}{\partial p} - \left(\frac{\partial y(p, \mathbf{w}^v, z_n)}{\partial z_n}\right)^2 \frac{\partial z_n(p, \mathbf{w})}{\partial w_n} \tag{28}$$

and from (22) and (2.67) we have

$$\frac{\partial y(p, \mathbf{w})}{\partial p} \geqslant \frac{\partial y(p, \mathbf{w}^v, z_n)}{\partial p} \geqslant 0 \tag{29}$$

which is a generalization of (3.20). From (25) we have

$$\frac{\partial z_i(p, w)}{\partial w_i} = \frac{\partial z_i(p, w^v, z_n)}{\partial w_i} + \frac{\partial z_i(p, w^v, z_n)}{\partial z_n} \frac{\partial z_n(p, w)}{\partial w_i} \tag{30}$$

$$\frac{\partial z_i(p, w)}{\partial w_n} = \frac{\partial z_i(p, w^v, z_n)}{\partial z_n} \frac{\partial z_n(p, w)}{\partial w_n} \tag{31}$$

so that, substituting (11) and (31) in (30):

$$\frac{\partial z_i(p, w)}{\partial w_i} = \frac{\partial z_i(p, w^v, z_n)}{\partial w_i} + \left(\frac{\partial z_i(p, w^v, z_n)}{\partial z_n}\right)^2 \frac{\partial z_n(p, w)}{\partial w_n} \tag{32}$$

and from (23) and (2.67) we have

$$\frac{\partial z_i(p, w)}{\partial w_i} \leqslant \frac{\partial z_i(p, w^v, z_n)}{\partial w_i} \leqslant 0 \tag{33}$$

a generalization of the result stated, but not proved, in chapter 3, that the firm's long-run elasticity of demand for an input is greater than the short-run elasticity.

All of these results can be extended to the case where several inputs are fixed in the short run, but it would be necessary to introduce some extra mathematical tools to do this. (We could also develop a general treatment of short-run cost minimization with several variable inputs and several fixed inputs, in contrast with the treatment of chapter 3 where there were only two inputs so there was no cost-minimization problem.)

Close scrutiny of the results obtained above reveals exact symmetry between inputs and output. Indeed we could formulate the profit maximization problem as

$$\text{maximize } px \text{ subject to } x \in X \tag{34}$$
$$\quad x$$

with positive entries x_i in x standing for outputs and negative entries standing for inputs, and the set X being the values of x which are feasible given the production function. (Thus in the case of the firm with production function $y = F(z_1, z_2)$, we would write $x = (x_1, x_2, x_3) = (-z_1, -z_2, y)$, $p = (p_1, p_2, p_3) = (w_1, w_2, p)$ and $X = \{x \mid x_3 \leqslant F(-x_1, -x_2)\}$.)

The solutions to this problem would be $x(p)$ and the function $\pi(p) = px(p)$ is the profit function. Results (4) and (5) are then both written as

$$x_i(p) = \frac{\partial \pi(p)}{\partial p_i} \tag{35}$$

This result, indeed, can be derived by an alternative proof to the one given above, a proof that makes no explicit reference to the Lagrangean conditions. Consider for any fixed p^0 the function $\pi(p) - px(p^0)$. It is non-negative by definition of $\pi(\mathbf{p})$ when $\mathbf{p} \neq \mathbf{p}^0$ and it is zero when $\mathbf{p} = \mathbf{p}^0$; that is, it is a function of $\mathbf{p}$ which is minimized at $\mathbf{p}^0$. The necessary conditions for minimization are simply (35) – hence the result. (Actually, this proof is just a version of the argument used in chapter 3 to prove (3.15).)

In this notation (2.64) becomes

$$(\mathbf{p}^1 - \mathbf{p}^2)(\mathbf{x}^1 - \mathbf{x}^2) \geqslant 0 \tag{36}$$

which implies that

$$\frac{\partial x_i(\mathbf{p})}{\partial p_i} \geqslant 0 \tag{37}$$

(which is (2.66) and (2.67)). In fact, a slightly more sophisticated proof of this result is possible too. It is easy to prove that $\pi(\mathbf{p})$ is a convex function of $\mathbf{p}$: that is, that $\lambda \pi(\mathbf{p}^1) + (1 - \lambda) \pi(\mathbf{p}^2) \geqslant \pi(\lambda \mathbf{p}^1 + (1 - \lambda) \mathbf{p}^2)$ for any $\mathbf{p}^1$ and $\mathbf{p}^2$ and any λ satisfying $0 < \lambda < 1$. It is fairly obvious that the second derivatives of a convex function are positive. Thus from (35) we have

$$\frac{\partial x_i(\mathbf{p})}{\partial p_i} = \frac{\partial^2 \pi(\mathbf{p})}{\partial p_i^2} \geqslant 0 \tag{38}$$

which proves the result. Finally we have

$$\frac{\partial x_i(\mathbf{p})}{\partial p_j} = \frac{\partial^2 \pi(\mathbf{p})}{\partial p_j \partial p_i} = \frac{\partial^2 \pi(\mathbf{p})}{\partial p_i \partial p_j} = \frac{\partial x_j(\mathbf{p})}{\partial p_i} \tag{39}$$

which is (10) and (11). All of this generalizes the previous theory to the case of a firm producing many outputs as well as using many inputs.

The reader with sufficient mathematical sophistication to have persevered thus far probably also has sufficient sophistication to have become increasingly worried about the fact that throughout these arguments we have assumed that all the optimization problems we have posed do have solutions and all the cost and profit functions we have defined are twice differentiable. (If you recall the problems that arose in the case of the profit-maximizing firm with constant returns, recall also that these problems were dealt with by looking at the cost-minimizing problem, and finally consider the results that were eventually derived for the profit-maximizing firm with constant returns, you should be able to see that there are problems with the existence and differentiability of the profit function in this case.) The next step in the formal development of this theory is to tackle the questions of when solutions do exist and when the solution functions are twice differentiable. Investigation of these mathematically deep questions is, however, beyond the scope of this book.

Exercises

A3.1   Derive the profit function for the example of section 2.10 and confirm that (4), (5), (10), (11) and (16) hold.

A3.2   The profit function for the example of section 3.3 is derived in (3.34). Confirm that (4), (5), (10), (11), (16) and (20) hold. (We have already confirmed in section 3.3 that (29) and (33) are satisfied.)

Investment and the Trade Cycle

In section 7.4 we looked at a dynamic multiplier model in which income, if disturbed, moved gradually towards its equilibrium value. Investment was exogenous. Let us now modify that model by recognizing that the purpose of investment is to provide capital for the production process.

Suppose that the capital stock K_t^* which producers want to have at time t is a linear function of output:

$$K_t^* = vY_t \tag{1}$$

where v is a constant, called the capital-output ratio. The fact that v is constant means that we are giving no role to prices and interest rates in spite of earlier discussion (chapter 2 and section 7.5) that suggests that input prices should affect input choices, and in particular that interest rates should affect investment decisions.

Now suppose that there is a one-period lag between the desire to have more capital and its installation so that $K_{t+1} = K_t^*$. By definition, investment is the change in the capital stock, so we have

$$I_t = K_{t+1} - K_t = v(Y_t - Y_{t-1}) \tag{2}$$

Assume there is also a lag in the consumption function:

$$C_t = c(Y_{t-1} - T) \tag{3}$$

so the equation of supply and demand for goods is:

$$Y_t = cY_{t-1} + v(Y_t - Y_{t-1}) + G - cT \tag{4}$$

Applying the standard method of dealing with such equations (left as exercise A7.1) gives equilibrium

$$Y_e = \frac{G - cT}{1 - c} \tag{5}$$

which equilibrium is unstable if $|(v - c)/(v - 1)| > 1$. Since it is reasonable to assume that the value of a machine exceeds the value of its annual output so that $v > 1$, it seems likely that the equilibrium is unstable: a rise in income above its equilibrium level will generate a rise in investment which, via the multiplier, causes a further rise in income which ... and so on. Output will move along the path depicted in figure A7.1.

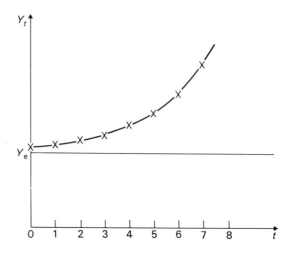

FIGURE A7.1   Explosive income growth

This instability is implausibly violent, but an apparently slight alteration will change the story. Suppose that there are limits both to the amount of positive investment and negative investment feasible in any year, but if desired capital stock is different from the actual stock the maximum amount of investment or disinvestment is undertaken, with a one-period lag as before. Thus

$$I_t = \begin{cases} B & \text{if } K_{t-1} < vY_{t-1} \\ 0 & \text{if } K_{t-1} = vY_{t-1} \\ -D & \text{if } K_{t-1} > vY_{t-1} \end{cases} \tag{6}$$

The consumption function (3) still holds. Suppose $K_0 = 0$ and $Y_0 = (G - cT)/(1 - c)$. Since $vY_0 > K_0$, $I_1 = B$ and

$$Y_1 = cY_0 + B + G - cT$$

$$= B + (G - cT)/(1 - c) \tag{7}$$

so that

$$vY_1 > vB > B = K_1 \tag{8}$$

which implies that $I_2 = B$. Let us suppose that investment is at the level B for t time periods: $I_1 = I_2 = \ldots = I_t = B$. Then

$$K_t = tB \tag{9}$$

and

$$Y_t = cY_{t-1} + B + G - cT \tag{10}$$

Our earlier analysis of the model of equations (7.34)–(7.39) immediately applies, to give

$$Y_t = c^t Y_0 + (1-c^t)(B + G - cT)/(1-c) \tag{11}$$

At $t \to \infty$, $Y_t \to (B + G - cT)/(1-c)$ and $K_t \to \infty$, so there must be some time t at which either $vY_t = K_t$ or $vY_t < K_t$. Let τ be the first such year and suppose that $vY_\tau = K_\tau$. Then $I_{\tau+1} = 0$, $K_{\tau+1} = K_\tau = B$ and

$$Y_{\tau+1} = cY_\tau + G - cT \tag{12}$$

Hence

$$\begin{aligned}
Y_\tau - Y_{\tau+1} &= (1-c)Y_\tau - (G - cT) \\
&= (1-c)c^\tau Y_0 + (1-c^\tau)B - c^\tau(G - cT) \tag{13} \\
&= (1-c^\tau)B > 0
\end{aligned}$$

and $vY_{\tau+1} < vY_\tau = K_\tau = K_{\tau+1}$ so that $I_{\tau+2} = -D$ and we enter an era of negative investment and declining capital stock. Capital decreases linearly but income decreases less than linearly, so eventually a 'floor' is reached at which the economy starts growing again. (The above argument assumes that $vY_\tau = K_\tau$; if instead $vY_\tau < K_\tau$ the only difference is that the era of negative investment starts one period sooner.)

The movement of income over time follows a cyclical pattern over time as illustrated in figure A7.2. Such a movement of income is called a *trade cycle*. This model of the trade cycle gives no role to prices: it is a very

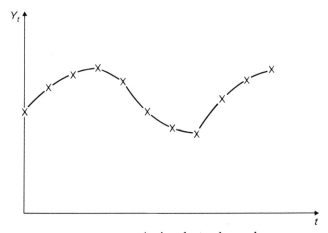

FIGURE A7.2   A simple trade cycle

direct extension of the simple multiplier model. It may seem strange that such an apparently simple model gives rise to such complex behaviour: the key is that investment depends on the *growth* of income, and as the multiplier effect of investment starts to settle down, the rate of growth of income slows down, which causes investment to stop, which makes income fall, which causes investment to become negative and the cycle enters a 'downswing' which continues until the slowing of the rate of decline causes a further reversal and the cycle goes into another 'upswing'.

Exercises

A7.1   Prove (5). How would the model of equations (2)–(4) be different if the consumption function had no lag?

A7.2   How can investment be negative? Why might there be a limit to the amount of negative investment in an economy in any year?

A7.3   How would the model with the investment function (6) be different if the consumption function had no lag?

Suggestions for Further Reading

The mathematics used in this book is almost exclusively calculus. Linear algebra has many interesting economic applications and a good introductory treatment is:

Geoffrey Heal, Gordon Hughes and Roger Tarling, *Linear Algebra and Linear Economics* (Macmillan, 1974)

Two books which partially overlap with the subject matter of this book, but which start at a higher level and cover interesting topics which are not covered here are:

J. W. S. Cassels, *Economics for Mathematicians* (Cambridge University Press, 1981)
Hal R. Varian, *Microeconomic Analysis* (W. W. Norton, 1978)

At a more advanced level for microeconomic topics useful references are:

Edmond Malinvaud, *Lectures on Microeconomic Theory* (North-Holland, 1972)
Kenneth J. Arrow and Frank H. Hahn, *General Competitive Analysis* (North-Holland, 1971)

An introduction to some topics which have not been treated here is given in:

Alan P. Kirman and Werner Hildenbrand, *Introduction to Equilibrium Analysis* (North-Holland, 1976)

A more advanced and rigorous treatment of duality theory is:

Daniel McFadden, 'Cost and Revenue Functions', Chapter 1 of M. Fuss and D. McFadden (eds.), *Production Economics: A Dual Approach to Theory and Applications* Vol. 1 (North-Holland, 1978)

For further work on imperfect competition from the point of view of game theory see:

James W. Friedman, *Oligopoly and the Theory of Games* (North-Holland, 1977)

A standard reference on game theory is:

R. D. Luce and H. Raiffa, *Games and Decisions* (Wiley, 1957)

See also:

Michael Bacharach, *Economics and the Theory of Games* (Macmillan, 1976)

On macroeconomics more extended and nonmathematical treatments of the topics covered in this book are in:

Rudiger Dornbusch and Stanley Fischer, *Macroeconomics* (McGraw-Hill, second edition, 1980)

or

Robert J. Gordon, *Macroeconomics* (Little, Brown, second edition, 1981)

Further macroeconomic analysis is in:

Arthur Okun, *Prices and Quantities: A Macroeconomic Analysis* (Blackwell, 1981)

An alternative approach to macroeconomic theory is found in:

Edmond Malinvaud, *The Theory of Unemployment Reconsidered* (Blackwell, 1977)

You should also read the classic work:

J. M. Keynes, *The General Theory of Employment, Interest and Money* (Macmillan, 1936)

For recent work along the lines briefly mentioned at the end of chapter 8 see:

David K. H. Begg, *The Rational Expectations Revolution in Macroeconomics* (Phillip Allan, 1982)

and

Robert E. Lucas Jr., *Studies in Business-Cycle Theory* (MIT Press and Blackwell, 1981)

Answers and Hints for Selected Exercises

Chapter 1

1.5 The techniques used in section 1.3 can be applied in this case to give $p^* = \alpha/(b + \beta)$, $q^* = b\alpha/(b + \beta)$ and

$$p_t - p^* = -\frac{b(1 - \gamma)}{\beta}(p_{t-1} - p^*)$$

You should discuss the effect of the size of γ on the stability of the equilibrium.

1.9 Differentiating the equilibrium equations with respect to t gives equations in $d\pi/dt$ and dp/dt which solve to give

$$\frac{dp}{dt} = \frac{px'(\pi)}{y'(p) - (1 + t)\,x'(\pi)}$$

$$\frac{d\pi}{dt} = \frac{py'(p)}{y'(p) - (1 + t)\,x'(\pi)}$$

whence

$$\frac{dq}{dt} = \frac{px'(\pi)\,y'(p)}{y'(p) - (1 + t)\,x'(\pi)}$$

1.10 The equations solve to give

$$p = \frac{\alpha - a}{\beta + b} - \frac{\beta}{\beta + b}t \qquad \pi = \frac{\alpha - a}{\beta + b} + \frac{b}{\beta + b}t$$

$$q = \frac{a\beta + \alpha b}{\beta + b} - \frac{b\beta}{\beta + b}t$$

Tax revenue is $T = qt$, and differentiating with respect to t shows that the revenue maximizing level of t is $(a\beta + \alpha b)/(2b\beta)$, at which level q is exactly half what it is when $t = 0$.

1.14   Differentiating (28) gives

$$\frac{dp}{dr} = \frac{-y_r}{y_p - x_p} \qquad \frac{dq}{dr} = \frac{-y_r x_p}{y_p - x_p}$$

Thus when r is low so that $y_r > 0$, a rise in r reduces p and raises q; while for high values of r when $y_r < 0$, a rise in r raises p and reduces q.

1.24   Since supply elasticity is infinite, the price suppliers receive is constant at its current level of 10p. Thus the price to consumers is $\pi = 10 + t$. If the demand function is $x(\pi)$, tax revenue is $T = tx(\pi)$, and the demand elasticity $\pi x'(\pi)/x(\pi)$ is equal to -1.2. Thus the effect of a tax change is

$$\frac{dx}{dt} = x'(\pi) = -1.2\,\frac{x(\pi)}{\pi}$$

$$\frac{dT}{dt} = x(\pi) + tx'(\pi) = x(\pi)\left(1 - 1.2\,\frac{t}{10 + t}\right)$$

When $t = 40$, dx/dt is negative and dT/dt is positive, so both objectives of the government can be attained by a rise in t. The tax-revenue-maximizing level of t, at which dT/dt becomes 0, is 50.

Chapter 2

2.3   The profit-maximizing inputs are $z_1 = 1$, $z_2 = 9$ so that $y = 3$ and profit is 9.

2.4   (a) The necessary conditions for profit maximization are

$$z_1^{-1/2}z_2^{1/2} - 1 = 0 \qquad z_1^{1/2}z_2^{-1/2} - 1 = 0$$

and *any* values of z_1 and z_2 satisfying $z_1 = z_2$ satisfy these equations.
   (b) The necessary conditions are

$$z_1^{1/2}z_2^{-1/2} - 2 = 0 \qquad z_1^{-1/2}z_2^{1/2} - 1 = 0$$

The first equation requires that $z_1 = 4z_2$, while the second requires $z_1 = z_2$. There are no values that satisfy both.

2.5   (i) (c) $(kz_1)^\alpha (kz_2)^\beta = k^{\alpha + \beta}z_1^\alpha z_2^\beta$, so this production function has decreasing, constant or increasing returns to scale according as $\alpha + \beta$ is less than, equal to, or greater than 1.

(d)

$$[(kz_1)^{-2} + (kz_2)^{-2}]^{-1/2} = [k^{-2}(z_1^{-2} + z_2^{-2})]^{-1/2} = k(z_1^{-2} + z_2^{-2})^{-1/2}$$

so this function has constant returns to scale.

(ii) (c) $\partial y / \partial z_1 = \alpha z_1^{\alpha - 1} z_2$ and $\partial y / \partial z_2 = \beta z_1^{\alpha} z_2^{\beta - 1}$, so the function has diminishing returns to z_1 if $\alpha < 1$ and to z_2 if $\beta < 1$.

(d)

$$\partial y / \partial z_1 = (z_1^{-2} + z_2^{-2})^{-3/2} z_1^{-3} = [1 + (z_1/z_2)^2]^{-3/2}$$

and symmetrically

$$\partial y / \partial z_2 = [(z_2/z_1)^2 + 1]^{-3/2}$$

so the function has diminishing returns to both inputs.

(iii) With $\alpha + \beta > 1$ and $\alpha < 1$ and $\beta < 1$ we have increasing returns to scale and diminishing returns to both inputs. There are values of α and β which satisfy this — for example, $\alpha = \beta = 2/3$. It is impossible, however, to find values of α and β such that $\alpha + \beta \leqslant 1$ and $\alpha > 1$ or $\beta > 1$ (recall that α and β are positive).

(iv) The isoquant is described by $(z_1^{-2} + z_2^{-2})^{-1/2} = 4$, that is, $1/z_1^2 + 1/z_2^2 = 1/16$, so it is asymptotic to both $z_1 = 4$ and $z_2 = 4$.

2.8   (c)

$$\frac{F_1}{F_2} = \frac{\alpha z_2}{\beta z_1}$$

which is a decreasing function of z_1/z_2.

(d)

$$\frac{F_1}{F_2} = \frac{(z_1^{-2} + z_2^{-2})^{-3/2} z_1^{-3}}{(z_1^{-2} + z_2^{-2})^{-3/2} z_2^{-3}} = \left(\frac{z_2}{z_1}\right)^3$$

a decreasing function of z_1/z_2.

2.11   (a)

$$\frac{w_1}{w_2} = \frac{\alpha z_2}{\beta z_1} \qquad \text{so} \qquad \frac{z_1}{z_2} = \frac{\alpha}{\beta}\left(\frac{w_1}{w_2}\right)^{-1}$$

and

$$\sigma = \frac{w_1/w_2}{z_1/z_2} \frac{d(z_1/z_2)}{d(w_1/w_2)} = \frac{-(\alpha/\beta)(w_1/w_2)^{-1}}{z_1/z_2} = -1$$

Thus

$$\frac{w_1 z_1}{w_2 z_2} = \frac{\alpha}{\beta}$$

which is constant, confirming (25).

(b)

$$\frac{w_1}{w_2} = \frac{(z_1^{-\alpha} + z_2^{-\alpha})^{-(1/\alpha)-1} z_1^{-\alpha-1}}{(z_1^{-\alpha} + z_2^{-\alpha})^{-(1/\alpha)-1} z_2^{-\alpha-1}} = \left(\frac{z_1}{z_2}\right)^{-(\alpha+1)}$$

so

$$\frac{z_1}{z_2} = \left(\frac{w_1}{w_2}\right)^{-1/(\alpha+1)}$$

and

$$\sigma = \frac{w_1/w_2}{z_1/z_2} \frac{d(z_1/z_2)}{d(w_1/w_2)} = -\frac{1}{\alpha+1}$$

$$\frac{w_1 z_1}{w_2 z_2} = \left(\frac{w_1}{w_2}\right)^{\alpha/(\alpha+1)}$$

so $w_1 z_1/w_2 z_2$ increases or decreases with w_1 according as $\alpha > 0$ or $\alpha < 0$, that is according as $|\sigma| < 1$ or $|\sigma| > 1$.

2.13 (c) This is a generalization of the example discussed in section 2.7. The solutions are

$$z_1(w_1, w_2, y) = \left[\left(\frac{\alpha}{\beta} \frac{w_2}{w_1}\right)^{\beta} y\right]^{1/(\alpha+\beta)}$$

$$z_2(w_1, w_2, y) = \left[\left(\frac{\beta}{\alpha} \frac{w_1}{w_2}\right)^{\alpha} y\right]^{1/(\alpha+\beta)}$$

$$c(w_1, w_2, y) = (\alpha + \beta)\left[\left(\frac{w_1}{\alpha}\right)^{\alpha}\left(\frac{w_2}{\beta}\right)^{\beta} y\right]^{1/(\alpha+\beta)}$$

(d) From the necessary conditions we obtain $z_2/z_1 = (w_1/w_2)^{1/3}$ so that

$$y = [z_1^{-2} + z_1^{-2}(w_2/w_1)^{2/3}]^{-1/2}$$

$$= z_1[1 + (w_2/w_1)^{2/3}]^{-1/2}$$

whence

$$z_1(w_1, w_2, y) = [1 + (w_2/w_1)^{2/3}]^{1/2} y$$

$$z_2(w_1, w_2, y) = [(w_1/w_2)^{2/3} + 1]^{1/2} y$$

$$c(w_1, w_2, y) = (w_1^{2/3} + w_2^{2/3})^{3/2} y$$

Because the production has diminishing marginal rate of substitution (exercise 2.8), these do give the true minimum. Average cost is $(w_1^{2/3} + w_2^{2/2})^{3/2}$, which is independent of y, reflecting constant returns to scale.

2.14 (and the relevant part of 2.18)   See section 3.3.

2.20   Initially, $y = 1000$ and profit is £9800. Grant (a) leaves y unchanged and raises profits to £10,800. Grant (b) raises y to 1050 and profit to £10,825. Grant (c) raises y to 1250 and profit to £10,425.

2.24 'Profits' measured by the taxman are $py - w_2 z_2 - w_3 z_3$, so the tax bill is $0.5(py - w_2 z_2 - w_3 z_3)$. The firm's true profits after tax are

$$py - w_1 z_1 - w_2 z_2 - w_3 z_3 - 0.5(py - w_2 z_2 - w_3 z_3)$$
$$= 0.5(py - 2w_1 z_1 - w_2 z_2 - w_3 z_3)$$

so the effect on behaviour is the same as the effect of doubling the price of capital.

2.36   The key to each of these questions is to split the postulated price change into two parts, one where all prices change proportionately, and one in which only one price changes.

Chapter 3

3.1   The relationship is

$$z_1 \frac{\partial}{\partial z_1}\left(\frac{F(z_1, z_2)}{z_1}\right) = \frac{\partial F(z_1, z_2)}{\partial z_1} - \frac{F(z_1, z_2)}{z_1}$$

3.2   You need to show that w_2 does not enter into *any* one of the three equations determining supply.

3.10   The (long-run) cost-minimization problem is solved by $z_1 = 3y$, $z_2 = 3y/2$ so that $c = 9y$, and $LRAC = LRMC = 9$. With z_2 fixed at 300, the short-run cost function is

$$c = \frac{300y}{300 - y} + 1200$$

The SRAC, AVC and SRM functions are now easily found. All three are asymptotic to $y = 300$; SRMC and AVC increase monotonically from $y = 0$, while SRAC is U-shaped attaining its minimum value of 9 ($= LRAC$) at $y_1 = 200$, where it also equals SRMC. Hence (14), (15), (16) are satisfied.

3.11 For the production function of the previous exercise, for $p \geqslant w_1$, we have $y(w_1, p, z_2) = [1 - (w_1/p)^{1/2}] z_2$ and $z_1(w_1, p, z_2) = [(p/w_1)^{1/2} - 1] z_2$.

3.18 Think about what happens to average cost as output becomes very small.

3.19 For all firms, marginal cost is $0.02y - 10$, but since $c(0) = 0$, there are no fixed costs and the firm will only produce if marginal cost exceeds average cost. The first 80 firms will enter at a price of 2, each with output 600; the next 80 at a price of 4, each with output 700; while the 140 come in at a price of 6 and output of 800. The industry's supply is 0 up to a price of 2; indeterminate between 0 and 48,000 at $p = 2$; $4000p + 40,000$ for $2 < p < 4$; indeterminate between 56,000 and 112,000 at $p = 4$; $8000p + 80,000$ for $4 < p < 6$; etc..

3.20 The higher cost firms will not produce.

3.24 If you know how to use differentials, it is easy to take the total differentials of (54) and (56) for given $\mathbf{w}$ and use (55) to give $dc = p\, dy$ which is the required result.

   Alternatively substitute (56) into (54) to give c as a function of $\mathbf{w}, y, y^2, \ldots, y^F$ and then use (55) to show that $\partial c/\partial y^f = 0$ for $f = 2, \ldots, F$ so that c is in fact only a function of y, with $\partial c/\partial y = p$.

Chapter 4

4.2

    (i) $x_1 = m/(2p_1)$, $x_2 = m/(2p_2)$

    (ii) $x_1 = 2m/(3p_1)$, $x_2 = m/(3p_2)$

    (iii) $x_1 = \alpha m/p_1$, $x_2 = \beta m/p_2$, $x_3 = \gamma m/p_3$

4.7 $\partial c(\mathbf{w}, y)/\partial w_i = z_i(\mathbf{w}, y)$, $\partial z_i(\mathbf{w}, y)/\partial w_j = \partial z_j(\mathbf{w}, y)/\partial w_i$

4.8 (i) (Compare exercise 2.14 and see section 3.3)

    $e(p_1, p_2, u) = u^2 p_1 p_2/(p_1 + p_2)$

    $x_1(p_1, p_2, u) = [up_2/(p_1 + p_2)]^2$

    $x_2(p_1, p_2, u) = [up_1/(p_1 + p_2)]^2$

The demand functions are given by (19) and it is easy to see that (33) holds. Differentiation confirms (29).

(ii)

$$e(p_1, p_2, u) = e^u \left(\frac{p_1}{\alpha}\right)^\alpha \left(\frac{p_2}{1-\alpha}\right)^{1-\alpha}$$

$$x_1(p_1, p_2, u) = e^u \left(\frac{\alpha}{1-\alpha} \frac{p_2}{p_1}\right)^{1-\alpha}$$

$$x_2(p_1, p_2, u) = e^u \left(\frac{1-\alpha}{\alpha} \frac{p_1}{p_2}\right)^\alpha$$

and we use (22) to confirm (33). Differentiation confirms (29).

4.9   The demand functions are (16), the compensated demand functions are (31). (35) can be confirmed for x_1 from

$$\frac{\partial x_1(p_1, p_2, m)}{\partial p_1} = -\frac{\alpha m}{p_1^2} = -\frac{x_1}{p_1}$$

$$\frac{\partial x_1(p_1, p_2, u)}{\partial p_1} = -(1-\alpha)\left(\frac{\alpha}{1-\alpha} \frac{p_2}{p_1}\right)^{1-\alpha} \frac{u}{p_1} = -(1-\alpha)\frac{x_1}{p_1}$$

$$x_1 \frac{\partial x_1(p_1, p_2, m)}{\partial m} = \frac{\alpha}{p_1} x_1$$

4.13   Differentiating with respect to m gives

$$\sum_{i=1}^{n} p_i \frac{\partial x_i(\mathbf{p}, m)}{\partial m} = 1$$

or

$$\sum_{i=1}^{n} \frac{p_i x_i}{m} \left(\frac{m}{x_i} \frac{\partial x_i(\mathbf{p}, m)}{\partial m}\right) = 1$$

so the income elasticities of all goods weighted by their shares in total expenditure must sum to 1.

4.14 (Compare exercise 2.36)   Think of this in two steps: all prices *and* income rise by 10%; and then income falls back to its original level.

4.19

$$x_1(p_1, p_2, m) = a_1 + \alpha(m - p_1 a_1 - p_2 a_2)/p_1$$

$$x_2(p_1, p_2, m) = a_2 + (1-\alpha)(m - p_1 a_1 - p_2 a_2)/p_2$$

$$x_1(p_1, p_2, u) = a_1 + \left(\frac{\alpha}{1-\alpha} \frac{p_2}{p_1}\right)^{1-\alpha} u$$

$$x_2(p_1, p_2, u) = a_2 + \left(\frac{1 - \alpha\, p_1}{\alpha\ \ p_2}\right)^\alpha u$$

$$e(p_1, p_2, u) = p_1 a_1 + p_2 a_2 + \left(\frac{p_1}{\alpha}\right)^\alpha \left(\frac{p_2}{1 - \alpha}\right)^{1-\alpha} u$$

a_1 and a_2 can be interpreted as essential minimum requirements.

4.24

$$x_1(p_1, p_2, w, m) = (m + 24w)/(12p_1)$$

$$x_2(p_1, p_2, w, m) = (m + 24w)/(6p_2)$$

$$L(p_1, p_2, w, m) = (24w - 3m)/(4w)$$

Clearly if $m = 0$, $L = 6$; while if $m > 0$, $\partial L/\partial w > 0$.

4.26   (i) and (ii) Initially, Mr D's budget constraint is

$$px + 2N = 376$$

and he chooses $N_1 = 148$, $x_1 = 80/p$. Then it becomes

$$px + 1.8N = 342.4$$

and he chooses $N_2 = 143$, $x_2 = 85/p$. Since

$$px_2 + 2N_2 = 371 < 376$$

and

$$px_1 + 1.8N_1 = 346.4 > 342.4$$

it follows that his choices are consistent, and he is better off in the first situation, as indeed is obvious from a diagram, or from the simple fact that all that has happened is that his wage has fallen.

(iii) Calculations like those above show that his tastes have changed: his behaviour is not now consistent with his previous choices.

Chapter 5

5.5   The elasticity of demand is $-1/b$. Consumer surplus is

$$\int_0^1 (x^{-b} - 1)\, dx = \begin{cases} \left[\dfrac{1}{1 - b}x^{1-b} - x\right]_0^1 & \text{if } b \neq 1 \\[2ex] [\log x - x]_0^1 & \text{if } b = 1 \end{cases}$$

However, $0^{1-b} = \infty$ if $b > 1$, and $\log 0 = -\infty$, so the integrals exist only when $b < 1$, in which case consumer surplus is $1/(1 - b) - 1 = b/(1 - b)$. In all cases, the price the marginal consumer is willing to pay rises towards infinity as x falls to zero, but if $b < 1$ (elasticity of demand exceeds 1) the rise in price is sufficiently slow for the area under the demand curve to be finite.

5.14   The value in cents of the bridge being open for free use is

$$\int_0^{1000} (100 - 0.1x)\, dx = 50,000$$

That is, its value is \$500 per day, which exceeds the cost of keeping it open. But there is no single price which will cover the cost, since the revenue-maximizing price is 50c which raises \$250 per day. Either price discrimination or taxes are needed.

Chapter 6

6.3   (a) Profit is

$$py - w_1 z_1 - w_2 z_2 = y^{-1} - w_1 z_1 - w_2 z_2 = z_1^{-1/3} z_2^{-2/3} - 8z_1 - 2z_2$$

and since the derivatives of this function with respect to z_1 and z_2 are negative there can be no maximum.

(b) $c = 6y$ is the cost function (see section 2.4 for the derivation). Revenue is $R = py = y^{-1}$. MC $= 6$, MR $= -y^{-2}$ so there is no value of y which equates the two.

(c) Since MC $>$ MR at all values of y, it is best to make y as small as possible. Profits are $y^{-1} - 6y$ which tends to infinity as y goes to zero. This is the consequence of the incredible assumption that even for very small y the elasticity of demand is $1/2$, so revenue rises as y falls.

(d) Now MR $= 12y^{-1/3}$ and profit is maximized when $y = 8$.

6.11   With a single price, profit as a function of price is

$$\pi = p^{-1} + p^{-2} - 0.6(p^{-2} + p^{-3})$$

which is maximized at $p = 1$, $y_1 = 1$, $y_2 = 1$. With price discrimination

$$\pi = p_1^{-1} + p_2^{-2} - 0.6(p_1^{-2} + p_2^{-3})$$

which is maximized at $p_1 = 1.2$, $p_2 = 0.9$, $y_1 = 0.69$, $y_2 = 1.37$. Note that it is in the market with the lower demand elasticity that price is raised in the discriminating case.

6.14   Joint profits are

$$p_1(y_1)\, y_1 + p_2(y_2)\, y_2 - c(y_1 + y_2) - g(y_2)$$

so to maximize joint profits we require

$$MR_1(= p_1 + p_1'(y_1) y_1) = MC_1(= c(y_1 + y_2))$$
$$MR_2(= p_2 + p_2'(y_2) y_2) = MC_2(= c(y_1 + y_2) + g'(y_2))$$

The subsidiary's profits are

$$p_2(g_2) y_2 - p_3 y_2 - g(y_2)$$

and the profit-maximizing rule is

$$MR_2 = p_3 + g'(y_2)$$

so to make this compatible with the joint-profit-maximizing rule, the parent should set $p_3 = c'(y_1 + y_2)$.

6.18   The reaction functions become $y_i = (a - c - by_j)/(2b + 2d)$.

6.19   Firms' profit-maximizing behaviour is independent of g so (27) and (28) still hold, and price is $a - bx = c + (a - c)/(n + 1)$. Firms will enter the industry only so long as positive profits are made, so n will be the largest integer satisfying $p \geqslant c + g/y_f$, that is satisfying $n \leqslant 1 + (a - c)/(bg)^{1/2}$. Note that this number decreases with b, c and g and increases with a, as one would expect.

6.20   If firm 1 is the leader, then (25) holds for $f = 2, \ldots, n$ which implies that

$$(n - 1)\left(a - c - by_1 - b \sum_{f=2}^{n} y_f\right) - b \sum_{f=2}^{n} y_f = 0$$

so that firm 1's objective

$$\underset{y_1}{\text{maximize}} \left(a - by_1 - b \sum_{f=2}^{n} y_f\right) y_1 - c_1$$

can be written

$$\underset{y_1}{\text{maximize}} \frac{n + 1}{2n} (a - c - by_1) y_1$$

and the equilibrium is therefore $y_1 = (a - c)/2b$ (independent of n) while $y_2 + \ldots + y_n = (n - 1)(a - c)/(2nb)$, $y_f = (a - c)/(2nb)$, for $f = 2, \ldots, n$, and $p = c + (a - c)/2n$.

6.23   It is easy to show that the condition corresponding to (52) is

$$c_i'(y_i) = {}'p_i \left(1 + \frac{y_i}{p_i} \frac{\partial p_i}{\partial y_i}\right)$$

but you then need to prove that $(y_i/p_i)(\partial p_i/\partial y_i)$ is not the same as $1/e_i$. The example used in (42)–(44) is sufficient: $\partial y_1/\partial p_1 = -2$, but if you rearrange the equations to get $p_1(y_1, y_2)$ you find that $\partial p_1/\partial y_1 = -2/3$. The outcome is therefore different.

6.25 $e_i = -2$ so $p_i = 2c$ for all firms and $y_i = (2c)^{-1}(n-1)^{-2}$ so the equilibrium number of firms is the largest integer n satisfying $c + 2cg(n-1)^2 \leqslant 2c$, that is $n \leqslant 1 + (2g)^{1/2}$.
   The demand function is decreasing in p_i and increasing in p_j, and, for given prices, decreasing in n. It is homogeneous of degree -1 in prices (which does not contradict standard consumer theory since the n goods produced in this industry are not the only goods available to consumers) so if all the prices rise proportionately, demand falls. All of these are reasonable properties.

Chapter 7

7.6   Equilibrium income is determined by

$$Y = c(1-t) Y + I + G$$

so savings is

$$S = (1-c)(1-t) Y = \frac{(1-c)(1-t)}{1 - c(1-t)} (I + G)$$

whence the effect of changes in c can be calculated.

7.7

$$\partial Y/\partial G = 1/[1 - (1-t) C_Y]$$
$$\partial D/\partial G = (1-t)(1 - C_Y)/[1 - (1-t) C_Y], \qquad \text{where } D = G - T$$

7.9

$$\partial Y/\partial G + \partial Y/\partial T = (1 - C_Y)/(1 - C_Y + M_Y) < 1$$
If $M = M(Y - T)$, $\partial Y/\partial G + \partial Y/\partial T = 1$.

7.10   (39) implies $Y_t = c^{t-1} Y_1 + (1 - c^{t-1}) Y_e$, but $Y_1 = Y_e + \Delta I$ since $Y_e = Y_0 = a + c Y_e + I$, whence $Y_t = Y_e + c^{t-1}\Delta I$ for $t = 1, 2, 3, \ldots$.

7.13   The value of T which satisfies the first-order and second-order conditions for a maximum is $T = [\alpha/(1 + r)]^2$. Since T may not exceed 1, it is optimal to set $T = 1$ if the present value is an increasing function of T at $T = 1$, that is if $\alpha \geqslant 1 + r$.

7.14   From (58) the annual payment must satisfy

$$100 = \frac{a}{0.05}\left(1 - \frac{1}{(1.05)^{10}}\right) + \frac{100}{(1.05)^{10}}$$

which implies $a = 5$.

7.17   The 'even' and 'odd' bonds have respective present values

$$PV_E = \frac{100}{(1 + r)^2 - 1} = \frac{100}{2r + r^2}$$

$$PV_O = \frac{100(1 + r)}{(1 + r)^2 - 1} = \frac{100(1 + r)}{2r + r^2}$$

so $PV_E + PV_O = 100/r$.

7.24

(i) $\dfrac{\partial Y}{\partial T} = \dfrac{-(1 - S_Y) L_r}{S_Y L_r + I_r L_Y} < 0 \qquad \dfrac{\partial r}{\partial T} = \dfrac{(1 - S_Y) L_Y}{S_Y L_r + I_r L_Y} > 0$

(ii) $\dfrac{\partial Y}{\partial G} + \dfrac{\partial Y}{\partial T} = \dfrac{S_Y L_r}{S_Y L_r + I_r L_Y} < 1$

The effects of T are opposite in sign to and smaller by the factor $(1 - S_Y)$ than the effects of G. The effect on Y of a balanced budget change is less than 1, because the balanced budget multiplier (the horizontal shift in the IS curve) is 1 but the effect of the increased interest rate is to dampen the multiplier effect.

7.28

$$\frac{\partial Y}{\partial G} = \frac{L_r}{S_Y L_r + IM_Y L_r + I_r L_Y}$$

and if $B = X - IM$

$$\frac{\partial B}{\partial G} = \frac{-IM_Y L_r}{S_Y L_r + IM_Y L_r + I_r L_Y} > -1$$

Chapter 8

8.1   In the long-run model, equation (1) and (2) with Y fixed at Y^* give

$$\frac{\partial P}{\partial T} = -\frac{(1 - S_Y) L_r}{I_r M / P^2} < 0$$

That is, $\partial P / \partial T = -(1 - S_Y)(\partial P / \partial G)$ where $\partial P / \partial G$ is given by (12), and the change in investment is

$$I_r \frac{\partial r}{\partial T} = 1 - S_Y < 1$$

In the short-run model equations (1), (2), (6) and (7) with W constant give

$$\frac{\partial Y}{\partial T} = -(1 - S_Y) \frac{\partial Y}{\partial G}$$

$$\frac{\partial P}{\partial T} = -(1 - S_Y) \frac{\partial P}{\partial G}$$

where $\partial Y / \partial G$ and $\partial P / \partial G$ are given by (21) and (22).

8.6   Differentiating (28) and (29) with respect to π with G, T and M/P constant gives

$$\frac{\partial Y}{\partial \pi} = \frac{-L_r I_r}{S_Y L_r + I_r L_Y} > 0$$

8.8   Use equations (45), (44) and (40) to show that Y_t constant and greater than Y^* implies accelerating growth of the money supply, accelerating inflation of both wages and prices (the inflation rate being faster than the rate of monetary growth) and accelerating inflation expectations (the expected inflation rate being slower than the rate of monetary growth).

Index